# FROM SNAKE OIL TO MEDICINE

# FROM SNAKE OIL TO MEDICINE

## PIONEERING PUBLIC HEALTH

## R. ALTON LEE

Healing Society: Disease, Medicine, and History
John Louis Parascandola, Series Editor

**Westport, Connecticut**
**London**

**Library of Congress Cataloging-in-Publication Data**

Lee, R. Alton.
  From snake oil to medicine : pioneering public health / R. Alton Lee.
    p. ; cm. — (Healing society : disease, medicine, and history, ISSN 1993–5938)
  Includes bibliographical references and index.
  ISBN-13: 978–0–275–99467–9 (alk. paper)
  ISBN-10: 0–275–99467–8 (alk. paper)
  1. Crumbine, Samuel J. (Samuel Jay), 1862–1954.   2. Public health
personnel—Kansas—Biography.   I. Title.   II. Series.
  [DNLM: 1. Crumbine, Samuel J. (Samuel Jay), 1862–1954.   2. Physicians—United
States—Biography.   3. Public Health—United States—Biography.   4. History of
Medicine—United States—Biography.   5. History, 19th Century—United
States—Biography.   6. History, 20th Century—United States—Biography. WZ 100
C956L 2007]
  RA424.5.C68L44   2007
    362.1092–dc22
    [B]                          2006038812

British Library Cataloguing in Publication Data is available.

Copyright © 2007 by R. Alton Lee

Library of Congress Catalog Card Number: 2006038812
ISBN-10: 0–275–99467–8
ISBN-13: 978–0–275–99467–9
ISSN: 1993–5938

First published in 2007

Praeger Publishers, 88 Post Road West, Westport, CT 06881
An imprint of Greenwood Publishing Group, Inc.
www.praeger.com

Printed in the United States of America

The paper used in this book complies with the
Permanent Paper Standard issued by the National
Information Standards Organization (Z39.48–1984).

10 9 8 7 6 5 4 3 2 1

# HEALTH
## (a Crumbine favorite)

Health is a state of physical, mental and moral equilibrium, a normal functioning of body, mind and soul. It is the state when work is a pleasure, when the world looks good and beautiful, and the battle of life seems worthwhile. Health is the antithesis of disease, degeneracy and crime.

The laws of health are as inexorable as the law of gravitation, as exacting as eternal justice, as relentless as fate, and their violation is the beginning and cause of disease, suffering and sin.

Health is the most desirable of all earthly blessings. When finally lost it cannot be purchased by countless millions, restored by the alienist, nor returned by the pulpit.

Health is that state of happiness, faith and love whose prototype was the first man—Adam; whose ideal is the Christ.

(Source unknown)

# CONTENTS

# PREFACE

At the turn of the twentieth century Samuel J. Crumbine became secretary of the Kansas Board of Health. His experience of two decades of medical practice in Western Kansas prepared him in various ways for this new role and he quickly established a statewide reputation for knowledge, honesty, integrity, and courage in confronting tough issues regarding public health. Both the older and newer definitions of public health are used here, that is, community action to avoid disease or other threats to health and that public health policy should actively promote health, not just maintain it. Crumbine's three decades in this field span the period when these definitions evolved. Born during the turmoil of the Civil War, his life spanned almost a century of sea change in medicine and he died during the rivalry of the Cold War, still thinking of means to promote his profession.

Crumbine dedicated his life to the betterment of mankind and as his field evolved, he grew with it, as do most individuals during their careers. He began his life's major work at the turn of the twentieth century at a time when most American doctors endorsed the germ theory and utilized the latest scientific methodology, although many in his profession were old-fashioned and only reluctantly accepted some of these new theories and discoveries. He gathered his evidence and then mobilized it effectively to achieve common sense goals. While the general public found it difficult to disagree with what these experts told them, embracing the thought that invisible things were making them sick did not come easily. Yet they did accept it sufficiently, at least superficially, to provide a broad market for popular patent medicines, such as the Microbe Killer.

Curiously, medical discoveries helped promote the patent medicine business by linking recent finds to a primitive cure. Texan William Radam promoted the Microbe Killer to appeal to a public misunderstanding of the dangers of germs. Consisting almost entirely of water with a minute amount of red wine, hydrochloric and sulfuric acids, it enjoyed a wide market because he promoted it as a cure-all for destroying germs internally. Lydia Pinkham's Vegetable Compound appealed especially to women as a welcome alternative to surgery to correct female disorders. Demand for this panacea remained high long after her death in 1883. By the turn of the twentieth century, Miss Pinkham was appealing to Victorian modesty to persuade women to refrain from consulting male doctors about their internal problems. Muckraking Progressive journalists helped the medical profession and Samuel Crumbine enormously by eradicating the deceptive nature of the patent medicine industry.[1]

American customs and habits of public spitting, using common drinking cups and towels, and ignoring disease-carrying insects such as flies and mosquitoes, were spreading these germs. Americans were freely dumping their sewage in open streams and water wells were dug without reference to drainage problems that polluted their community drinking water. It fell to Dr. Crumbine to educate the public to these dangers that surrounded them, to teach them the necessity of quarantine from killer diseases such as tuberculosis or cholera, and to take precautionary measures when epidemics struck. All the great scientific advances would be of little benefit until Crumbine and his colleagues developed a far more effective public health system to spread these messages than that which was in place at the turn of the twentieth century. Americans of the twenty-first century are as appalled at the ignorance of these obvious facts of life as was Samuel Crumbine a century earlier. It was his special task to educate Kansans and the rest of the world in these basic public health principles. And as a noted authority on Kansas medical history expressed it, Samuel J. Crumbine "was the most skilled educator the state has ever known."[2]

Crumbine's successful educational career coincided with a noticeable increase in public acceptance of doctors during the Progressive Era. Before the turn of the century, common wisdom among rural folk, who were Crumbine's largest constituency, was that there was "considerable difference between a good doctor and a bad one, but hardly any difference between a good doctor and none at all." Building on the advances in public hygiene and bacteriology, use of scientific instruments such as the stethoscope, and improved infant feeding and care, the public became increasingly confident in the scientific judgment of their professional physicians. Crumbine's popularity and educational campaigns contributed much to this process in Kansas.[3]

The modern person has specific questions on these ancient developments now taken for granted. How did people of the turn of the century period come to believe there were living microbes they could not see with the human eye? How did this new knowledge affect their everyday lives? How did they come to enjoy the benefits of a flush toilet, drinking pure water, enjoy uncontaminated food? Samuel Crumbine would explain these and a myriad of similar questions with the germ theory and teach them certain protective behaviors to avoid these "invisible" killers by providing a guide for how they circulated. But old customs and traditions die hard and they retarded acceptance of this hygienic enlightenment that only education conscious scientists could generate. One of Crumbine's favorite media was use of poetry, ditties, and limericks to spread his gospel.[4]

Samuel Crumbine's life was rooted in the soil of Kansas, a state he dearly loved. His exploits were a legend in his own time in the Sunflower State. He was a big fish in a small pond until he moved to New York City and became a small fish in a large pond, as the folk saying goes on the Great Plains. Yet he made his mark indelibly on both worlds. Much has been published in the history of American public health in the last two or three decades. While several awards are given annually in Crumbine's name for pure food controls, advancing the work of public health, promotion of consumer containers, and the like, in all this secondary material, curiously, Crumbine is rarely quoted or indexed. It is the national story almost exclusively with examples coming from the Northeast. Presumably this is because historians of that section of the country are writing about their experiences in public health developments and overlooking the possibility that major advances in that area might also occur in more remote regions of the nation where identical problems and needs arose and were successfully met. This man and his triumphs should not be lost from the annals of the public health movement.

I owe debts to many people who helped produce this study. The staffs of Hale Library at Kansas State University and the Manhattan Public Library were indispensable. Dawn McInnis of the Clendening Library of the University of Kansas Medical School went beyond the call of duty in uncovering bibliography and sources of research for me, and Billie Broadus of the Cincinnati Medical Heritage Center responded professionally to inquiries about that medical school in the 1880s. To those myriad other unnamed librarians and archivists who generously, as is their nature, answered my queries during the gestation of research and writing, I extend my heartfelt thanks. Professors Jo Ann Carrigan of the University of Nebraska, Omaha and Robert P. Hudson of the University of Kansas Medical Center were generous with their time in reading the entire manuscript and offering their perceptive comments and criticisms to make this a stronger study. While the book is much better because of their efforts, I, of course, retain responsibility for the errors that remain, despite their suggestions.

# ONE

# THE WILD WEST

The first Krumbine in America, Leonard, landed in Philadelphia in 1754, farmed on the far western frontier of Pennsylvania, and fought in the Revolutionary War. He and the maternal Mull family ancestors had migrated from Germany, along with thousands of fellow "Pennsylvania Dutch," to enjoy the religious freedoms found in Penn's colony. The Krumbine family bible records that Samuel Jay was born to Samuel Jacob and Sarah (Mull) Krumbine on September 17, 1862, coinciding with the time of the battle of Antietam, General Robert E. Lee's first thrust north to the Mason–Dixon Line. The son arrived in a log cabin in Emlenton, County of Venango, Pennsylvania, on the Allegheny River some fifty miles east of Youngstown, Ohio. The elder Samuel was a blacksmith and farmer and when the Civil War broke out he left his pregnant wife and daughter Mary to become First Sergeant of Company 14 of the 101st Infantry of the Union Army. A short time later he was captured by Confederate forces and died soon afterward in Libby prison in Richmond, Virginia, a month before the birth of his only son. Giving birth to him in a log cabin, the mother thought, was a good omen and she wistfully observed to the grandmother, "maybe this means that my baby has a chance to be more than a blacksmith like his father." Death of the father left the widow and her two small children with two options: she could accept charity from neighbors or "work out," as it was called in that time and place. Rugged, independent Sarah chose the latter course and, for the first eight years of his life, Samuel was raised primarily by his grandmother Mull.[1]

It was a hardscrabble life, though nurtured in love and care. The grandmother might be able to replace the mother that he seldom saw but what of the unknown father who was to impose discipline, teach moral values, and serve as a masculine role model? Grandmother Mull, also a widow who had to raise eight fatherless children, knew how to cope with life. "A God-fearing, thrifty disciplinarian," she made Samuel do his share of the work, which for a small boy included driving the cows in for their milking morning and night, brushing off the flies while the milking was being done, cutting kindling for starting cooking fires, churning butter, helping with the sheaves of oats and wheat at harvest time, and harvesting the farm's produce. The family cultivated the usual vegetable garden of that age, including a corner for flowers. They ate simple but wholesome food and were one of the few in the area to eat tomatoes, a daring feat because at that time it was commonly believed that "love apples" caused cancer—a common old wife's tale that many were disputing. In the autumn, following the first frost, the rolling hills and heavy forests of Western Pennsylvania produced an abundance of chestnuts, walnuts, butternuts, and hazelnuts for the family members to gather by the bushel and to bury in pits lined with straw. Apples, corn, and various fruits and vegetables were stored in the cellar after being sun-cured or oven-dried. Passenger pigeons lived in numbers still so great that they cast a heavy shadow on a bright sunny day as they flew by on their way to roost in Forest County, northeast of Venango.[2]

Grandmother Mull had little formal education but she had an abundance of common sense. Like many of her neighbors, she had no problem in making a boy wear secondhand clothes without complaining and seeing that he behaved, while showing affection when praise was due. After helping with the weekly wash and on baking day, he could expect the reward of a small cake to enjoy or a pat of approval for a job well done. She was the first to aid a neighbor in need or condemn a shiftless man for neglecting his needy family. She loved her corncob pipe and dispensed much common sense while enjoying a rare moment of relaxation and indulging in her pleasure after a long day of work. She knew how to make a boy feel wanted and a part of the family, not merely endured, reminding him to wash his feet after he went barefoot in the summer, pulling briars from the bottom of his feet, and tending his cuts and bruises. Her examples made a deep impression on the growing lad. "God-fearing parents," he wrote later, "gave me mental and spiritual health while they were building up my physical welfare with simple, wholesome food, and hard work on the farm." But at age eight he was old enough to leave this loving, sheltering environment and venture out into the world of schooling.[3]

Mercer school, to be built some thirty miles west of Emlenton, initially for educating destitute children of slain Civil War soldiers, would admit qualified orphans between ages eight and sixteen. Crumbine later expressed his ceaseless gratitude to those pedagogues who gave him the rudiments of an education for the next eight years. Their "patience, devotion, and loving kindness" reminded him of the Scripture "inasmuch as ye have done it to one of the least of my children, ye have done it unto me." Mary White, Josephine Smith, Anne Wilson, Bill Orr, Almira Marstellar, Amelia Lynch, Sadie Lynch, Harriet Petite, Alice Bogle, and William Bogle were among the teachers who made a great impression on the minds of the children entrusted to their care. After eight years of their pedagogy, students were prepared for college. Crumbine continued to attend the school reunions as long as he was able. There is a description of the school's location in the records:

> The situation is a beautiful one and is as well adapted to the purpose as any that could have been selected. A spring of soft pure water gushes from the base of Bald Hill on the east. The west is fringed by a wandering stream, the excess water from many streams. A beautiful grove ornaments the property and offers an excellent and delightful playground for the children.

His experiences during this formative period in this gorgeous setting remained with him for a lifetime. He received a diploma indicating that he attended the boarding school from September 11, 1869, until September 17, 1878, his sixteenth birthday, "having studied diligently during that time and bourne a good moral character." Legend has it that his friends and sister early nicknamed the little fellow "Crummie," and he and teachers subsequently began spelling his name Crumbine. It is unknown when this change took place but his Mercer diploma certifies "Samuel J. Krumbine" as the recipient.[4]

Small, wiry, and strong from farm work, self-reliant, with an education far superior to most Americans of the time, at age sixteen young Samuel Crumbine was ready to challenge the world and repay his state and school for its tender, loving care during his formative years. His mother believed that, having been born in a log cabin, as was Abraham Lincoln, would make her son something special. "Maybe this means that my baby has a chance to be more than a blacksmith like his father," she had observed wistfully when he was born. Grandmother Mull derided this notion, telling her daughter to "bring him up in the fear of God and the rest is up to him." But where to begin, now that he was prepared to face the world? "Crummie" had always been fascinated by the bottles and other paraphernalia displayed in the Mercer drugstore and he loved watching the pharmacist while he mixed his prescriptions. This instilled in the youth a determination to become a doctor. One June day in 1873, when he was eleven, he stood in front of the Old Corner Drug Store with a friend, David Hanna, inhaling the odors of spices, herbs, drugs, and perfumes coming from within. "Gee, Crummie," David exclaimed, "when I grow up I'm going to be a doctor." "I am too," responded the lad, "and I'm going to have a drug store, too, with big blue, red and yellow bottles in the window, just like this one." The school physician, "the lovable Doctor Hosack," who was talking to the pharmacist at the time, also served as an ideal role model for youthful ambition to become a doctor. Both boys managed to fulfill these dreams, David in Stoneboro, Pennsylvania and Crummie in Dodge City, Kansas. After graduating from Mercer, he found a job in nearby Sugar Grove, in a drug store operated by a Dr. Phillips who, typical of those in the profession at that time, had to have a second vocation to supplement his income from his medical practice.[5]

There were close ties in the nineteenth century between doctors and pharmacology. Numerous physicians prepared their own medicines. Many found it necessary to have a second occupation and a pharmacy seemed natural, as did midwifery and treating sick animals, especially in small towns and on the frontier. Druggists, in turn, often went to medical school with their store supporting their education, as was the case with Crumbine.[6]

The medical profession in the latter half of the nineteenth century was a curious, and in many ways dubious, profession. One authority has noted that at the turn of the twentieth century a person with a medical problem "stood only a fifty-fifty chance of benefiting from an encounter with a random physician." This quandary resulted from scientific medicine and pharmacology being in their infancy when Samuel Crumbine contemplated becoming a doctor. It also came from an oversupply of unqualified doctors because medical education was relatively cheap before the turn of the century and licensing requirements in most states were lax or nonexistent.[7]

Sectarianism was strong at this time. There were at least five medical philosophies, or schools of thought in current vogue. Homeopathy was based on the conviction that diseases could be cured by drugs producing similar symptoms, or "the law of similars." Their effect could be heightened by small doses. The "regular" doctors, or allopaths they were called, insisted that contravening drugs were the only answer. This branch would come to dominate the American Medical Association and eventually, after many struggles over several decades, succeed largely in driving the other sects out of business, although in recent times homeopathy is making a resurgence in popularity. Osteopathy held that illness was caused by a malfunctioning in the blood or nervous systems, especially the small bones of the back. Chiropractic borrowed heavily from osteopathy. Finally, eclectics were basically herb healers who utilized the best from all the other theories. Being empiricists, they argued that medical practitioners should use whatever worked. All these schools taught conventional medical science courses in their schools and differed primarily in their therapeutics. Most doctors, though, whatever their beliefs and practices, had to have some second source of income because of the public's widespread suspicion of their profession and an oversupply of ill-trained physicians. They had to farm, be a pharmacist, midwife, or some combination thereof, to supplement their medical income. In addition, when they received a fee in rural communities, doctors often had to accept payment in kind because of the scarcity of currency.[8]

Crumbine's employment as a clerk and "handy boy" in the drug store included keeping the store and equipment clean and, later, to open the store and close it, morning and evening, and dust the merchandise after opening. He also had the opportunity of learning from the owner Corydon J. Phillips, a combination physician/pharmacist. For his work in the store, and care for the doctor's cow and horses, he received his room and board. He was too small to learn to milk a cow as a boy on the farm and now he and the cow developed a personality conflict and someone else had to milk her. After six months of apprenticeship, he received a meager salary and, by his third year, was entrusted with preparing prescriptions of tinctures, elixirs, and plasters. As many of the preparations required local gums and resins, the boy had to gather these, and he learned a great deal of medicine vicariously through these experiences. He occasionally had the opportunity to assist Dr. Phillips with minor surgeries and to accompany him on night calls.[9]

With this background of three years, and his satisfactory performance, Samuel was offered the opportunity of studying with a preceptor in Cincinnati. It was standard procedure at the time to study under a recognized physician and one of the benefits was access to the doctor's library, which, in this case, was surely a good one. The location also allowed him to attend an allopathic school, the Cincinnati School of Medicine and Surgery. Dr. W.E. Lewis, who was a professor of anatomy at the Cincinnati College of Medicine and his preceptor, proved to be both kind and crucial to the aspiring young medic. But after less than two months of study, Crumbine announced he was ready to quit! He told his mentor he was just too "dumb" to understand "the lectures and demonstrations." Rushing across the room, Dr. Lewis shook his hand vigorously saying, "Congratulations! Unlike most students, you've learned unusually early that you know nothing about medicine. That should give you a head start, put you at the head of your class, for it takes the average medic at least a year to find out what you have discovered in two months." The aspiring doctor reported that "I never experienced, before that moment nor since, such a sudden reversal of outlook, such a stiffening of determination, such exaltation of spirit." This inspired him to continue with his studies, as he expressed it, "no matter what happened."[10]

He ate only two meager meals daily, but his savings evaporated rapidly in the big city. He answered a want ad for "an energetic young man to take samples to drug stores and pass handbills." He received the job but, much to his dismay, found the samples to be Piso's Consumption Cure, a patent medicine condemned by the medical profession but popular with some physicians and many people at the time. Swallowing his pride and medical ethics, he accepted the work and the $25 weekly, which permitted him to remain in school. While on the streets he was careful to hide when he saw a colleague from medical school approaching. By then he had acquired an additional reason for wanting to complete his medical studies. Living in a boarding house, he came downstairs one day to complain about the towel situation. With hands dripping, he was terribly embarrassed when the matronly owner introduced him to a pretty young roomer she was chatting with, "a red-cheeked, brown-eyed girl, a vision that left me breathless." Miss Katherine Zuercher of Springfield, Ohio was training to become a foreign missionary but her doctor would not let her go to India until she recovered from her bronchial problems. She invited him to accompany her to services at the Vine Street Congregational Church. They began to see each other regularly but he was hesitant about pressing her to become serious as his mother and grandmother had taught him to regard missionaries as "saintly people" and he wanted to provide for her properly. Only after establishing a medical practice and graduating from medical school, would he ask for her hand in marriage.[11]

Despite pushing Piso's Consumption Cure, the young student was chronically short on funds. After two years of school, a friend wrote him about a business opportunity in Western Kansas. Traveling to the area by freight train, a hayrack ride, and on foot to investigate, he decided to purchase a half-interest in a drugstore in Spearville, a small village on the Atchison, Topeka, and Santa Fe Railroad, twenty-one miles east of Dodge City. He worked there as a pharmacist for a year and later during vacations and summers, with the co-owner deducting from his salary to pay for his half-interest. He landed in Spearville with "a good start on a beard" and $35, most of which he spent on a pair of buckskin ponies. With his medical school background and the absence of medical practice laws in Kansas at the time, people began consulting him for advice and he added to his medical knowledge and reputation. Using funds from his pharmaceutical enterprise, he returned to Cincinnati for further medical courses and peddling Piso's Cure. He must have cut an interesting figure on the campus after months in the Wild West. His western experience added many picturesque expressions to his vocabulary, such as "howdy, pardner," "ornery cuss," "pull your freight," and similar cowboy idioms.[12]

His periodic medical trips around Spearville took the young practitioner to Dodge City. He developed an attachment for the cowtown and, when he returned from Cincinnati in 1885, he decided to locate there. He hung out his shingle and began to practice but it was not until 1889 that he received his M.D. from the Cincinnati College of Medicine and Surgery. Dodge City was acquiring some respectability by that time, although still considered rough by Eastern standards.[13]

This medical school, established in 1851, sought to produce "competent general practitioners" and offered two courses of study to achieve this goal: three years with two terms of lectures and one of medical experience, or a graded course of three lecture terms. In the latter, the first and second terms included anatomy, histology, chemistry, and materia medica (therapeutics), with midwifery and the practice of medicine added to the basic courses in the second term. The third term in this option included practice of medicine, surgery, obstetrics, gynecology, and ophthalmology. The second option was recommended and Crumbine chose it, completing the last term when he returned to school. Fees included "general ticket" $40; matriculation $5; "demonstrator's ticket" $10; laboratory $5; "hospital ticket" $5; and graduation fee $25, all of which had to be "*paid strictly in advance*" Board and lodging ranged from $3 to $6 weekly, "according to style and accommodation."[14]

As a wild and wooly cattle town on the edge of the frontier, Dodge City enjoyed and endured the same experiences as Abilene and Wichita had earlier. Although Hollywood has glamorized and exaggerated its wildness, the actual cattle town milieu was truly exciting and dangerous, and it seemed especially so to easterners who wrote home about it. Guns were everywhere, as were tempers aggravated by plentiful whiskey, life seemed cheap. Merchants were reluctant to curb the brutality as it was profitable and they steadfastly refused as long as possible to hire marshals to "tame" their town. Stanley Vestal tells the story of a mother alone in the house with her child, who saw a dirty, drunken tramp approaching. Although her husband's gun was not loaded, she prepared to bluff with it to defend her honor and her baby. Then she remembered her husband's admonition never to "pull a gun unless you aim to use it," and dropped the weapon in the child's crib. The vagabond entered the house and when he found only a woman, prepared to make himself at home. He staggered toward her, then looked down at the baby in the crib. He paled, turned, and ran out of the house, heading for the prairie. The baby was teething and the drunk decided to have nothing to do with a town where the children cut their teeth on a revolver. Samuel Crumbine would experience firsthand this western reliance on guns. When he stepped onto Front Street, he must have wondered if the Chicago reporter was correct when he observed that "there is no law west of Chicago and no God west of Dodge City."[15]

The buildings on Front Street had high false fronts and wooden awnings stretching out over wooden sidewalks. The wide street was ankle-deep in dust and horse dung and a moderate rain made "an adventure of crossing Front Street." It was not until a year before Crumbine arrived that Front Street had "a continuous walk along the major business block." The south side was lined with saloons, dance halls, and cheap rooming houses. On the north stood gambling halls, nicer restaurants and drinking establishments, and the hotel, the Dodge House. Prostitutes invaded the cowtowns in great numbers. The "soiled doves" came from homes of various types but, contrary to the legend of them marrying and becoming good housewives, they enjoyed their work for the most part and when they married they often missed their former "trade." Though frequently beautiful, they were normally as hard and dangerous as the cowboys and buffalo hunters. There were, of course, exceptions. As coroner of Ford County, Crumbine once had to investigate the story of a sad suicide.

The girl was an only child, sheltered from all of life's problems but dominated by her parents who continually quarreled over who would control her. All this left her feeling possessed rather than loved and wanted. She met a well-dressed lady one day who won her confidence and persuaded her to run away from home and make "plenty" of money in "a glamorous way." The life of prostitution soon soured for her, and with no one to turn to the girl sought escape through suicide. This was not an uncommon story on the frontier and Crumbine placed the blame on the parents who quarreled over possession of her rather than giving her the love and guidance she so desperately needed.[16]

Civilization came slowly to Dodge City. Over time churches and schools were built, leading merchants were converted to the need for law and order, various professionals were arriving to offer their services, and the "better elements" finally "tamed" their town. The year after Crumbine moved there, the town installed its first telephone system and the city council slowly had the numerous hogs and other wandering livestock removed from the streets. The blizzard of 1886 ruined the open range and cattle drive industries and a devastating fire in town the previous year destroyed most of the business district on Front Street. But when Crumbine moved to Dodge City in 1885, Bat Masterson had just replaced Wyatt Earp as marshal and, while it was still a little wild, as he well knew from his experiences in Spearville, the town gradually acquired some refinement.[17]

Soon after he arrived there, Samuel Crumbine met the resident doctors, all allopaths. Because Dodge City, with over 5,000 inhabitants, was the only major town in the area—in fact Denver was the nearest city—there were five other physicians because their practices covered a seven-county region. The rural population was sparse and this meant they traveled long distances to see some of their patients—by horse, horse and buggy, and by train. Dr. A.E. Choteau practiced alone. Drs. Thomas L. McCarty and C.A. Milton were partners, as were J.J. Plummer and A.O. Wright. Crumbine was the youngster at twenty-seven and Plummer was only ten years older. They assured him there was plenty of work for all, considering the vast area they had to cover.[18]

Dr. Wright, a Civil War surgeon, warned him of the pitfalls in the Wild West for the unwary tenderfoot, which he was not, strictly speaking, as he had lived in the vicinity for two years. Then Plummer offered a tour of the "dens of iniquity," assuring Crumbine that "keeping in touch with the town sports, male and female," constituted an important part of their job. They entered an unfamiliar social world at the first dance hall at about 10:00 PM, when the evening's action was beginning to accelerate. Amid peals of happy laughter, the loud rhythmic chants of the caller, cowboy whoops, and shuffle of heavy boots on the wood floor, the patrons were whirling in a square dance, accompanied by a small orchestra of banjo, guitar, and fiddle. The bar was at the other end of the hall. The men were mostly cowboys and sports and the ladies were house entertainers, many of whom worked as ranch servants during the day, and "members of the local demimonde." A couple of girls asked the doctors to dance and Plummer accepted while Crumbine begged off and, instead, absorbed the gaudy sights. Guns and holsters were checked on a shelf behind the bar. Groups of men were exchanging stories and one bunch was talking loudly and began gesticulating wildly. Fortunately, Plummer returned at that point and suggested they "hit the road" before violence erupted.

A visit to the Long Branch saloon came next, the "Fifth Avenue" of Dodge City, where cattle deals and other important business were consummated and "gentlemen gamblers" congregated to play cards with the sports and reckless cowboys. The fashionably attired gamblers here wore the currently popular Prince Albert coats. Crumbine was fascinated with the "guarded movements" of the gamblers, with no emotion showing on their frozen faces.

Next came the eye-opening "red light" district. Plummer explained that most of his medical practice came from these women and "all you need to do is be reasonably friendly and normally human and understanding with them." "When they're in trouble," he added, "they'll listen to your advice, if you are sincere and they trust you." They also passed Boot Hill where men who died with their boots on were buried when they had no one to claim their bodies.[19]

Their last visit that night was a sobering and enlightening experience. As they passed a house full of Plummer's patients, the door opened and some of the girls were urging a cowboy to leave, but he was resisting. He wanted to sing. "If he stays longer," the girls explained, he would pass out on them and "we'll have to keep him here all night while he sleeps it off. That is not good for business. But if he sings in the open he'll get air in his lungs and recover." They finally guided him into the street, singing "Oh My Darling Nellie Grey." The doctors followed him down the street to make certain he did not harm himself, and then went home for the night. "What a novel way to treat acute alcoholism," the Eastern doctor marveled, "just get air in your lungs by singing." "Quieter folks," Crumbine later discovered, "lived on the hillsides, in one-story wooden cottages, although I saw several sod houses left over from when the town was new." It was there on a hillside that he would begin his married life five years later.[20]

Living in Dodge City allowed Crumbine to take advantage of some of the customs and benefits of his rural Western surroundings. When he used a buggy on his extensive trips, he carried his shotgun and would occasionally stop to shoot prairie chickens, plover, and rabbits. After treating one farmer in his home, he was rewarded with some shooting at the man's "private chicken flock" and he took home five birds as a bonus! Often he was thrown from his horse and left to walk to the nearest house. His horse suddenly stopped one night, throwing him through the barbed-wire fence he could not see, and leaving him incapacitated for several days. Another time he got out of his buggy to snap his whip at a snake. His strawberry roans were startled and ran away, leaving him stranded on the prairie. These experiences taught him to take a driver along, when he could find one, for assistance in an emergency. As with other frontier doctors he ate and slept when and where he could, sometimes stopping at a farmhouse for a short nap before pressing on. He learned to enjoy a good cigar and he would occasionally take a drink of whiskey, although he never became convinced of its efficacy for medicinal purposes, even for snakebites as his patients argued.[21]

The vastness of the prairie sometimes overwhelmed him and Crumbine often found himself lost at night. "One real dark night," he related, a man living fifteen miles from Dodge City asked him to look at his sick baby. They hitched up the buggy and tied the man's horse on behind. They finally crossed a creek and the man said "just follow the bend of this creek for half a mile and you will get to my house." They drove for half an hour and still no house. The man said they were not there yet so they drove on. Finally, the doctor decided to return to the creek and start over. They began again and soon passed a house, the man insisting it was "So and So's place." They wandered another half hour and decided to begin again at the creek. They came again to "So and So's" house and Crumbine insisted the man ask directions from "So and So." "Oh hell," he replied, "I know this country." The exasperated doctor said he would enquire then, so the man grudgingly went up and knocked on the door and started to ask his wife how to find his house.[22]

The beauty of the Kansas prairies also developed an aspect of his personality that greatly enhanced his life's work later. As he spent much time crossing the prairie in his horse and buggy making his calls, it gave him "hours of time to think about and study" his patients and their problems. "Age-old customs and superstitions were, sometimes, as necessary to combat as the disease from which the patient suffered." Thus he "learned very early that we often suffered from ignorance and that we may escape through knowledge." He discovered he would have to educate his patients and the public to overcome their superstitions, old wives' tales, and plain lack of common sense about themselves and their body's enemies.[23]

Crumbine fought one such battle against the widespread acceptance of the old wives' tale that sassafras tea was a good spring tonic to "thin the blood." He finally found that ridicule was an effective weapon against superstitions such as this and he wrote for his health bulletin a story that he entitled "Sassafras Days":

> The sassafras days are here, the happiest of the year. The late winter with its sulphur and molasses did not bring the joy of living to the average boy as did the appetizing aroma of the sassafras days of spring, for nothing in all the world compares with the redolent odor of this nectar brew.
>
> Speaking for myself, it seems altogether likely that Ponce de Leon was really looking for a brew of sassafras tea when he searched this country for the fountain of perpetual

youth. Yes, indeed, for what harrowing trouble can sit at the same table with sassafras tea? What brooding misery can successfully cope with its uplifting enchantment? What dyspeptic pessimism can continue in the presence of its stimulating optimism? What accumulation of years can count the passing seasons when vivified with this elixir of youth? It simply can't be done!

The essay was widely reprinted with occasional editorial comment. The *Kansas City Star* said, in part,

Dr. Crumbine has joined the ranks of the higher medical critics who speak of sassafras tea with irreverence and tries to discredit it as a "spring tonic." It will do no harm to drink it, says the doctor, but it will not thin the blood or purify it. Right in the sassafras season, too!

It is well for the doctor that the recall is not in use in Kansas just now, for from thousands of firesides will go up a protest against having a man in the important office of Secretary of the State Board of Health who does not believe that sassafras tea, the old favorite, does not thin the blood and purify it; prevent the 'ager;' relieve rheumatism, and clear the complexion. As well tell the old-fashioned folks who were using sassafras tea when Dr. Crumbine was in knee trousers, that carrying a 'poke' of asafetida about the neck will not prevent diphtheria or the croup. As many an old-fashioned mother will say when she reads what Dr. Crumbine has to say about sassafras tea, 'and him a doctor, huh.'[24]

The fellows often made their own entertainment, which sometimes involved a hoax played on a, "tenderfoot," a newcomer to town, or especially habitual drunks. Crumbine recalled one trick that boomeranged on the perpetrators. A wealthy easterner wanted to participate in an antelope hunt, but asked his cattleman-host if they would be safe from Indian attack. His apprehension suggested a joke to the fellows and they arranged for an Indian raid during the outing. Some twenty cowboys and hangers-on at the dance halls dressed up in war bonnets and native American trappings for themselves and their horses with souvenirs left from the battle of Adobe Walls. The group lay in wait in an arroyo for the party of eight hunters, who occasionally were suggesting to the visitor the dangers they could encounter momentarily. They made certain the "dude" was on a docile, slow horse that would not spook easily. Suddenly the "Indians" rushed from their hiding place, screaming and shaking their weapons. "My God, run for your life," yelled the host and the easterner soon fell behind his friends. As the attackers drew closer, he saw his life flashing before his eyes and was certain of capture, at the least, recalling the tales he had heard of horrible torture at the hands of the natives. Suddenly he jumped off his horse and began firing at the attackers. His first shot came too near the "chief's" head for comfort and the "Indians" beat a hasty retreat. When the fellow finally arrived in town on his slow horse, the tale of his bravery had already made the rounds. The sports set up drinks for everyone and the tenderfoot's friends gave him a memorable dinner that evening.[25]

One evening during his dinner at the Dodge House, Crumbine heard "screams of terror, mixed with shouts of laughter." An Italian organ-grinder had arrived in town that day with his pet black bear. One of the town characters was dead drunk, sleeping in a room just off the bar. Some of the local sports rented the bear and put him in the room with the fellow but nothing happened. Then they thought of honey and smeared some all over the hapless sleeper. The bear immediately went to work on it and his rough tongue awakened the drunk. The poor fellow thought he was being devoured. Up he jumped, running and screaming with the bear chasing him in hot pursuit because he had not finished his dessert. Down Front Street the man ran, yelling "kill him; my God, shoot him, someone! Help!" The Italian finally caught his bear after a block or so and the fun was over. But the town drunk was the butt of jokes for a week.[26]

Entertainment sometimes came at the expense of infrequent visiting preachers, as happened when Crumbine described the first "prohib" speech in Dodge City. One day news spread around town that a "meetin" would be held that evening in the Methodist church to hear a strange crusader speak on the evils of John Barleycorn. The cowboys turned out en masse with quiet demeanor and angelic faces, apparently ready to listen and reform. The tall, lanky preacher, dressed in a Prince Albert coat, white shirt, and glossy black scarf wrapped around his high Henry Clay collar, mounted the pulpit and in a thunderous voice began his oration. Soon a screeching catcall arose, then another, soon bedlam, and the minister could not be heard above the uproar. Then a sloppy paper wad hit him in the nose, then a hymnal, then various missiles. He quickly retired to the anteroom and emerged with a tall, silk stovepipe hat, while the crowd moved outdoors. As soon as he appeared, a revolver exploded and the hat went tumbling. The Methodist brethren finally got the fellow into a rig and to the depot, the cowboys in hot pursuit. The preacher leapt on the train and disappeared. The cowboys searched thoroughly for him, to no avail, and as the train pulled away, they gave it a good send-off with catcalls and gunshots. When safely out of town, the lid to the passenger car's coal bin rose slightly, then opened. Out crawled the minister, dirty as a chimney sweep, but with a happy heart that he had escaped the savages. He never returned to Dodge City.[27]

With medical expertise of any variety so rare in the frontier area, doctors often were called upon to treat sick animals as there were no veterinarians in the early years. Crumbine eventually established an enviable record for treating livestock around Dodge City. Frank Wellman, an early pioneer in Southwest Kansas, drove through Spearville soon after Crumbine arrived there, on his way to settle a farm. One of his horses was sick. Wellman pulled the team into the livery stable and persuaded Crumbine to treat the horse until it was well enough for the family to depart. The

Stubbs brothers, who operated a general store in town, were so pleased with his care of their horses that they named a racehorse after him. The locals enjoyed a good joke at the doctor's expense when a St. Louis newspaper headlined the results of a horse race with "Dr. Crumbine Wins!" The wags promoted the rumor that their feisty doctor had made a killing at the racetrack.[28]

Once he hung his shingle, Dr. Crumbine was busy with patients, as the older doctors warned, with visits sometimes lasting twenty-four or more hours. On one such visit he discovered the role of guns in his adopted culture. A cowboy rode in one day from a ranch thirty-five miles away reporting that his boss lost an argument with a bucking broncho and had a broken leg needing attention. After a four-hour ride, they arrived at the ranch house and the doctor set the fracture. Curious about the large ranch, Crumbine looked around for three hours, then prepared to ride back to town. "Stay here," the rancher said harshly, his face paling as he spoke, and told his foreman to take his Springfield down from its rack. Pointing it at the startled Crumbine, he thundered, "Jim, take good care of the doctor's horse and see that he gets a good night's sleep." Protesting that he had patients in town needing his attention, the befuddled doctor was notified that he was "*not* leaving here until tomorrow and that's final." The next morning he examined the rancher and rode back to town. A few days later the patient came in for a checkup and gave him a generous fee. The doctor persuaded him, with little effort, to rent a hotel room so he could check periodically on his progress while the leg healed. Never argue with a gun pointed at you in the Wild West!

Samuel Crumbine adjusted quite well to this frontier environment. When he nursed Big Bill Tilghmann, a noted marshal, through a severe case of pneumonia, he found him to be as "obedient and humble as a child." He related the story of how a gang threatened to "ride him out of town" for some unknown reason. For some time thereafter, when called out at night, he walked down the middle of the street with a six-gun strapped to his side, dressed in his usual Prince Albert coat and plug hat. He was glad that Bat Masterson, who had just replaced Wyatt Earp, was his friend. The little doctor seemed fearless and was always willing to set any patient straight, no matter his size, if he refused to follow instructions. To many of his fellow citizens he was the "fighting Bantam rooster," although they were careful not to say this within his hearing. As one source expressed it, "he had no qualms in telling off his patients about the errors of their ways, regardless of size or character. The residents, both the good and the bad, accepted Dr. Crumbine's bullying meekly [because] mainly he was concerned with good health rather than morals." One of his associates observed that Crumbine "is a deceptively mild man. When he says no most people think he means maybe. What he actually means is Hell, no."[29]

On the other hand, the doctor occasionally received a dressing down from a patient. He often had to substitute as a dentist and one day a young cowboy with a toothache asked him for help. He finally pried loose and pulled out a single-root tooth. It turned out to be the wrong one! After a "severe lambasting such as few men have ever heard," the doctor politely asked, "why don't I try to put it back in?" He was successful, amid great pain, in sterilizing the molar and tapping it back in place, apparently, because the cowboy and tooth were fine a month later when the fellow checked in with him before he headed west.[30]

Along with his usual black bag, the doctor also carried in his buckboard or saddle bags, a hammer and wire-cutters for moving through barbed-wire fences, a kerosene lantern for night travel and for dimly lit homes where he had to operate, a shovel for digging out of snow banks or into one to catch some sleep before traveling further, while the storm raged. He also, of course, carried a water bag, some food, and a blanket roll. His black bag held his instruments, ipecac for an emetic, calomel for a cathartic, opium for painkiller, and a variety of items such as mercury, copper, iron, arsenic, and nitric acid for mixing prescriptions.[31]

On New Year's Day, 1886, Dodge Citians celebrated as usual. The bars offered free "Tom and Jerry" drinks to their regular customers and there was merry singing of "He's a Jolly Good Fellow." Crumbine and three of his young friends, dressed in their Prince Alberts and top hats, "young bloods," the cowboys called them, "improvised a tallyho from a two-seated spring wagon with a four-horse team." They drove up and down Front Street delivering their calling cards to friends, printed specially for the occasion with their names at each corner and a large sunflower in the center. Before they had completed their rounds, the wind turned chilly and huge dark clouds swooped down from the northwest. This was the first of the great blizzards of 1886–1887 that devastated the western ranges. The north wind roared at over forty miles an hour and the snow began to pile up so that a man could get lost just making his way from barn to house. The storm raged until the next morning when people began to dig tunnels to get out of their houses. The snow was packed deeply and one could walk across the countryside right over fences, gates, and even low buildings. Trains were stuck in deep drifts, further isolating the town. Some two hundred men and boys dug for days to clear the right-of-way. A ration train was stalled but its cargo was finally delivered by mule train. No mail, no news from the outside world. Then a second blizzard hit, again isolating the town. The air was so heavy with atmospheric electricity this time that telegraphic messages were sent out without batteries. Then another storm came, and still another until there was twenty inches of snow and the Arkansas River was frozen solid with twelve inches of ice. The dry, powdery snow filtered through shingles on the roof, through keyholes, or window cracks, to pile up in drifts on the cabin floors. When it all melted in the spring the prairies were dotted with livestock and wildlife, the shelterless animals piled up against the fences, desperately seeking refuge from the elements. Even the ubiquitous jackrabbits almost became extinct. Men, women, and children perished, or were so badly frostbitten they lost limbs. The range cattle industry and trail drives moved further westward that spring.[32]

Crumbine almost lost his life during one of these storms in 1886. Out on a call, his horse fell into a snow-filled hollow and threw the doctor and his driver into a snowdrift. They finally got the buggy righted and the horse settled down. If the horse had run away, they would have frozen to death as did many others that night.[33]

Samuel Crumbine discovered early in his practice the danger of waiting too long before calling for help. One case in particular demonstrated this problem and also of operating under primitive conditions. A couple called him one night to treat their twelve-year-old son. When he arrived the boy was semiconscious, blue, and breathing with difficulty. His left lung had collapsed and the cavity had filled with fluid, pushing his heart to the right of his chest. He should have had attention much sooner and the doctor had to act immediately! He sterilized his instruments while the mother brought clean sheets and towels, and the father rearranged the kitchen furniture. They laid the boy on the table and Crumbine punctured his left chest. This released the pressure and the fluid "came out like a geyser," drenching the apron Crumbine was wearing as a surgical gown. Despite this great shock to his body, the lad's sturdy constitution helped him to survive the ordeal. The father, a Methodist minister in the small town, had so little income that Crumbine did not charge him for his ministrations. The story had an unhappy ending, though, as the young fellow later studied to be a missionary. Before his missionary board allowed him to leave for the Orient, they required a vaccination for smallpox. He refused on the grounds that he was going about the Lord's work and He would protect him. After a year in India, the young missionary contracted smallpox and died because "he confused blind ignorance with faith," Crumbine concluded, and "closed his mind to all understanding of scientific truth, the wisdom God had permitted us to acquire."[34]

His moral judgments sometimes also overcame his natural reticence about becoming personal with patients when pregnancies were concerned. A young, beautiful girl came west with a "gentleman gambler." She asked the doctor, "with tears in her eyes," to save her from disgrace by ending her pregnancy, an event not uncommon on the lawless frontier. When he refused, the gambler first tried bribery, then threats. He stood his ground, explaining "more or less brutally," the physical and moral hazards of abortion and finally persuaded them to let the pregnancy continue. On another occasion a Santa Fe conductor telegraphed ahead to Spearville "Woman in labor. Must remove from train." When they arrived at the depot, Crumbine found the woman too far advanced in her labor to be moved. He persuaded the conductor to hold the train, clear the car of passengers, and recruit a woman volunteer. He prepared an accouchement table with a plush back of a seat placed on top of the coal box. When the baby girl soon arrived, he suggested the name of Santa Fe, to which the mother acquiesced.[35]

At that time most of a physician's work involved house calls and the frontier doctor had to ride the Santa Fe for fifty miles on either side of Dodge City to tend his patients. He recalled vividly one train ride on the branch line that connected with the Rock Island Railroad in Bucklin. It was a daily mixed train of freight and passenger cars, called the "sand-bur express." With wheat and cattle to pick up along the way and two flag stops, it often was six hours late on its thirty-mile run. Even more so if a covey of prairie chickens was flushed and the crew downed some. Then the train had to stop while the men retrieved the birds. One Sunday the wife of a railroad fireman in Bucklin was badly burned. Her local doctor was absent so the fireman asked the division supervisor to run a special train from Dodge City to Bucklin. The crew hooked a freight engine to a caboose and away they flew with Doctor Crumbine aboard, over the uneven rails. Even the conductor feared for their lives and when they arrived, remonstrated the engineer, "were you trying to kill us?" "Hell, no," came the reply, "but the superintendent said it was a matter of life and death, so I let her have all the steam she could stand—did my damnedest." The woman survived, but might not have if they had reached her much later.[36]

Crumbine had some unusual experiences while serving two terms as county coroner of Ford County. He investigated deaths by gunshot, by kicks of horses or other animal attacks, and an occasional suicide. An unusual case he found difficult to report legally involved an inmate of the county jail. The toilet had an elevated seat and the fellow raised it, put his head in the bowl, then lowered the seat until it encircled his head, and jammed his head down until the flow of water drowned him. Testimony showed the man to be mentally disturbed but Crumbine concluded that "he certainly had an inventive mind."[37]

During his first year in Dodge City, Crumbine staked a claim to a homestead and planted a crop of wheat. The climate of Western Kansas determined that this was too small an acreage to be profitable, but the farm came in handy when he was paid in kind. He credited cashless patients with 25 cents per chicken, $1 for turkeys, barley at 35 cents per bushel, wheat 20 cents, honey 5 cent per pound, ham 11 cents per pound, and butter at 12 cents—prices for which he could exchange the goods with the local merchants. At one time he had accumulated a herd of sixty-five cattle. He even took in a donkey, harness, and cart for his children for $20. When the terrible drought hit Western Kansas in the 1890s, one farmer owed the doctor $35, which he could not pay. He offered him his farm instead, which had a small mortgage on it, but Crumbine refused. A few years later the farm sold for $5,000.

In addition, he enjoyed income from his half interest in the Spearville drugstore and he later shared a similar interest in a drugstore in Dodge City. He fulfilled in a big way his boyhood dream of having drugstores. Ledgers he kept for Crumbine and Dorsett in Spearville indicates that the store included more than the usual sundries as he entered items such as flour, eggs, butter, chickens, potatoes, and other commodities found in a rural general store in the late nineteenth century. In small towns such as Spearville, merchants tried to meet all the mercantile needs possible for their customers and they also accepted these commodities for credit on purchases. In addition, in January 1888 he and John Stewart purchased the J.M. Wright and Company Drug Store in Dodge City. A brief history of Spearville notes that at the time Dr. Crumbine "had considerable other business interests." He made an effort to visit the town where he began his career in the West on every Friday afternoon to see patients and check on his business enterprises. John Stewart also operated the Eagle Pharmacy in Dodge City, which despite the competition from two other drug stores there, grew to the point where the partners needed larger quarters in 1888. During these years, Crumbine "applied himself diligently to his profession and soon built up a reputation as a skilled physician with a large and lucrative practice."[38]

Katherine was present to witness the glorious moment when he finally received his diploma and his gold medal for placing first in his class. With his degree and worldly affluence in pharmaceuticals, Samuel Crumbine at last decided he could support his "saint" from Ohio. The *Dodge City Times* announced one day in September 1890 that "Dr. S. Jay Crumbine left for the east this week. There is a sly rumor of interest concerning the trip." Another local newspaper, under the headline "Married," soon reported that Dr. S.J. Crumbine had wed "Miss Kate A. Tuercher [*sic*] on Wednesday September 17th (his birthday), 1890 at Springfield, Ohio." "The groom has resided in Ford County for a number of years," the editor added, and "he has hosts of friends who are pleased to congratulate him on his Matrimonial Venture." Two weeks later the newspaper proclaimed that Dr. Crumbine and his wife would arrive in Dodge City early "next week" and "a reception will be tendered them by the Phoenix Club." The newly-weds enjoyed a lengthy visit with friends and relatives in Pennsylvania and Ohio for their honeymoon. This included a family reunion dinner for twenty-four people with group pictures, hot cakes and smoked sausage for breakfasts, and a series of fried chicken dinners. Then came a steamboat ride down the Ohio River to Cairo, Illinois, followed by a train to St. Louis and another on to Dodge City.

The first thing Samuel did when they arrived home was to take Katherine on a tour of Front Street to expose her to the seamier types of his patients so she would get a firsthand view of the still primitive town. After that the Eastern bride would seldom be shocked at anything. Samuel and Katherine established their residence in a six-room house on one of the hillsides north of the city, looking down on Front Street, with the railroad and the river in the background. Here they raised their children, Warren Jay, born on January 29, 1892, Kansas Day, and Violet Ruth, born on March 5, 1896. Their residence became known widely for its fruit trees and flower and vegetable gardens. Crumbine built a tree house in the backyard, which he dubbed "the crow's nest." It was a great place for friends to play when they visited Warren and Violet. Katherine was quickly initiated into the life of a frontier doctor's wife because immediately after their arrival in Dodge City, he was gone for twenty-four hours, involved in a difficult childbirth.[39]

His long trips, sometimes fifty miles away from home, gave him a variety of experiences that had an impact on his development as a medical doctor. On one occasion in the springtime he decided to save time by cutting across a large pasture (in Western Kansas large pastures sometimes meant several miles across). During the drive he saw several "magic circles" ranging from a few feet to one hundred feet across. The rings were bands of dark green buffalo grass, in contrast to the surrounding pale, gray-green turf. The bands were taller, more dense, and appeared as though fertilized, which they were. When the buffalo cows and their calves were attacked by coyotes or prairie wolves, they would circle around their young, often for hours at a time, keeping the marauders at bay. Their droppings were trampled into the sod and made the grass more lush than previously. On this occasion he drove over a rise and saw a bunch of cows circled around their calves, periodically bawling and charging at a wolf, trying to hook him with their horns before he could hamstring a calf. Crumbine's sudden appearance distracted the wolf and a cow saw her opportunity to charge the animal and toss him a few feet. He ran limping away and soon the herd resumed their grazing. The scene reminded him of how often he wished that humans would care for their young in such a collective sense.[40]

By the end of the nineteenth century most doctors accepted the germ theory, but not all of the American public did, at least those on the frontier. Smallpox arrived in Dodge City in the 1890s. The school board wisely ordered all children to be vaccinated or they could not attend school. Crumbine had two patients, twin girls, whose oldest sister did not go to school because she had lost an eye in an accident. The twins' vaccination scabs had become infected and the older girl was dressing them and, at the same time, taking out her glass eye and then replacing it, thus infecting the socket. Her mother, too, had not only infected her chapped hands with the disease but also an ear that she had burned. They simply did not follow his instruction to use disinfectants. Crumbine had to fight this problem and many other frontier superstitions, such as night air being dangerous so keep the windows closed while sleeping, or hanging a bag of asafetida around a child's neck to ward off diphtheria. He concluded that his prairie patients often waited far too long before finally calling for a doctor when the patient was desperately ill, rather than seeking help much earlier. He had to combat these perplexities on a large scale later in his work with the state department of health.[41]

In the late nineteenth century, the Harvey House became an institution on western railroads. Fred Harvey met the culinary needs of travelers by building a chain of restaurants located at strategic points on railroad right-of-ways. He hired college girls as waitresses, most of whom soon found husbands in the West where females were in short supply. Crumbine the bachelor usually took his meals at the Dodge House where he could easily be found if needed. Fortunately, when Front Street and the Dodge House burned in 1886, Harvey Houses were being built on the Santa Fe with one at Topeka, Florence, and Dodge City. Crumbine began dining there immediately but, remembering the care the Dodge House took with selecting, storing, and preparing its food, he was disappointed with the way the Harvey House served their milk to customers. It came by the pitcher and the diner poured his own from this common jug. The containers were open and, to Dr. Crumbine, this appeared to be most unhealthy and dangerous, especially in the summertime with flies and other insects everywhere. He had a long discussion with "Mr. Benjamin, General Manager of the Fred Harvey Dining Car Service" and persuaded the company to bottle fresh, whole milk and serve it in these individual containers. This was the first time milk was sold in this manner and proved to be Crumbine's first notable achievement in improving public health.[42]

Samuel Crumbine sincerely believed that professional people should participate in community life through service to organizations. On arriving in Dodge City, Katherine immediately assumed the burden of superintendent of the Sunday School at the First Presbyterian Church and Samuel became one of her teachers. He also sang bass in the church choir. In addition to the Crumbine family contributions to the church, Samuel joined the Masonic fraternal order and by 1892 had worked his way through the various offices to become Worshipful Master of the local lodge, an office he held for two terms. His long rides in the countryside to visit patients gave him ample opportunity to memorize the lectures and ritualistic work of the fraternity by practicing on his horses. Katherine became a member of the Masons' sister organization, the Order of the Eastern Star, and was elected Worthy Matron while Samuel served as the local order's first Worthy Patron. He was also appointed medical examiner of the Grand Lodge of Kansas as well as for applicants for insurance with the Ancient Order of United Workmen, a very popular group in Kansas in the nineteenth century and, as noted, he served as Ford County coroner.[43]

Crumbine was always ready to fight for his principles. In 1881 Kansans amended their constitution to provide for prohibition, the first in the nation to do so. It proved difficult to enforce. The change was not good for business on Front Street but the saloons remained open with the owners each month marching down to city hall to pay their $50 fine. Some citizens went to the district judge and obtained an injunction to close the bars. City officials called a town meeting to discuss the issue. Three citizens—the Reverend J.M. Gillette, School Superintendent Warren Baker, and Crumbine—spoke vehemently against the practice of tolerance and fines. Believing the law to be sacred, Crumbine spoke of the hypocrisy of keeping the saloons open in violation of the state constitution. Reverend Gillette based his sermon the following Sunday on the same principle. He was not asked to return to the church the following year, Superintendent Baker was not reelected to his post, and Crumbine lost some of his "friends" as a result of this crusade. The issue continued to simmer and finally his friend, the mayor, was impeached for renting rooms in one of his buildings for a "joint." Someone overheard Crumbine saying the mayor was guilty of this because the area had been the doctor's suite of offices before he was asked to evacuate and make room for the saloon. The doctor was immediately called as a witness and, through his testimony, the mayor was evicted from office. The mayor was reelected several times thereafter and refused to speak to Crumbine until sympathy overcame his antipathy. He heard one day the doctor was ill and could not keep anything on his stomach. He knocked at the door and gave Katherine a bottle of champagne, expressing his wishes for a speedy recovery, and soon the two reconciled. The town eventually closed the saloons officially (with them still operating illegally as before) and Samuel Crumbine was able to maintain his self-respect even though it cost him some "friendships" temporarily.[44]

The new fad of hypnotism caught people's interest in the 1890s. Dr. Franz Mesmer of Paris insisted at that time that he could cure medical problems with wands and magnets. During the course of his experiments he added a word to our vocabulary when, by serendipity, he discovered the basis of hypnotism while trying to help a blind girl. Hypnotism quickly became a fad in America. A listing of magnetic healers through this process of "suggestive therapeutics" in Nevada, Missouri, required a half-page in the city directory in 1900. The craze eventually faded but not before Crumbine experimented with it because he thought he saw a therapeutic in it. As he noted in his autobiography, traveling showmen and medical quacks exploited the public interest with various types of demonstrations, but the Dodge City doctor proved to his own satisfaction that, contrary to legal defenses that a person would commit a crime because he was hypnotized and told to do so, you cannot make a person perform an act by hypnosis if it was contrary to his innate sense of ethics. After hypnotizing patients and curing their constipation by suggestion, and relieving headaches and neuralgia in a similar way, he experimented with a woman by trying to get her to take a silver dollar because no one could see her do it. The hypnotized girl tentatively picked up the coin then suddenly put it back. When she came to, of course, she remembered nothing of the trial. To him this proved that an honest person could not be hypnotized and persuaded to commit a crime. The "antics of traveling showmen made hypnotism unpopular," however, and he eventually lost interest in its possibilities for medical therapy.[45]

He never completely forgot his interest in hypnotism, however, and some time later he became engrossed in mental telepathy for personal, rather than medical, reasons. He had been suffering from a duodenal ulcer and, when he was on a business trip in the East, he suffered such a severe attack that he found himself forced to enter the Crile Clinic in Cleveland for an operation. Katherine believed he was still in Trenton, New Jersey on his business, and he worried about not telling her of the ordeal. She sensed something was wrong, hundreds of miles away, and was "suddenly seized by an overwhelming foreboding, and insistent impression that [Samuel] was in grave danger." She desperately needed company and called her friend, Mrs. C.F. Menninger, wife of a local physician and one of the founding fathers of the Menninger Clinic in Topeka. They took a drive in the countryside, but her worry persisted. When they returned to town, she had a telegram waiting for her from Dr. Crile, explaining that the operation was successful. When Samuel came home, she agreed that he had meant well by not letting her worry about the operation, but she "still knew something dreadful was happening." How, he wondered, "is there any other answer to such a baffling experience except telepathy?"[46]

It was a dangerous operation that required some time from which to recuperate. Crile removed a section of the stomach, spliced in some tubes, and put what Crumbine called a "time lock" on the remainder. He sewed up about half of the remaining stomach to let it rest for a while. The stitches dissolved in a few months and let the stomach open up to full size without a further operation. When it opened up, he could feel "the machinery begin to grate and grind, and notice the unoccupied end of his stomach tug and pull in an effort to get back into the game and enjoy a square meal once again."[47]

He later recalled another strange experience of mental telepathy with living things. He was hunting ducks early one morning in a swampy area a half-mile from Hoisington. He bagged a number of birds and was preparing to go to town for breakfast when he heard a Canadian goose honk. He immediately dropped to the tall blue-stem grass but the flock was too distant for a possible shot. He began to whisper "come over this way . . . over here . . . over here . . . come . . . with all the intensity of his being." Usually geese "fly to their objective in a straight line, the gander leader giving an occasional honk or none at all, except in night flying," he related. While he whispered, the flock suddenly became agitated, they all began to honk, and the leader turned and headed straight for where he lay waiting. He was so excited over the birds' behavior that he failed to get any geese, although the opportunity was excellent. No one witnessed this event and he never discussed it with anyone. He could not explain it as "it just happened so," but it seemed "to be incredible even to myself," and he concluded it was "the result of my tremendous concentration of mind over a living animated thing." The occult sciences declined in popularity, as showmen exploited them and he dropped them from his study on advice from friends that it might otherwise hurt his medical practice.[48]

Crumbine believed that everyone should, if possible, schedule an annual vacation and his family tried to do this. These trips rested him, or as he put it, "it will electrify your health." Following his ulcer surgery, he met the family in Chicago and they traveled to Little Twin Lake in Wisconsin for two months of convalescence. He loved fishing and hunting and his forced inactivity quickly led to restlessness. Finally he

Crumbine the Hunter [Courtesy of the Clendening History of Medicine Library, University of Kansas Medical Center]

could stand it no longer and persuaded his son, Warren, to take him for a boat ride. He surreptitiously took his fishing tackle along and soon hooked a large "fighting Muskie." His surgery had been only a week previously and by the time he landed the fish he was exhausted. But he was mentally refreshed because such an experience "crowds health into you." At the end of two months at the lake he was eager to return to work.[49]

These were eventful years for him and by this time political events in the state capital began to push Samuel Crumbine into the relatively new field of preventive medicine. As he indicated in his memoirs, in his twenty years of medical experience on the frontier, he had learned three lessons that were to be of great benefit to him in this new endeavor. First, he had learned to practice medicine without the benefit of trained nurses, laboratories, or hospitals and therefore discovered he could improvise to meet his needs. Secondly, he could recognize the dangers of "nostrums and the advice of professional grannies" and this had convinced him of the absolute need for sanitary precautions. Third, he "had learned what superstitious people took seriously, and something about their sacred taboos and customs." Of course, he had acquired many other important principles he would follow for the rest of his medical career but these, he believed, were of greatest import.[50]

At this point, medical knowledge was expanding rapidly and it was an exciting time to be in the profession. The germ theory was becoming widely accepted. This combined two related propositions: animal and human diseases were caused by microorganisms present in air and water and they did not arise spontaneously but came from a previous case. One by one the various bacillus were discovered. John Tyndall became aware that the "floating matter" he found in the air actually contained germs. In France, Louis Pasteur, having lost two daughters to typhoid fever, was preaching the necessity of immunization, Robert Koch of Prussia uncovered the bacillus of tuberculosis and the source of cholera. Others were revealing the causes of bubonic plague, diphtheria, and typhoid fever, and American Edward L. Trudeau established Saranac Laboratory for the study of tuberculosis. The great English doctor, Joseph Lister, was emphasizing the overweening medical concept of antiseptic surgery. In building the Panama Canal, William C. Gorgas and others conquered yellow fever in the region by exterminating the virus-bearing mosquito. As an authority on Kansas medicine noted, "the reign of the microbes had begun." These discoveries, though, were basically preventives; cures or effective therapy lay in the future, later in the twentieth century. Samuel Crumbine would join this assault on exploring the frontiers of public health, beginning with his appointment to the Kansas State Board of Health in 1899, a rather recent addition to state government.[51]

In 1859 the territorial legislature authorized the establishment of the Kansas Medical Society, an organization that fought for legislation to control the practice of medicine, a development that occurred in all frontier areas. The society in 1885 petitioned the state to create a board to promote better health, as other states were doing. This, it was thought, would help bring about controls over improper medical practice and also it would gather correct vital statistics. The society had persuaded the legislature to set standards for medical practice in 1870 by requiring a degree from "a respectable school of medicine" and to be "of good moral character." The law proved to be disappointing, and the legitimate members of the profession hoped the board of health might provide the answer to this ongoing problem. That same year Governor John Martin passed on to the state legislature a grave warning from the National Department of Health that a wave of Asiatic cholera sweeping Europe was expected to arrive soon in America.[52]

On the Kansas frontier people were apprehensive over epidemics of malaria, diphtheria, scarlet fever, and typhoid (called the "filth disease,"), but smallpox was also dreaded, and even more than any other, the danger of cholera. To prepare for this impending epidemic, states were urged to establish some type of health department if they had not already done so, as had Louisiana in 1855 and Massachusetts in 1870. By this time only Kansas and four other states had not taken this action. The legislature that session passed a concurrent resolution to approve a measure drawn up by the Kansas Medical Society to create a board of health composed of nine members. Appointed by the governor, they were to chose one of their own as chairman. The major opposition to such an organization came from a split between the eclectic and the allopath (regular) doctors over representation on the board.[53]

The legislative fiat resolved this division by requiring that no branch of medicine could have a majority on the board, so usually governors appointed three eclectics, homeopaths, and allopaths each for every year. The secretary would receive $2,000 annually, a sum raised by $500 the following year. Due to a clerical error, however, this was later lowered to $1,200, which meant that the doctor had to have a small medical practice on the side to survive financially. The board was directed to investigate the causes of diseases, "especially epidemics," and to advise on "the location, drainage, water supply, disposal of excreta [*sic*], and heating and ventilation of all public buildings." Most important, the board was ordered to gather statistics and supervise the registration of births, deaths, and marriages. All doctors were required to keep records of deaths that occurred in their practice. To achieve all these tasks, the legislature stingily placed a limit of $5,000 annually for expenses for the unpaid members. All practicing doctors were required to register with the board and they had to have two "full courses" (years) of instruction, and graduate from "some respectable school of medicine." Those who had been practicing for ten years or more were grandfathered in and those with five years were allowed a grace period of two years to take the necessary required courses. Each county was strongly urged to appoint a health officer but, unfortunately, it was several years before all 105 counties complied with this suggestion.[54]

The board reported the following year that it had assisted the towns of Topeka, Atchison, Paola, Centralia, Emporia, Holton, and Marion and the counties of Shawnee, Atchison, Miami, Nemaha, Lyon, Jackson, and Phillips in fighting epidemics of smallpox, scarlet fever, and diphtheria. The report called attention to the fact that the state was "exceedingly fortunate to escape the visitation of that dread disease cholera," but conceded that this happy news was due to the diligence of authorities in American and foreign ports. Interestingly, the account listed the causes of death that year as reported by physicians. Because there was no standard nomenclature, eleven tied for first place with 175 deaths each, including exhaustion of various types and hiccoughs. The number two killer at 174 was "sudden–cause not stated."[55]

The new board was beset with problems from the start. At its first meeting in Topeka on June 14, 1885, the members adopted a number of resolutions designed to implement what they considered a proper exercise of their powers. But the state attorney general decided otherwise. He concluded they had only advisory functions and could not assume the initiative in protecting the health of the citizens or issue punitive decisions. He further ruled that they could not require children to be vaccinated before attending school or to impose quarantines for contagious diseases, all of which rendered the board powerless.[56]

The board had to do its work under the most trying circumstances. Critics, both disgruntled doctors and dissatisfied politicians, kept up a drumfire of criticism and it had to survive the biennial attempts to abolish it immediately after its creation. In 1893, for example, a cholera threat again surfaced and the danger prompted the legislature to appropriate $10,000 to combat it, a large amount for this time period. The invasion "veered away from the Midwest" eventually, but the board, always underfunded, spent $2,200 of its money in sanitary work, mostly in Atchison, to fight a smallpox invasion and scarlet fever in other communities. Soon there were blaring headlines in various hostile newspapers about the board wasting the remaining some $8,000. The Populist secretary of the board felt compelled to devote several pages in his next report in explaining and justifying the board's actions. "He (health secretary Henry Dykes) Almost Smells Cholera in the Air," screamed one headline in the *Topeka Daily Capital* (a journal that especially despised Populists), and the *Topeka State Journal* declared that the board of health "isn't worth ten cents to the people of the State." Many saw no value in its work and sought to transfer its functions to the state Board of Medical Examination and Registration when the 1870 law creating it was declared constitutional in 1890 and the board began to function. Many doctors resented the reports required of them. But the board persevered, helping establish county health officers, gathering vital statistics, and working for unpopular quarantine regulations and enforcement, stoutly resisted in some quarters. Some physicians even condemned the concept of immunization with one deploring the injection "into the arms of our dear ones of the decomposition products derived from some animal perhaps half rotten with tubercle, anthrax, glanders, or some other foul disease." The board was assisted in 1893 when another cholera epidemic threatened and the legislature authorized the establishment of quarantine stations against infectious diseases.[57]

The board of health barely survived the even more hostile reign of the Populists. Then in the election of 1898 Republican William E. Stanley ended their control of the state government by being elected governor. Ford County Attorney Edward H. Madison campaigned for Stanley and, following his victory and his stated desire to "clean house," Stanley told him he would appoint any good man Madison named to a position in his administration. It helped that Samuel Crumbine was a staunch Republican. One day soon after the election results were known, Madison walked into Crumbine's office, handed him an envelope, and said "here is an expression of my thanks to you. It's the first time I've really been able to express myself since you saved my baby's life two years ago." Inside was Samuel J. Crumbine's appointment as a member of the state board of health in 1899. He accepted the assignment with good grace and outward pleasure, although it meant spending some time away from home occasionally, and it was no great honor or political plum. By that time the board had a small room in the basement of the capital building for an office and its secretary normally spent an hour daily in answering the mail. With all its difficulties, the board had achieved only moderate successes, although its gathering of statistics alone was worth its existence.[58]

The board, with Crumbine present, organized and elected officers but the Populist secretary, H.Z. Gill, refused to leave his office. The governor ordered his personal possessions moved into the hall and had a new lock installed on the office door. The determined Populist brought in a table and chair and continued to keep office hours in the huge corridor. It was not until the end of the month when the state auditor refused to pay him that he finally surrendered.[59]

A crisis arose in 1900 that led to a significant change in Samuel Crumbine's life in the field of preventive medicine. During his second year on the health office board, an epidemic of smallpox hit the town of Pratt. Located some seventy-five miles east of Dodge City, the population of this railway division point was dependent primarily on the railroad for its livelihood. Board of Health Secretary William Swan telegraphed Crumbine to proceed there, investigate, and take proper action. The doctor found some fifteen cases of smallpox and many unvaccinated railroad people who had been exposed to the scourge. Crumbine daringly decided not to quarantine all these exposed people in a "pest house" as usual, but to try a revolutionary new approach. He quickly quarantined in their home the cases he found, vaccinated all those who had been exposed, and released them contingent upon their reporting to a health officer periodically. This allowed the schools, businesses, and railroad workers to function as normally as possible. His treatment of the crisis was widely publicized and endorsed. At least one man expressed his gratitude for the quarantine and described a typical experience when he wrote the doctor that "my wife caught up with her sewing. We had three square meals a day, as no one came in and she was not permitted to leave.

Best of all, a cousin and her four children, who had arranged to visit us, saw the smallpox sign and left town so scared they will never come back. Thanks!"[60]

When Dr. Swan accidentally drowned in 1901, the board met after his funeral to choose a successor. They selected Crumbine because his wise handling of the smallpox crisis had proven to them that he was the "man for the job." Protesting that he did not want to leave his home and practice, they gave him time to reconsider. Katie was to become Worthy Grand Matron of the Eastern Star the next year so they agreed to let him postpone his decision until she had completed her term of office. Katherine's annual report as Grand Matron focused on the disastrous Kaw River flood in 1903. She toured the area, appointed committees to investigate, and appealed to the state chapters to aid the victims. They "responded immediately and generously."[61]

The decision was not to be made lightly. Dodge City was where he began his medical practice, where he brought his new bride to make a home, where his children were born, where the family had their closest friends. His practice was a lucrative one and he was highly respected in the community. Yet the four-year drought in the 1890s had depopulated the area and his fees were increasingly being paid by barter. And he saw challenges in the field of public health, frontiers that could be better conquered in the capital city. Finally, in 1904, with Warren ready to enter high school and with Violet especially interested in music, he decided the opportunities for him and his family would be much greater in Topeka than in Dodge City so he agreed to move to the capital.

Pulling up stakes and moving to a new life, however, can be a wrenching experience. In this instance he was leaving his practice, home, and friends of twenty years to face an unknown future on a new frontier. But he reported the event ended up being "lightened . . . by a laugh." He took his small daughter to see his new office in the capitol building and after seeing the marble floors and high dome, she responded, "Papa, when I grow up and get married I am going to have a home just like this."[62]

In July 1904 the Crumbines moved to their new residence at 1303 Tyler Street. To mark the change in his life, Samuel shaved his beard, leaving his moustache, which was to become legendary, along with his bushy eyebrows that made him a cartoonist's delight. Victorian American styles required a beard to demonstrate manliness but, by the turn of the century, less facial hair was becoming more fashionable. Also, at that time physicians were shaving their beards for "convenience and safety," because the hair might be a haven for germs.[63]

When the department of health met that summer of 1904, the state's largest newspaper, the once critical *Topeka Daily Capital*, described their gathering "in the opinion of those who attended [as] the most important meeting of the kind that has been held in the state." The doctors discussed the regulations they were preparing to request of the legislature: (1) provide for fumigation of railroad cars; (2) more

Young Crumbine [Kansas State Historical Society]

comprehensive collection of vital statistics; and (3) prevent the spread of tuberculosis with the establishment of a state sanitarium in the high, relatively dry climate of Western Kansas. Outgoing Governor Josiah Bailey addressed the gathering and S J. Crumbine read a paper he had prepared entitled "Quarantine and Necessity of Enforcing Same." He was subsequently elected, officially, secretary of the board.

This part-time position would require his developing a limited practice on the side, and he opened a medical office on Kansas Avenue for three years until his workload at the Board of Health required his attention full-time. The board's annual appropriation in 1904 was $3,080 and from this meager sum he was to receive only $1,200 in salary. The biennial report he submitted to the governor for the board requested a raise from $400 to $1,000 for the state bacteriologist to compensate for his expected increase in activity and a raise in the salary of the board's stenographer to $900 to put her on a par with the other state secretaries. He explained that "with the rapidly increasing work of the Board, and the large amount of statistical tabulation it requires an accurate, painstaking and competent stenographer to fill the position, and such services should be properly compensated." Crumbine requested no increase for himself despite the "rapidly increasing work." Among other projects, he would change the board's annual or biennial report to a monthly one to facilitate more rapid response to outbreaks of disastrous plagues. The following year he wrote to the new Governor Edward W. Hoch that

> I take it that the health and life of the people of this splendid commonwealth are quite as important a matter as one could well think of, and it is my desire and my efforts has [*sic*] been directed toward the accomplishment of making the State Board of Health of real value and service to the physicians and people of the state, and it is along these lines that I desire to make some suggestions.

He was to be full of suggestions over the next two decades and eventually to win the hearty support of the governor and legislature to implement them. Samuel Crumbine was ready to embark on an immense undertaking that would bring world fame to himself and to the State of Kansas in the field of public health.[64]

# TWO

## PROMOTING PUBLIC HEALTH

At the turn of the twentieth century, when Crumbine moved to the state capital, Americans supported a reform movement, during what was called the Progressive Era, that transformed many of their institutions over the next two decades. Surprisingly, given their conservative bent for the remainder of that century, Kansans were on the cutting edge of this regenerative movement and provided outstanding leadership in many categories. This crusade was the epitome of what the federal system should be whereby the states assumed the lead in improving the lot of the common man, experimenting with social change. Demonstratively workable reforms developed in the forty-eight state laboratories, were then applied at the national level. During this time span the Kansas legislature enacted laws to establish small debtor courts, child and convict labor restrictions, workmen's compensation, protection of female workers, employer liability, all legislation directed at benefiting the working classes. Kansas was also in the forefront in protecting and improving its public health.[1]

The rise of the germ theory and the more favorable evaluation Americans placed on the medical profession by the turn of the century, in conjunction with the direct contact physicians had with urban poverty and misery, promoted an increase in sanitation control and what people consumed. Much of this interest was also stimulated by the ubiquitous epidemics that plagued Americans. Weather was obviously a factor with summer fevers and winter respiratory infections, demonstrating its connection with public health. Communities began controlling the freedom of livestock and the uncontrolled dumping of garbage in their streets, piles of manure in their alleys, and the disposal of human waste. These problems led to the need to regulate water supplies, promote proper drainage, and construct sewage systems to fight malaria. typhoid, cholera, diphtheria, and other scourges arising from their filthy environment. Reformers of the Progressive period sought to control unhealthful food and drink. Houseflies and mosquitoes were regarded as insects whose only danger was their bite, the fly being viewed almost as a cute, friendly source of amusement. Public health work would cover the spectrum of bacteria, chemicals, and all types of contaminants.[2]

The first national efforts at regulating foods came from agrarian pressures to protect their interests and these laws utilized the congressional power to tax as a regulatory device. Congress, in other words, taxed out of existence commodities that farmers and their organizations deemed "impure." Manufacturers in the later nineteenth century, for instance, were mixing beef stearine or cottonseed oil into rancid lard to achieve a firmer texture and were selling it as "refined" lard. Not only did hog producers protest this debasement, but foreign exports of American lard declined drastically as Europeans complained about this adulteration. The power of meat packers and Southerners proved too powerful, though, and Congress failed to legislate against this practice. At the same time the legislators took action against the practice of mixing flour. A goodly amount of the wheat flour produced in America contained alum that whitened the product, especially when cheaper corn flour was mixed with it. An even more questionable practice was revealed with the discovery that mineraline, a white clay of North Carolina, was being ground up and mixed with an inferior grade of wheat flour. "No civilized country in the world ... gives so little protection to the consumers of food and drink ... as in this country," proclaimed Senator William Mason of Illinois. With his leadership, in June 1898 Congress forced the labeling of "mixed flour" with a small tax and this ended the practice. American "filled" cheese also occasioned European cheese buyers to protest and in June 1896 Congress levied a prohibitory tax on that product. A short time later Congress responded to the dairy interests by taxing heavily the process of renovating rancid butter and the artificial coloring of oleomargarine to make it resemble butter in May 1902.[3]

The problem of impure food, drink, and drugs in the early twentieth century, however, extended far beyond dairy products because of the development of scientific processes to adulterate and to preserve foods. Food processors became ever more adept at adulterating their products to make them more marketable—and sometimes more dangerous. Reformers of the period, beginning at least in 1880, agitated for controls. They were immeasurably assisted by what are now called investigative journalists, then labeled Muckrakers, who wrote articles and books of description and exposure. Ida Tarbell exposing the nefarious tactics of Standard Oil, Lincoln Steffens describing the corruption of machine politics in control of the governments of large cities, or David

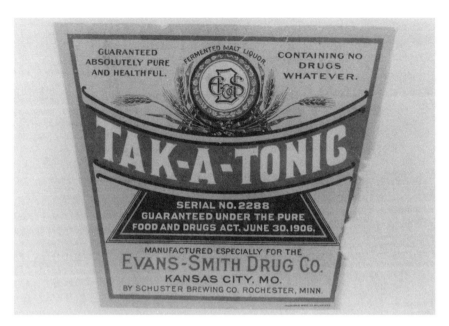

Tonic Label [Courtesy of the Clendening History of Medicine Library, University of Kansas Medical Center]

Graham Phillips' book *The Treason of the Senate*, describing how the upper house managed to defeat changes, aroused widespread public indignation and demands for action. Food and drugs, too, had their proponents of reform, but change did not come quickly.

Reporter Samuel Hopkins Adams, though not a doctor, was familiar with medical matters and became indignant over the products of the patent medicine business. He methodically studied their advertising, gathered samples for his chemist to analyze, and asked experts if the ingredients could result in the curative claims made by their manufacturers. In 1905 the Muckraking journal, *Colliers*, carried the first of his series of exposures entitled "The Great American Fraud." Eighty million Americans, who spent $75 million yearly for patent medicines, consumed vast amounts of alcohol, narcotics, and dangerous opiates in their efforts to achieve good health. Lydia Pinkham's Vegetable Compound was one-fifth alcohol, accused Adams. Peruna, widely advertised nationally as the surest cure for catarrhal diseases and endorsed by fifty congressmen, contained 28 percent alcohol, he claimed. A one-dollar bottle cost the manufacturer about 15 cents to produce. Liquozone, whose advertisements were carried in William Jennings Bryan's journal, *The Commoner*, was a nostrum promising to cure problems ranging from dandruff to dysentery. It contained 99 percent water and 1 percent sulphuric acid and traces of hydrochloric acid. Adams discovered that a good dose of soothing syrup really pacified the baby but it also made her an alcoholic. Some contained significant amounts of opium. Country doctors such as Samuel Crumbine spent much of their time trying to cure alcoholic babies who received their temporary habit inadvertently from their health-conscious mothers. Muckraker Adams had the following conversation with a public health official:

> Let us buy in large quantities the cheapest Italian vermouth, poor gin, and bitters. We will mix them in the proportion of three of vermouth to two of gin with a dash of bitters, dilute and bottle them by the short quart, label them *'Smith's Revivifier and Blood Purifyer*; dose one wineglass before each meal; advertise them to cure erysipelas, bunions, dyspepsia, heat rash, fever and ague, and consumption; and to prevent loss of hair, smallpox, old age, sunstroke, and nearsightedness, and make our everlasting fortunes selling them to the temperance trade.

"That sounds to me," Adams responded, "very much like a cocktail." "So it is," the health official agreed, "but it's just as much a medicine as Peruna and not as bad a drink."[4]

The pure food movement found an effective ally in the national department of agriculture. Harvey Washington Wiley trained to be a medical doctor but eventually found that his real interest and life's work lay in analytical chemistry. He taught chemistry for several years at the fledgling Purdue University, but left this post in 1883 to become chief chemist in the department of agriculture and began a two-decade struggle for better food laws. At first he specialized in promoting sorghum sugar production in an effort to make America independent of foreign sugar sources, but the national problem of food and drugs soon captured his attention, especially after the Muckrakers began their investigations. Wiley was concerned for the remainder of his career, not so much with adulterants, but with the fact that many food labels did not tell the purchaser what should be known about the ingredients. The consumer had the right to freedom of purchase, he believed, but should be protected by labels that described honestly what he was consuming. Beginning in 1902 he recruited his famous "poison squad," twelve young men who worked in the department of agriculture and who pledged to follow his rules for a special program of food consumption. First they determined the quantity of food each of their bodies required in order to maintain normal health and weight, followed by a testing period for the effects of substances they consumed, then a follow-up to correct disturbances that had taken place, if any, to the body during the experiment. All this required a great deal of laboratory work in analyzing and weighing food and bodily wastes. These trials continued for five years, with the testing of preservatives and additives and publishing the results in a series of bulletins made available to health officials across the country.[5]

Congress engaged in lengthy and sometimes bitter discussions over his findings for several years. Both sides in the debates organized their lobbying forces for the coming struggle. The National Wholesale Liquor Dealers Association, the Proprietary Association (patent medicines), the National Food Manufacturers Association, the National Baking Powder Association, and lesser groups, along with the publishers of their advertisements, mounted a huge offensive in Washington to lobby Congress for their persuasion. Wiley was indefatigable in cultivating the support of the American Medical Association, the National Retail Grocers Association, the National Association of Dairy and Foods Departments, the Consumers League, and especially influential, the powerful General Federation of Women's Clubs, to rally support for the reform effort. The struggle continued for several years until a significant turning point came in 1906 when Upton Sinclair published *The Jungle*. This novel, originally written to promote socialism, described in stomach-turning detail the incredibly filthy practices in the Chicago meat-packing industry. The book prompted President Theodore Roosevelt to appoint a special investigatory commission whose report verified Sinclair's description of conditions. Roosevelt then threw the considerable support of the White House behind the reform movement and July 30, 1906, Congress enacted both the meat inspection requirement and the pure food and drug law. The latter prohibited the manufacture, sale, or transportation of adulterated or fraudulently labeled foods, drinks, or drugs in interstate commerce.[6]

As usual with significant reforms, it was one matter to secure the law and quite another to enforce it. The law of 1906 authorized state health officials to report violations, thus providing the machinery for federal–state cooperation for implementing it. The tremendous widespread public interest generated by the national effort to obtain a pure food law redounded to the struggles on the state level, led by Samuel J. Crumbine in Kansas, for a similar one. The movement was severely handicapped by the fact that, at the turn of the century, there were no full-time public health services worth mentioning west of the Wabash River or south of the Mason–Dixon Line. But Crumbine would change this.

Soon after becoming its secretary, Crumbine surveyed the work of his health department in the nineteenth century, through its reports. In its second annual report in 1887 the secretary, Dr. J.W. Reddin, had noted that the board and local health officials were at work in "the broad fields of hygiene and sanitary science." The secretary warned of the dangers of typhoid and malarial fevers from polluted water wells that contained "dangerous invisible essences" (an archaic term). Crumbine found his report "interesting" because at that time neither the typhoid bacilli nor the identification of mosquitoes as carriers of fevers had yet been discovered. That year Reddin called the first state conference on sanitation held in Wichita. Mary Elizabeth Lease of Wichita, the famous Kansas Populist, was a former school teacher and addressed the meeting on school hygiene. She quoted Dr. Oliver Wendell Holmes who said that "all the diseases and ills which humanity inherits can be cured, but that with many of them we must begin two or three hundred years before the patient is born." Therefore, she observed, "we cannot begin too soon with the children of today who will be the men and women of tomorrow. Out of the school systems of today are to come the perfect physical race of a new era." The doctor concluded that she was a "prophet" when she observed that mankind was unaware of "the wonders that science will reveal in the future [but] there is little doubt that at the close of the 20th century the foul disease that affects humanity will be under the control of, and many of them stamped out by the scientific physician."[7]

The fourth annual report in 1889 noted that all 105 counties in the state were organized and eighty-three of them had established some kind of a health board or agent. Secretary Reddin emphasized the demand for and distribution of literature and of his annual reports that came from across the state. "It seems clear," Crumbine concluded, "that Dr. Reddin was fully conscious of the need to instruct the people in the plans, needs, and objectives of the newly organized state and local boards of health." He also gave high marks to the secretary's paper at the annual meeting that year, entitled "Salus populi, suprema est lax," or "The health of the people is the supreme law," as being "very good." Crumbine thought both the title and the education of the people was quite important. The following year he emphasized the work of the state sanitary commission and the papers presented at its convention in Lawrence. "Sewage and Drainage of Lawrence" by Professor F.O. Marvin, "Polluted Water" by Professor F.N. Snow, and an address on adulterated food and drugs by Professor L.E. Sayre, with comments by Professor E.H.S. Bailey "made it much easier for me to get the legislative actions looking to their correction" later, he believed. Dr. Reddin encountered many problems in enforcing the rules of quarantine and the issue of abatement of sanitation nuisances. They were difficult to implement and often were simply ignored because of the lack of knowledge of public health necessities, and this attitude was encouraged by "some malicious and uninformed doctors living in total ignorance of the laws of sanitation."[8]

C.F. Menninger later described one of Reddin's experiences to Crumbine. During a scarlet fever epidemic, a health officer "in the southern part of the state" acted severely in quarantining a family "with a light case." Scarlet fever had claimed two lives in the community, but the man of the house resisted the strict ruling. The health officer then took him to court. The judge supported the law and fined him, threatening a jail sentence if he broke it again. The fellow had "a good deal of political influence" and won support from others in a similar situation with regard to the unpopular quarantine law. He appealed to the state legislature and "quite a ruckus was raised about it." Menninger recalled that this resulted in some doctors opposing Reddin "because of the mildness of this case and the rigidity with which the health officer insisted on the quarantine."[9]

The opposition to the board of health was strong enough that the legislature again considered abolishing it. The "courageous Daniel" of the board resigned as secretary that year rather than be "cast into the den of lions," Crumbine concluded, because of these "vicious attacks from certain doctors and laymen opposed" to the action of enforcing the board of health rules. "I think I felt, at times," the doctor later admitted, "something of the hidden opposition and jealousy, especially from certain doctors and violators of the food laws." In 1891 the board of health appealed to the governor and sent a memorial to the legislature to enact a strong statute compelling counties to organize boards of health and to enforce compliance with the state board rules and orders. Crumbine summed up the board of health's frustrations in enforcing orders and his own public philosophy by observing,

> In the administration of public health service, it is necessary at times, to invade the exclusive territory in which the doctrine of individual rights and the sacred personal liberty dominate in the rule of action. Arguments and admonitions are alike futile.
>
> Every encroachment is strictly resisted. This Kingdom, too, must be taken by violence.

Dr. Crumbine would follow this philosophy in enforcing food and drug laws, along with a careful effort to educate the public to demand compliance with the health statutes and board rulings.[10]

Based on this background and his own experiences as a doctor, he took four important steps over the next several years to ensure his campaigns for public health improvement were successful. First, he established his board of health report as a monthly publication, not only to keep doctors throughout the state as current as possible on medical developments, but also to propagandize the public into supporting his reforms. As he noted, "we have outgrown the mimeographed page" of the bulletin previously published. He announced in his first issue in 1905 that the state bacteriologist would make available "mailing tubes and sputum boxes" in every county and he asked county health officers to designate "a responsible druggist to be the repository" for them. Specimens would be analyzed in the state laboratory in Topeka by Dr. Sara E. Greenfield, the current state bacteriologist who received $75 monthly for this work. If a specimen tested positive, the news was telegraphed back to the submitting doctor for immediate action. Second, Crumbine organized the county health officers as a significant force in his campaigns and thus made "the state's capitol, not the 105 county seats, the center of health related decisions." Thirdly, he utilized scientists from the state university and agriculture college to good effect in his tests and his propaganda campaigns. Finally, he secured and maintained political support across the state for two decades by keeping his department out of politics and thus ensuring the sustenance of key politicians who approved his nonpartisanship approach.[11]

Crumbine later wrote that "support or popular approval for any work must be based on three fundamental principles: first, that it meets a public need; second, that the public is made acquainted with that need, and with the means and measures used to meet adequately the situation; third, that the work be conducted impartially, judiciously, fearlessly, and justly to all interests and persons concerned, consistently keeping in mind the objective to be obtained rather than the persons who may be involved." He followed these precepts objectively, not only in pursuing food and drug controls, but in all his campaigns for improving public health.[12]

One warm September afternoon he was sitting in his office with nothing in particular to do. The stenographer and the secretary had finished their letters and the quarterly report of the department. Crumbine's job was primarily to compile the monthly reports on births and deaths, which he had completed. Looking for something to occupy his time, he began thumbing through a Kansas statute book. Suddenly a paragraph caught his eye—it was the dormant pure food law of 1889. This chance discovery transformed his lethargic office into one of bustling activity. It "changed Kansas from a state where practically nothing was done for the health of its people to one where the death rate is perhaps the lowest in the United States," wrote one editor. "It also enlarged his office in the next few years to one of thirty-five employees." For the next six years the doctor was "laughed at and jeered more than almost any man in Kansas. But he doesn't mind," the newspaper account asserted, "because he knows what he is doing and because he is accomplishing results and bringing health to his state."[13]

The statute everyone had forgotten was the only law in Kansas at that time that provided for regulation of food and drugs. Proponents of national pure food and drug laws in the late nineteenth century generally were frustrated but finally managed to persuade the Congress to enact a limited one in 1888. Modeled on the English law of 1875, the act attempted to prohibit the manufacture and sale of adulterated food and drugs in the District of Columbia (DC), over which Congress exercised complete control. The following year the Kansas legislature enacted a primitive control program based on the DC law. It prohibited the manufacture or sale of adulterated food, drugs, and drink if they (1) differed from the standards of strength, quality, or purity of the *United State Pharmacopoeia*; (2) had substances mixed in, or extracted from them to lower, depreciate, or injuriously affect their quality, strength, or purity; and (3) "consisted wholly or in part of diseased, decomposed, putrid, infected, or tainted substances." The act also outlawed the staining, powdering, coloring, mixing, or coating of these products in order to conceal damage or inferiority and provided penalties of $25–$100 fines and/or imprisonment in county jail for thirty to one hundred days.[14]

It was not until two years later that the "first prosecution, so far as it is known," was undertaken under the law. C.L. Burnham of the Burnham-Krupe Grocery of

Topeka sold one pound of Broken Turkish Mocha and Java Coffee on July 31, 1891. N. D. Church, analytical chemist for the city, described it as about 50 percent broken coffee berries and 50 percent chicory root and parched peas, with two parts chicory and one part peas. The defense introduced witnesses who testified that "every grocer in town sold large quantities of similarly adulterated coffee." The grocerman argued, to no avail, that the compound was "recognized as an ordinary article of food" and its label notified the purchaser that "it was not a pure article of coffee." The grocer was found guilty and fined the minimum of $25 and court costs. Enforcement of this weak law was spasmodic, though, and eventually nonexistent.[15]

This was the statute Crumbine hoped he might enforce when he discovered it some fifteen years later. He first sought the state attorney general's opinion on August 31, 1904, asking "who is the proper authority to enforce the adulteration of foods, drinks, and drug laws?" State Attorney General C.C. Coleman replied, "the statute does not make it the duty of any particular officer to enforce the pure-food laws. The duty of enforcing these laws is with the general executive officers of the State, the same as other laws." Crumbine also asked him whether or not he could use some of his board's meager expense money to purchase food for adulteration tests. The response was an emphatic "NO." As a current observer noted, he was "gentle and quiet, always pleasant and smiling, but he has a six-inch vein of fight in him when he gets on the right scent." Crumbine boldly decided he was one of the "general executive officers" and took $20 of his own hard-earned money to purchase some commonly used groceries. He sent the samples for analysis to the board's official chemist, Professor E.H.S. Bailey, chairman of the chemistry department at the University of Kansas. This began the great cooperation between Crumbine's board and university scientists that was later extended to the University of Kansas Medical School and Kansas State College of Agriculture in Manhattan. Bailey found the foods to be loaded with adulterants, preservatives, and colorings and he published a startling report on them in January 1906. Bailey also wrote a pamphlet on procedures for women to use in simple kitchen tests to detect common adulterants in foods and drinks.[16]

Among other irregularities, Professor Bailey found that about three-fourths of the flour sold in Kansas had been bleached to a more appealing bright white with nitrous oxide, the substance that peroxide blondes used on their hair, or laughing gas for an anesthetic. The process added nothing to the product but made its appearance more appealing to the housewife. But the doctor warned consumers that the bleaching rendered the flour so antiseptic that it resisted digestive juices, thus presenting a health menace. Fruit bleached with burning sulphur had to be labeled and sold as bleached fruit and Crumbine insisted that the same rule must apply to this bleached flour.[17]

Crumbine also conducted his own tests. He was concerned over the "embalmed beef" of Armour and Company that soldiers of the Spanish–American War claimed killed more men than Spanish bullets. He borrowed three young canines from the city pound and put them on a special diet. He fed one dog meat laced with borax, a common preservative at the time; he fed another dog meat with benzoate, another widely used preservative; and the third was given meat with no preservative added. The neighbors complained about the howling and yapping of the canines, but he assured them it was an important experiment and the animals would soon disappear. After six weeks on this diet the dog consuming borax gained one pound, the one with benzoate three pounds, and the one with fresh meat gained a pound a week. This convinced him that preservatives should not be used or at best sparingly. He noted that manufacturers argued that climate differences and long shipping routes necessitated these adulterants in order to preserve the products. Most of the preservatives used, he maintained however, were to conceal inferior products and to prevent further deterioration of the items. Crumbine would permit a limited use of coal tar dyes in food and drinks but, like Wiley, would insist on honest labeling of the kind and amount of adulterants used.[18]

Dr. Crumbine particularly made sensational news with his campaign for pure oysters. Kansas is about as far as one can get from oceans, but for some reason oysters were highly popular in the state at the turn of the century. As C. Robert Haywood notes, "oysters whole, smoked, scalloped, fried, in soup, or on the half-shell, were excuse enough for a party, celebration, benefit, or simply dining out." They were the specialty of Hall's Oyster Bay in Wichita but churches and lodges in small towns especially featured oyster suppers for fund raisers. "Perhaps the remoteness of Kansas from the oyster banks of the coast," Haywood added, made Kansans "crave them as special, exotic delights." There also was the widely accepted myth on the frontier, of course, that the sea food was a strong aphrodisiac. Some were shipped to Kansas and canned but they were most popular when brought in fresh in wooden tubs. The forty-eight-hour trip by railroad, with the oysters packed in ice, provided ample opportunities for careless handling and exposure to contamination.[19]

Normally the ice melted during the long trip and had to be replaced. Oysters are at their best when taken from ocean beds and eaten fresh when they are a dull-gray and thin. When packed in ice for shipment, they absorb the melted water and turn white and plump, gaining weight in the process. One day a railway clerk, told Crumbine about an incident that occurred in an express car that he felt compelled to report. Crumbine described the episode well:

> At a certain station it became necessary to re-ice the oysters; a dog was tied next to these tubs; one of them upset; its contents spilled on the dog and on the floor. One of the expressmen said, "here's a hell of a mess! What are we going to do?" The other replied, "they say oysters are dumb; so I guess they won't tell if we put them back in the tub."

After that the two scooped up the oysters with their dirty hands and a broom, put them in the tub along with a cake of ice that had been laying on the floor, then fastened the lid on the tub. After this they had a good laugh, scrubbed down the dog, and washed their hands.

By the time my friend had finished this story I was mad as a hornet.

Crumbine quickly found that he had to deal with only two express companies who were the consignees of all the oysters shipped into the state. He notified them immediately that they were in violation of the pure food law and all such shipments and similar incidents must cease at once. When company officials proved willing to listen to reason, he suggested replacing the wooden tubs with metal containers with their tops securely fastened and to refrigerate the oysters with ice outside those containers, a process that became known as "seal-shipt," and this would prevent adulteration from the melting ice water. It would also result in the oysters arriving in their natural condition. Ice at that time was of doubtful purity as it was cut from rivers and ponds in the winter and packed in sawdust until used in warm weather. The companies agreed to the new packaging plan and proceeded to use it across the country. Kansans thus pioneered in a new national process of shipping fresh seafood that not only benefited themselves but other people located some distance from oceans.[20]

After getting used to them in their natural state, Kansans began to enjoy oysters as they were eaten on the East Coast, thin and gray. Dr. Crumbine estimated that his fellow citizens consumed 180,000 gallons of this seafood annually and, with a 20 percent content of water previously, this meant, among other things, a savings of $54,000 for them. These negotiations required several conferences and before they were completed Crumbine expected a court case to result. To prepare for this, he charged Professor J.T. Willard of the Kansas State College of Agriculture with analyzing samples of oysters from towns across the state. The chemist found traces of copper in all of them, leading to the conclusion that they needed oyster samples from all of the shipping points on the East Coast for further analysis and comparison. The close of the oyster season ended the study temporarily but in the fall with the new season, Willard traveled to Washington and secured some samples and made arrangements for agents to forward specimens from Philadelphia, New York, and Baltimore. After extensive research, expecting the copper to have been added as a preservative, they discovered that the metal was a normal constituent of oysters and that a trace of copper is important for nutritional health. Based on this research, the Kansas board of health established a new minimum standard for oysters; it required them to be "not less than 10 percent of total solids." Many shippers then sent them to Omaha, Kansas City, Missouri, or St. Joseph in the same old process, and some of them were repackaged according to Kansas standards and forwarded to the Sunflower state. As usual, it took some time to convince all shippers on the East Coast to package them properly but over time they adopted Kansas criteria for their shipments. Kansas thus became the first state in the Union to take this action and to establish proper standards for shipping that prevented them from becoming adulterated.[21]

As Dr. Crumbine observed, "we had to blaze our own trails. In that period people would believe anything, buy anything, eat anything, drink anything—and with the sorriest kind of results." He and his chemists investigated many foods, drinks, and medicines and published their results in the department's monthly bulletin. They found that Dr. Turner's Shaker Neurogen was guaranteed to be "an absolute cure for all nervous troubles" but contained 75.3 percent alcohol and "nothing else of benefit to the nervous system." Many people with whom the doctor discussed the value of the potion were forcing themselves to drink a bottle of it daily. Cook's Gold Bond Oil claimed to be a cure for eighteen diseases, "some of which," the bulletin reported, "are ordinarily considered incurable." Trying to be helpful, Crumbine noted that its high percentage of turpentine might make it "useful in thinning paint." Burke's White Pine Balsam claimed "to be a cure for all throat, lung, and chest diseases," but he questioned its curative powers because of its large amount of chloroform. The Chicago manufacturer of a very popular gingersnap claimed he was being persecuted when Crumbine denounced the cookies for containing broom straw, splinters, and mouse hair. A pepper popular with cooks was found to be 90 percent ground olive pits. The Wolff Packing Company of Topeka was accused of using borax to preserve sausage. Several laboratory reports noted that alum was a common ingredient used in baking soda. Otto and Huehne Company of Topeka produced "Silver Leaf" tomato catsup that contained salicyclic acid and either benzoic acid or sodium benzoate as preservatives.[22]

Crumbine even helped enforce the Prohibition law when he swore out a warrant in 1908 for a Kansas City brewer who shipped a load of beer to Junction City. Its labels showed a lower percentage of alcohol than the analysis found. "This is the first seizure of goods in Kansas for alleged violation of the pure food act," one newspaper reported.[23]

A tragic accident occurred before the legislative session of 1907 opened and gave Crumbine a valid reason to ask the solons to tighten up the regulations they were considering. During play a sixteen-month old child, Lois Closen of Ellenwood, secured a bottle of medicine that one of the elders of the family was taking to relieve kidney problems. It was Vesitone and the wrapper described it as a "combination of simple and harmless vegetable or herbal remedies that affects in a most wonderful manner the change desired." It was advertised as "A wonderful Cure of kidneys and bladder weaknesses." The father was uncertain about the number but believed the baby had swallowed some ten tablets by the time he discovered the accident. He tried first giving her soothing syrup for relief. The child continued to remain "rigid" and became unconscious, so he attempted to induce vomiting with a mixture of salt water and mustard. This was too late. Lois remained unconscious until she died forty-eight minutes after swallowing the tablets. Crumbine sent them to Professor Sayre who analyzed them and found they contained a grain of alkaloid material, most of which was strychnine. Sayre, a member of the national committee revising the *United States Pharmacoepia*, and his colleagues planned to ask Congress to amend the law to require honest labeling on drugs. He and the doctor cleverly appealed to the state legislators to amend the state pure food and drug bill they were currently considering to require accurate labels on all medicines containing dangerous poisons. They argued, successfully, that they were not "advocating this amendment to the bill because we are physicians, but for protection to our families." They insisted that if the bottle had been honestly labeled, the parents of baby Lois would have kept the bottle out of her reach and "there is every reason to believe the child would be alive today."[24]

Fred A. Snow, chairman of the legislative committee of the Kansas State Pharmaceutical Association, said he received telegrams and telephone calls "all day long" from druggists who objected to adding "caffeine, or other alkaloidal substances, or active poisonous principles" to the list of prohibitions. They argued that this would "have the effect of driving the patent medicines from the State" and would "prevent the druggists from compounding their own, even such as face lotions, cough medicines, etc." To drum up opposition, the manufacturers sent messages "throughout the state," mobilizing their forces. Druggists then sent in the following telegram to their legislators: "House bill #30 detrimental to our interests. Will appreciate your efforts against it." Country newspaper editors, who profited from patent medicine advertisements, wired the following message: "label clause in food and drug bill should be amended to conform strictly with national law or great confusion will result. Please look after it and greatly obliged." Fortunately, they lost this campaign and the measure passed. Crumbine now had a law with some teeth that could be enforced.[25]

Crumbine made innumerable presentations to wholesale grocers and groups of retail dealers, informing them he was trying to prevent, not punish, wanting to make certain they understood the law and did not unintentionally violate it. He instructed his agents to use tact and restraint, and his approach paid off. The public gradually became aware that he was not a sensationalist, but was trying to help and protect them. He staged a pure food show at the Kansas Mid-winter Exposition of 1907, with John Kleinhans, "an expert on foods and knows the tricks of the trade," preparing much of the exhibit. They used pairs of foods, one pure and the other in the condition in which it was purchased, to show how the food should be if the law was obeyed. The doctor employed dramatic techniques of microscopic demonstrations of food to women's clubs across the state. Glazed coffee, colored vinegar, mislabeled beer, drinks of lemonade were analyzed. He met the Ringling circus at the railroad station in

Topeka and warned them not to sell their usual combination of citric acid and water as lemonade. He threatened legal action against butchers who were selling hamburger spiced with embalming fluid. He sent warnings to mothers that their cough syrups really were soothing their babies because they were getting gloriously drunk from the high alcoholic content. Mrs. Winslow's Soothing Syrup contained morphine and sulphate, he advised, and Dr. Moffett's Teethina Teething Powder contained powdered opium. Along with these exposures came a drive by the Kansas Medical Society to remove patent medicine advertisements from newspapers. Editors fought this bitterly because this was a principal source of their revenues. Arthur Capper was adamant about retaining them in his publications until he ran for governor. Every medical society in the state pledged to work for his defeat and his loss by twenty-nine votes permitted them to claim they had succeeded.[26]

With this mass of scientific evidence of adulterated products and widespread public support for his cleanup campaign and the need for more authority, it was easy for Crumbine to persuade the legislature to enact a meaningful pure food and drug law, especially after Congress passed its national law in 1906. In March 1907 the state legislature reenacted basically the provisions of the Kansas law of 1889, along with some significant additions that provided for adequate enforcement. The major objection to the measure came with an attempt to postpone it going into effect until October 1, but this effort lost and there was no opposition on final passage. The state board of health was authorized to make, publish, and enforce rules and regulations on adulterated food, drugs, and drink as long as they conformed to the regulations of the national department of agriculture. The University of Kansas School of Pharmacy was assigned the task of examining drugs based on the standards established in the *United States Pharmacaoepia*. The University of Kansas and the Kansas State College of Agriculture were delegated similar functions in testing food and drink and the institutions were authorized to employ additional chemists for this purpose. The law instructed the governor to appoint four food inspectors, one of whom was to be "a practical dairyman," and these people would investigate conditions and forward samples to the chemists for analysis. The salaries of the four could not exceed $100 monthly each and expenses and the board's secretary, their supervisor, had his salary raised to $2,500. The senate approved the measure thirty-two to zero and the lower house vote was seventy-seven to three.[27]

Also in 1907, the legislature enacted a water control law whereby the board of health was to establish standards for public water systems and municipal or private companies were required to file certified copies of plans and surveys of proposed water systems with the board for its approval. The statute forbade the discharge of untreated sewage into water systems and authorized the board of health to inspect and force current public water plants to comply with its regulations. The proposal cleared the senate thirty-six to one and the house sixty-three to one. An additional measure authorized the board of health to contract with the U.S. Geological Survey to study Kansas waters with a time limit of two years and expense of $1,500. The survey would determine the nature and condition of natural water, sewage and industrial waste, and water-borne diseases in water systems already in existence and sources for the future.[28]

The board of health met with its secretary days after the food law was enacted and agreed upon rules and regulations patterned after those established by the department of agriculture. To make certain they were on sound footing before proceeding further, Crumbine forwarded the list to the attorney general for his opinion concerning their legality. C.C. Colemen replied:

> I have given this matter some consideration, and have compared carefully each of the rules in connection with the section of the statute upon which you state you have founded them. I agree with you in every particular as to the powers of the Board and its duty in the premises. I find the rules are each and all authorized by the law. I think this move on the part of the Board is fully warranted by the circumstances now existing in the State, and you will have no trouble enforcing the rules pro-mulgated under the provisions of the law as it now exists.

This gave Crumbine the green light to proceed with his plans to clean up food and drink in Kansas. By this time he was so occupied with his public health work that he had to abandon his private practice in 1907.[29]

It was not long before a food company challenged these rules, carrying the case to the United States Supreme Court. The Corn Products Refining Company, an Illinois business, produced "Mary Jane" corn syrup, composed of 80 percent glucose, 15 percent molasses, and 5 percent sorghum. The company based its complaint on a decision arising in Indiana that protected companies from revealing the contents of their product, which would assist their competitors. The Indiana board of health had a number of pure food restrictions that went beyond national standards. In *Savage v. Jones*, the Supreme Court struck down these extensive rules of Indiana on the basis of the power of Congress exclusively to control interstate commerce. The court reasoned that the Indiana rules contained an unconstitutional requirement to force the company to reveal the contents of its products, a stipulation not intended in the national regulations.[30]

The Kansas board of health required products containing glucose to be labeled as a "compound" and the Corn Products company sought to have this rule struck down on the basis of the *Savage* decision. In *Corn Products Refining Company v. Eddy*, however, the high court sustained the Kansas rule on the basis it followed the national guidelines "almost literally." The national code forbade forcing the manufacturer to reveal his formula except for securing "freedom from adulteration or misbranding."

Syrup Label [Courtesy of the Clendening History of Medicine Library, University of Kansas Medical Center]

The justices decided that the Kansas code containing the phrase on compounds that followed the national requirement, "or the rules and regulations of the State Board of Health and its subsequent extension requiring labels on compounds," to be legal in regard to requiring glucose to be labeled as a compound. This point overrode any company rights to avoid revealing the contents of their product.[31]

The governor appointed Harry Bell of Kansas City, Kansas, A.G. Pike of Ft. Scott, and John Kleinhans of Topeka as state food inspectors and A.H. Robey of Stafford as dairy inspector. The statute made Crumbine, or the current secretary of the board of health, chief investigator. The group met in Topeka soon after the law was approved to plan strategy and approach to enforcement. They decided to send notification to dealers that they had until November 1907 to dispose of goods not in compliance with board regulations. Among other requirements they mandated that grocers could not display foodstuffs, fruits, and vegetables, or any food that did not need to be peeled for use, in open air in front of their stores without glass covers. In May 1907, Crumbine began traveling across the state, holding meetings to explain the new law and regulations. His powers of explanation and persuasion contributed much to compliance with the law and his crusade to purify food and drugs for Kansas consumers.[32]

These conferences often resulted in those concerned with the law organizing to govern their industry. As an outcome of Crumbine's visit to Wichita, for example, the local dairymen organized into the Dairymen's Association of Wichita to help enforce the law. Crumbine had urged, in an interview with the *Wichita Eagle*, that the city appoint a local inspector to enforce the state dairy laws. A few days later food inspector John A. Kleinhans followed up his chief's visit with an outline of the board's health rules, resulting in the meeting to form the association. The group agreed to try and raise the quality of milk in the area to the law's standard of three and one-fourth percent butterfat for milk and eighteen percent for cream. Their primary motive in organizing, obviously, was to make certain all cows and milking facilities of dairy producers, "dairymen or families," be inspected by the same standards of sanitation because they believed, often correctly, that those of the "private families" were not as high as theirs.[33]

On the other hand, Crumbine's attacks on patent drugs, called proprietary medicines, was strongly opposed by the Proprietary Association of America. Sensing huge financial losses if the doctor went unchecked, "they responded by pouring thousands of dollars into a campaign to discredit Crumbine's work," and this was where the doctor's political acumen was rewarded. The medicine men insisted that the governor silence "this thorn" and when he supported the doctor instead, threatened to fund an opponent in the upcoming election who would respond to their demands. The powerful interests were not accustomed to taking no for an answer. They sent a politician to talk to Governor Edward Hoch who gave the man "a half-humorous lecture on ethics and handed him his hat." They then sent a lawyer to threaten Crumbine with a lawsuit. "You are interfering with legitimate business," the lawyer thundered at the secretary." Crumbine, who was busily engaged in examining some brackish pickles, took him out into the hall and said, "you want to file a suit? Two floors down, third door on the right" and he would find the clerk of courts for filing his case. With the governor's support in this crucial showdown, "the age of the drug charlatan had ended. Medical enlightenment had replaced 'snake-oil.'"[34]

The meeting of Crumbine and professors E.H.S. Bailey and L.E. Sayre of the University of Kansas with the merchants of Lawrence was typical of the secretary's campaign to enlighten food retailers of the new rules. Bailey first explained the law, then gave some examples of what the inspectors, who would arrive in the city sometime the next week, would check for illegality. They would "look in ice boxes, under counters, in the cellars, and in the dark corners. Street displays had better be taken in." Bailey listed examples of adulterated food the investigators might encounter. He mentioned pepper that often had a "50 percent mixture of cocoanut shells and cracker crumbs; jams or jellies made from the refuse from cider mills treated with sulphuric acid, flavored with glucose and colored with analyne dyes and preserved with chemicals . . ." He reminded them that it was forbidden to put substances into milk to keep it from souring, maple syrup could not be made of cane sugar and flavored with hickory bark or walnut; butter and cheese could be colored but must be labeled accordingly. Crumbine then assured the merchants that it was not the intention of the board of health to harass them but to help them comply with the law. He asked the audience for response and "the merchants were greatly interested and asked a number of questions."[35]

The same trio held a meeting in Independence a few days later, and the local newspaper, headlining it "An Interesting Meeting," described the proceedings. Professor Bailey reminded the audience that the law required ice cream to contain 14 percent milk fat and if other articles were sold as substitutes, they must be correctly labeled as ice milk, frozen milk, or whatever. "Flour bleached by an electrical process, sugar whitened with bluing, butter mixed with too much water, pickles hardened with alum, pure cider vinegar made of a malt substance and colored with burnt sugar, lemon extract made of diluted alcohol and passed through the shadow of a lemon and colored with coal tar yellow. . . . chocolate icing made of brown paint and glucose and flavored with chocolate or minilic, and copper in coloring vegetables," were common examples they would be checking. Sayre, dean of the pharmacy school, discussed adulterated drugs and told retailers who had soda fountains they should publicly label the flavorings that were "assimilated and what were pure." Crumbine warned that undrawn game or poultry could not be put in cold storage and in places selling food, merchandise must be kept in a sanitary condition. Again he noted "we are here to get people right on the pure food law and not to gather evidence against them. We are here to help, not to find fault," and reminded the audience that the law "would not injure trade but would better it."[36]

His crusade was contagious and continuous once it gained momentum. In 1915, the Topeka city sanitation manager organized his five inspectors and recruited an additional two nurses from the Topeka Public Health Nursing Association to inspect 120 grocery stores, 16 bakeries, 13 hotels, 42 drug stores, 22 restaurants, and 11 confectionary stores in the capital city for a fly count. At the same time, they checked the general sanitary conditions of the businesses, but the main purpose was to estimate the number of flies as an indication of cleanliness, and they would publicize the entrepreneurs who had the fewest and encourage the public to patronize them.[37]

A Crumbine inspector discovered that a butcher was using "freezum" to preserve meats. "This practice must be stopped," the diligent doctor declared. "The preparation is made from a sulphate injurious to the health and its use will not be permitted." He promised first offenders notification they were violating the law but second-time violators would be prosecuted.[38]

Crumbine began a "war" on the state's twenty-two slaughterhouses, ordering county commissioners to investigate those establishments under their jurisdiction. If they found unsanitary conditions they were to give the meatpacker five days to correct the situation or face arrest. This decision resulted from complaints received from Wellington residents about their local butcher. The doctor could scarcely believe their descriptions and decided on making a personal inspection. Here is what he found:

> The situation in that slaughterhouse is beyond description. I never saw anything to equal it. The slaughterhouse is on piling several feet from the ground on a slope. The butchering is done on the inside and all the offal that does not run through the cracks in the floor run down the side of the hill to a depression in the ground. Here it gathers in a great mass. Everything that is not utilized goes into this dump where it decays and exudes an odor that is simply unbearable. To make matters worse a herd of hogs is permitted to feed around the slaughterhouse and fatten off this decay and matter. They have wallows in the pond and lay in them these hot days. Then the man who owns the slaughterhouse contracts with the city to take care of all carcasses. He hauls these to this slaughter yard and the hogs feed on them. In the end the hogs are butchered and sold to the man's patrons.

Crumbine ordered the mess cleaned up in five days or face prosecution, although he thought it could not be done in "fifty days."[39]

This experience convinced the doctor that other slaughterhouses probably needed inspection and he instructed his food investigators to check on some of the worst offenders. John Kleinhans soon "stirred up more trouble in the little town of Paxico in one day than could be quieted in one week." When on an inspection trip in nearby Alma, he was informed that the butcher in Paxico had sold meat that caused some people to be sick. Upon investigation he discovered that John, Frank, and Sam Schilling had skinned a dead steer and sold half of the carcass to the Paxico butcher, telling him that the animal had choked to death and they had bled it immediately. Actually, Kleinhans discovered, the steer was sick and a witness saw it "cough and blood and water ran from its nose" before the critter drowned in its own fluids. He swore out warrants for the arrest of the suspects and predicted the three would receive the maximum penalty.[40]

Crumbine's experience here led him to conclude that if Upton Sinclair had investigated the country slaughterhouses, he would have "found ample material for another Jungle." He discovered that, after the national meat inspection law went into effect, it covered only about half the livestock processed nationwide, the remainder being in intrastate commerce. Shippers who had sick animals would send them to the country slaughterers, knowing they would never pass national inspection, but the odds of them being discovered and condemned locally would be small. This development meant an increase in the activities of local houses, which were notoriously more unsanitary than the large ones in the cities where scrutiny was more regular. Dr. Crumbine read a paper at the national conference of State and Provincial Boards of Health in DC in 1908, begging for an extension of the meat inspection act to cover those in intrastate commerce, but this important change did not come about for several decades. Crumbine was many years ahead of his time here, as he was in many categories where he demanded clean food.[41]

Occasionally state officials found themselves at odds with each other over food regulations, disputes occurring between those concerned with health and those with production. Part of this division also arose over Wiley's interpretation of the national law that conflicted with that of Secretary of Agriculture James Wilson and President Wilson who supported his Cabinet member over his chemist. The case of a preservative was an issue in point. At an early joint convention of food inspectors for the state boards of health and those for state boards of agriculture in Denver, the two groups stalemated over the issue of using benzoate of soda in meats and foods. As some of the health officials began to drift off to a luncheon, the agricultural representatives hastily elected a supportive president. While they were celebrating their victory, Dr. Crumbine led the health forces to retaliate by naming one of their men to the important post of secretary. This "battle of Denver," as it was labeled, left the two sides in strained relations until they met again at Mackinac Island where all the participants became violently ill from eating poisoned whitefish. Crumbine and other physicians in attendance had to tend both factions as best they could and more cordial relations resulted from this crisis. The representatives of agriculture thenceforth were more understanding of the goals of the health officials.[42]

In the summer of 1908 Crumbine was appointed an inspector for the U.S. Food and Drug Administration (FDA). This was a major step in his goal of cleansing Kansas of impure foods because, heretofore, he had to report violations of the federal law to U.S. inspectors. Now that he was one, he could take direct action.[43]

Generally, canned and bottled foods were of no great concern for national or state investigators. But occasionally a death from botulism created a public scare. In 1916 some cases of the disease arose "apparently . . . from string beans and spinach processed in a Kansas factory." Then in 1919 a series of deaths was traced to black olives, a very popular dinner treat at that time. The National Canners Association had already begun investigating the procedures of its members and immediately concentrated its focus on this crisis. But not before the scare almost destroyed the ripe olive business in the United States. Most important, the issue "gave a much needed jolt to food processing technology" and thenceforth the industry more carefully regulated itself.[44]

Throughout his life Samuel Jay Crumbine detested the common housefly. As director of the Kansas public health program he was in a position to do something about the pest and he launched a spectacular campaign in 1905 that resulted in the world forever associating his name with his slogan, "Swat the Fly." This provided an obvious way to alert the public to the dangers of spreading germs. Household insects, especially flies, were clear "signs of unsanitary living conditions," so emphasize this link between them and disease. As a result of Crumbine's campaign and the work of other health officials, the fly was transformed from a friendly domestic insect into a threat to life and health. "It was portrayed as horrific, in fact physically repulsive and its dangers were exaggerated. . . ."[45]

His crusade began when he requested a copy of a military study. The Army had commissioned doctors Walter Reed, Edward Shakespeare, and Victor C. Vaughn to make a study of the devastating effects of typhoid fever on soldiers encamped at Chickamauga Park in Tennessee, during the Spanish–American War. They discovered flies with lime, used to disinfect the latrines, on their hairy legs, feeding on food in the mess tent. If the ubiquitous fly could carry lime to the men's food, it was obvious they also could carry millions of deadly bacilli from fecal matter. They verified this elementary deduction with biological testing of samples. Crumbine noted that this news was not exactly new. In a book published in Rome in 1658, Kercher had observed "there can be no doubt that flies feed on the internal secretions of the dead and dying, then flying away they deposit their secretions in the food in neighboring dwellings and persons who eat it are infected." The doctor found it "to be regretted" that people ignored this warning and now, two-and-a-half centuries later, investigators were confirming Kercher's theory. "The report made a deep impression on me," Crumbine observed, because with this evidence he "could formulate a plan of action": first, an intensive public health education program; second suggestions on eliminating the fly within buildings with screen wire, which was just coming into use; and third, eliminating the fly's breeding grounds.[46]

First, the public needed a thorough indoctrination on the problem. Crumbine proceeded to achieve this with his most famous campaign of propaganda. But he faced a Herculean task of overcoming widespread apathy over the annoying but "harmless" fly. A rhyme in an elementary reader in the nineteenth century instructed children

Busy, timorous, thirsty fly
Drink with me, and drink as I;
Welcome freely to my cup–
Wouldst thou sup, come sip it up.

The fly in that century was "depicted as the innocent victim of the spider's scheming invitation to come into my parlor." Americans inculcated with this philosophy would find it difficult to suspect the common fly as their dangerous enemy. Crumbine even met with outright opposition. One fellow wrote that " house flies never bite so don't introduce pizens rather draw it out which is the right way," and offered to eat a quart of the insects if anyone would donate $1,000 to an orphans' home. First, Crumbine wrote the U.S. Public Health Service for literature on the life cycle of the fly and its

Flies [Kansas State Historical Society]

habits. Then he published a story in the monthly bulletin and a special Fly Bulletin, a four-page leaflet that would accompany all outgoing public health correspondence for the next several years. His leaflet contained this gem of warning: "the fly, born in a dunghill, is tasting your coffee, taking a bath in the cream, playing Bre'r Rabbit and Tar Baby in the syrup." He sent out large 10x16 posters to be displayed in post offices and public buildings.[47]

His ten-page article on the fly for the *Bulletin* traced the origin and habits of the insect. The incubation period was ten days and the "maggot or worm" was the "chief attraction of the barnyard fowl who, as it is well-known, has a predilection for scratching in manure heaps." The average female laid 120 eggs, and assuming half were female and this reproduction was compounded thirteen times in the average season, which was normal, then the progeny was enormous. Just think what you could do for your community by killing just one fly! "One eminent biologist," he noted, had counted 5,000 tuberculosis germs in a single fly speck, and another found the living bacilli fifteen days after they had been passed from flies feeding on tubercular sputum. The state bacteriologist, Crumbine announced, was surprised recently to find that tubercular sputum contained live larvae of the ordinary housefly. He told the story of the Topeka baker who left his lemon pies uncovered near a manure pile. The baker insisted that the brown specks on them were burnt sugar but analysis showed them to be fly specks. Crumbine suggested rewriting Tilton's poem to

> Baby bye, here's a fly
> Let us swat him, you and I.
> He carries filth upon his toes,
> Which he wipes on baby's nose.[48]

The average citizen might not be able to comprehend the function of the scientist with his microscope but he could understand the language the doctor used in explaining the menace. His catchy doggerel was contagious. The *Caney News* responded with

> Baby bye, here's a fly;
> Let us swat him, you and I.
> See him crawl up the wall;
> Ain't he got a lot of gall?
> Now he goes on his toes;
> Tickling baby's nose.
> Baby bye, swat the fly
> Smite the villain hip and thigh.
> He is like Pandora's Box,
> Full of mumps and chicken pox.

See he scatters in his wake,
Germs of croup and stomach ache.
Get a sheet of tanglefoot (flypaper),
Screen upon the window put.
Do not let the baby fly
In the room with baby bye.[49]


Crumbine had an amazing stroke of luck or serendipity one day in 1905 when he received a letter from Frank H. Rose, a public school teacher from Weir City. Rose had just organized a boy scout troop there and had read of the department of health's "clean up, paint up" campaign for towns. Could his scouts help? "This was like manna from heaven," Crumbine exulted, because "we could use an alert group of boys under interested leadership, to test the validity and effectiveness of our anti-fly campaign." He sent literature, plans, and a model anti-fly ordinance to the teacher. Rose divided the town into districts with a group of scouts assigned to each one with rakes, hoes, and shovels. The city fathers provided wagons to haul away the debris and piles of manure from the streets and alleyways. By nightfall Weir City was almost spick and span. Scoutmaster Rose was not finished with this cleanup campaign. He bought a roll of screening wire, cut it up into small squares and tacked them on sticks of wood made from advertising yardsticks he scrounged from the local druggist. His boys then delivered one to each house in town. Rose managed to persuade some of the scout fathers to make fly-traps, which were placed around town, and he had the scouts write essays on the dangers of the fly. They read some of them before the municipal council and the city dads enthusiastically enacted the recommended anti-fly ordinance. Crumbine contacted scores of other scout leaders around the state with suggestions they could follow if they were of like mind. Local newspapers carried stories of these activities, which gained further publicity. Gradually dead animals, piles of garbage, manure, and other refuse disappeared from the streets of Kansas towns and the effects, both aesthetically and healthwise, were immediately apparent. The doctor concluded from this episode that people, or a community, or a city would cooperate in any reasonable or feasible health project, if competent and capable leadership was provided. Crumbine was greatly assisted in his cleanup program when the legislature in 1907 authorized his board of health to require "removal of nuisances," or sources of filth and causes of sickness on private property and waterways.[50]

Teacher Rose brought his contrivance to hit flies to Topeka to show the doctor, calling it a "fly bat." Soon thereafter Crumbine was attending the opening professional baseball game of the Western League between Wichita and Topeka, an intense rivalry that he enjoyed. In the last half of the ninth, with one man out and one man on third, and needing a run to win, a hometown batter strode to the plate. Fans began yelling "a sacrifice fly," "hit a fly," then a stentorian voice roared "swat a fly." "That's it," the doctor thought immediately and jotted the phrase down on an old envelope for future reference. Thus the great slogan was born, "Swat a Fly," and it and Dr. Crumbine became immortal. The phrase swept the country, crossed to Europe, then Asia, and around the world. The modern flyswatter was born! A short time later Crumbine met Dr. Woods Hutchinson of England in Washington, D.C. The Englishman greeted him with "I'm glad to meet you. You are the man who made 'Swat the Fly' famous— and it was great work." Crumbine's name was forever associated with this catchy slogan. The doctor was able to turn the common fly from a friendly creature for children into one of public health's greatest villains.[51]

Popular journals joined in the offensive against the fly, soon making it a national crusade. They described how households could fight the menace with repellants, flypaper, and traps. In Cleveland school officials organized children from sixth through eighth grades to serve as "Junior Sanitary Police," roaming their districts to report unsanitary areas where flies were breeding. Encouraged by these articles, Washington, D.C., organized a two-week campaign that netted 7 million flies. The *Washington Evening Star* offered a $25 prize for a fly-killing sweepstakes. A thirteen-year-old boy won with a kill of 343,800. He had organized twenty-four friends to help and they split the prize money. Imagination used in writing these stimulating stories made the fly's "elimination or suppression . . . the panacea for most human ills," though, and the public "gradually grew tired of sensational publicity in which repetition was the most outstanding feature."[52]

Samuel Crumbine loved poetry, ditties, epigrams, and catchy limericks and used them extensively to promote his programs. He wrote a housefly catechism:

### Swat The Fly

*Where is the housefly born?* In filth, chiefly in horse manure and outhouses.

*Is there anything too filthy for the fly to eat?* No.

*Does the fly like clean food, too?* Yes, and it appears to be its delight to wipe its feet on clean food.

*Where is its favorite place of feeding?* The manure heap, the privy vault, and the spittoon.

*What does he do in the kitchen, dining room, and bedroom?* He wipes his feet on the food, bathes in the milk, and annoys the sleeper.

*How does he spread disease?* By carrying infection on his legs and wings, and by 'fly specks' after he has been feeding on infectious material.

*What disease may the fly thus carry?* He may convey typhoid fever, tuberculosis, cholera, dysentery, and "summer complaint."

*Did the fly ever kill anyone?* He killed more American soldiers in the Spanish-American War than the bullets of the Spaniards; and was the direct cause of much of the typhoid that hit Kansas last year.

*Is the presence of flies an indication of nearby filth?* It most certainly is, and that is disgraceful.

Swat the Fly [Kansas State Historical Society]

*How may we successfully fight the fly?* By destroying or removing his breeding place, the manure pile; making the privy vault fly-proof; and keeping your yard clean; by screening the house, by use of the wire swatter, and sticky fly-paper.

Crumbine's campaign caught on and Kansans began in earnest to clean up their environment. As the *Salina Evening Journal* noted eight years after he initiated it, "Shoulder to shoulder a bold citizenship has swatted with telling effect," the newspaper reported, "and the general disposition of the people has made the great indoor and outdoor sport of exterminating the pest peculiarly popular."[53]

Crumbine and the board of health promoted the anti-fly campaign in many ways. Club women throughout the state received packets of materials, including cards with blanks to fill in: "Flies carry unnameable filth to food. I counted __ flies in your place of business. Date _____, Customer _____" to be filled out and mailed to the merchant involved. As late as 1923, a women's club in Eskridge presented a program on "The House Fly." Some of the topics discussed were "Diseases that Flies Carry," "Preventative Measures," "Control Measures," and "What a Club Can Do." County health officials offered bounties for pecks of flies brought in by children. In Hutchinson a cup full of flies gained admission to an amusement park and a hundred flies let them into the movies free. In one week the children of the city of 10,000 population turned in thirty-seven bushels, or 224 and one-fourth pounds of dead flies! In time few Kansas children would want to share their food or drink with "the busy, timorous, thirsty fly." Some time later the secretary of the Merced County Merchants Association of California wrote Crumbine asking him for the Kansas strategy for attacking the fly. "We have heard excellent reports of the work you have done in Kansas to exterminate the fly," he noted, "and would appreciate your bulletins on the subject, also your plan of campaign." The nationwide demand for the fly bulletins had almost exhausted his supply but the doctor forwarded some of them along with a copy of the card he recommended customers to use to pressure grocermen into action against the dangerous pest. He believed it to be "very efficacious in inducing merchants to comply."[54]

From the fly it was an easy move to "Bat the Rat." In 1914 Crumbine suggested a nationwide crusade against the rodent. In another educational program he discussed the rat's menace to health and advised on exterminating them. The press assisted him nobly in his cause with one headline reading "Kansas Spends Four Million on Rats Says Crumbine."[55] Rats in cities, Crumbine noted, were as numerous as people and in rural areas they outnumbered humans ten to one. They ate what grain they needed and destroyed about the same amount. More important, they presented a threat as carriers of disease. The fleas, or parasites of rats, carried the bubonic plague or Black Death, which had destroyed between one-third and one-half the population of Europe in the Middle Ages. Crumbine feared a bubonic plague of some kind in this country, as happened on the West Coast in 1919 and the Gulf Coast in 1920. His Bat the Rat campaign, however, came up against too much public indifference and, as he admitted, this was one of his public health efforts that failed to mobilize public opinion, as did the more dramatic fly campaign.[56]

In the decade of the 1920s, writers satirized and debunked many American values and heroes, including sanitarians such as Samuel Crumbine. Some of the more exaggerated claims and foolish health posters that arose across the country led Sinclair Lewis to caricature them in his 1925 novel *Arrowsmith*. The official of a midwestern city health department, Almus Pickerbaugh, publicized some of his campaigns with posters on "Swat the Fly Week," "Can the Cat," and "Doctor the Dog." He wrote silly jingles, such as "Boil the milk bottles, or by gum, You better buy your ticket to Kingdom Come." In fact, Lewis labeled Walt Mason, the Kansas writer, as one of Pickerbaugh's "favorite poets." Lewis fictionalized biochemist Jacques Loeb as Max Gottlieb who "advanced a mechanistic conception of life and predicted that life processes would be ultimately reduced to chemical and physical explanations."[57]

In 1926 Paul de Kriuf continued this exaggeration in his *The Microbe Hunters*, a ludicrous account of the pioneers of the germ theory from the invention of the microscope to Salvarsan. His presentation exalted the new generation of scientists who debunked "the silly sanitarian" and investigated the "real" world with an attitude of skepticism. "Science is cruel," de Kruif asserted, "microbe hunting can be heartless." Ignoring these barbs of satire, Crumbine continued his relentless pursuit of improved public sanitation.[58]

The doctor's inspectors seemed to appear everywhere. J. Floyd Telford, assigned to investigate living conditions among railroad "gandydancers," reported that the situation varied from gang to gang. One group of painters he visited fared rather well. The foreman provided them with meals for 20 cents each, the railroad made bunk cars available, as well as good water. The men provided their own bedding and their quarters were clean. Another gang of Greeks, though, lived eight to ten in a bunk car, refuse was strewn all about their cars, and if they wanted to bathe they had to use a creek with stagnant water a mile away. For a grade building crew, the cars were dirty, full of bugs and flies, and the bedding was so filthy, worn, and old that if one tried to clean it "it would all fall to pieces." The "dirty and greasy" kitchen car was not screened and the meat, bread box, and flour were covered with dead flies. The cook indignantly assured the inspector that he "sifted them out." The inspector found a hundred pounds of bad meat and ordered it destroyed, which created a tense situation as the meat cost the men "eleven cents per pound." Crumbine took up these matters with the management of the railroads and they promised reform. The difficulty in this type of work, as the inspector noted to the doctor, was that the crews and their quarters were constantly on the move and follow-up inspections were nigh impossible. The skilled painters were difficult to recruit and were treated well, while the hapless immigrant laborers were not.[59]

One never knew where Samuel Crumbine might appear personally for a sanitary inspection. After receiving complaints about the condition of the Cowley County jail, Governor Edward Hoch sent the doctor and an assistant attorney general to Winfield to investigate. Crumbine reported being "at a loss to express my surprise at the filthy and unsanitary condition" he found there. Eight or nine persons were incarcerated on the second floor. The walls were black and dirty and the ceiling was "festooned with ancient cobwebs." The back wall was encrusted with tobacco juice and expectorations "covering a period of years." The floor was "a mass of filth and dirt." The toilet bowls were "in such a vile and filthy condition as to be beyond description." Leaking sewer pipes permitted septic gas to accumulate and the bedding was "filthy." Both prisoners and jail officials complained of the smell when the cesspool was pumped out every night or two. The famous labor agitator, John Ireland, was being kept there and his physical condition was terrible. His mother and a brother had died of consumption and a sister and another brother currently were suffering from tuberculosis. Ireland was "of the tubercular type" and Crumbine found his confinement in these quarters to be deplorable. The doctor and the local county health officer filed "a remonstrance" with the county commissioners and they hoped for "speedy action" in making the jail habitable.[60]

Crumbine also discovered lamentable conditions at the state prison in Lansing. When the territory of Oklahoma was organized in 1890, the new government signed a contract with the state of Kansas to incarcerate its extensive number of criminals. Territorial authorities paid no heed to their treatment, being happy to have them elsewhere, but stories began to filter back after a few years that the Kansas penal institution was "a relic of the dark ages," a system based on revenge, not reformation. Kate Bernard, commissioner of charities and corrections in Oklahoma, paid an unexpected visit to Lansing in August 1908. Despite prison authorities proving uncooperative, she managed to inspect conditions in the coal mines, prison factories, punishment, physical care, and other reported problems. Lansing housed 562 men and 12 women from Oklahoma for which the Sooner state paid 40 cents each daily. She estimated the food, clothing, and other maintenance averaged 48 cents but the men worked in the prison mines, factories, and contract work for about 50 cents daily, so this was a profitable arrangement for the Sunflower state.

While working in the mines took its terrible toll on the men convicts, it was the punishment by the guards that particularly caught her attention. The infamous "water cure" was the worst, where convicts were chained down and a garden hose turned on them until they were near suffocation before being released. The "crib" was a coffin-like structure where recalcitrants were chained and locked into it for periods of time long enough to be temporarily paralyzed. She found "fourteen black inky dungeons with small openings that admitted little air." The men laid there at night, then were chained to sprockets on the wall in a standing position during the day. This, with a diet of bread and water, broke a man's vitality until he was unable to mine his daily quota of coal.[61]

Bernard's report shocked the public in both states. A prisoner wrote her some time after her visit to say that, as a result, the *Topeka Daily Capital* had exposed these sordid conditions and "today all Oklahoma papers were confiscated—we are wondering why." The convicts referred to her lovingly as "Our Kate." Governor Hoch and Governor C.N. Haskell of Oklahoma both appointed investigating committees that were to cooperate with each other's work. F.D. Coburn, secretary of the state board of agriculture, chaired the Kansas committee composed of Crumbine, the famous Reverend Charles M. Sheldon of Topeka, state mine inspector Frank Gilday, and F.W. Blackmar, professor of sociology and economics at the University of Kansas. Governor Hoch later added Professor E.H.S. Bailey to the group upon their request. He asked them for an "absolutely fair and impartial, thorough and complete" investigation of Bernard's charges on sanitation, food, punishment, and attitude of prison officials. He also instructed them to visit the federal penitentiary at Leavenworth for a comparison because its warden was "one of the most eminent criminologists and penologists in the United States." By the time the committee arrived at the Lansing facilities, they were assured the "crib" and "water cure" were obsolete and no longer in use. The committee requested the two be destroyed and they watched the vicious instruments being burned.

The committee reported "two monumental errors of public policy" regarding the state penitentiary: it was operated as a money-making institution, and it "had been subservient to partisan politics." The investigators concluded that it was "a real mistake" for Oklahoma to send their convicts and for Kansas to accept them. Otherwise, food and sanitation conditions were satisfactory, except for the need for special care for the sick, the insane, and the tubercular patients. The water supply from the Missouri River was "of good quality" and sewage disposal adequate, although modern cells should be constructed with sanitary closets and lavatory facilities similar to those provided for the female prisoners. The committee saw nothing wrong in requiring the prisoners to labor, although they urged the contract system be abolished and an eight-hour workday be established. The members also objected to the concept that the penitentiary should show a profit. Finally, they recommended an appropriation for educational purposes that was at least as large as the one for the inmates' supply of tobacco.[62]

Soon after, many county jails, in addition to Winfield's, came in for a good measure of justified criticism. When members of the IWW (Industrial Workers of the World) were arrested by federal agents during World War I, they had to be incarcerated in county jails as there were no federal facilities for holding them before trial. Some of these jails were in a disgraceful condition and the situation of the Wobblies, as they were called, caught a reporter's attention. He published a vividly descriptive article about them in *Survey*, a national journal. This embarrassed the Kansas government sufficiently for Governor Henry J. Allen to appoint investigators for the county jails in Wichita (Sedgwick County), Topeka (Shawnee County), and Kansas City (Leavenworth County), the three most offensive facilities widely used by federal authorities. Allen asked Samuel Crumbine, Dr. T.D. Tuttle, state epidemiologist, and Dr. Florence B. Sherbon, state child hygienist, to inspect the Shawnee jail. They were appalled at the unsanitary conditions they found. The jail was built in 1886 and it was "a rather bad example of penal architecture of thirty years ago," they said. The plumbing was "very dirty," particularly an unenameled iron bathtub that "was black as a boiler" and "could not be made sanitary or safe by even scrupulous care." The metal floor under it had rusted through and "doubtless quantities of water and filth had run in between the floor and the cage below." The dungeon in the basement, used for "recalcitrant" prisoners, had a very small hole in the double metal door to let in a bit of light and air. When the door was opened, "a flock of enormous cockroaches scuttled about." The padded cell for the violently insane had "filthy mattresses." The group agreed they could find nothing to criticize about the "large, airy room" that had been remodeled for the female prisoners, but the remainder of the jail had to be remodeled and updated.[63]

Coinciding with these myriad efforts came the doctor's work in giving effect to the other public health laws enacted with the pure food act, the measures to clean up the drinking water in Kansas. Water studies were in their infancy at this time and they usually came as a result of studying the sources of outbreaks of cholera and typhoid. The Asiatic cholera epidemic of 1832 prompted New York City to improve its water supply, for example, and the yellow fever scourge in New Orleans in 1854 caused that city to study its drainage and sewage problems. It was not until 1893 that Hiram Mills of the Lawrence Engineering Laboratory, developed the first open slow sand filter for producing safe drinking water. By 1911, some 20 percent of the urban population was drinking filtered water and chlorine was beginning to be used to treat water. As cities increasingly utilized water reservoirs outside their boundaries, the problem of waste disposal became greater. Most large cities simply dumped their sewage into adjacent streams or rivers. Two nineteenth-century beliefs contributed to this problem: filth was the basic cause of infectious disease and running water purified itself.[64]

In 1903 the Kansas or Kaw River and its tributaries flooded Northeastern and Central Kansas, and the resulting catastrophe of deadly epidemics of typhoid fever especially hit hard the large communities of Topeka and the two Kansas cities. Crumbine estimated from the deaths from typhoid in Kansas City, Kansas, and Topeka that there were probably 1,500 cases in those two cities alone. When he became board secretary the following year, he found there were no state laws under which the board of health could assume control over water supplies and sewage systems in Kansas. He made himself an authority on water resources in the state and published an important paper on the topic in 1910. Rainwater, he noted, washes out the atmosphere and in the process collects "enormous quantities of dust, smoke, and gases, so that bacteriologically speaking, it is exceedingly doubtful that any rain water is absolutely pure." Then it comes in contact with "the living earth," which is "teeming with myriads of all sorts of germ life," until it becomes a part of underground water. Wells in densely populated communities along the Arkansas and Kansas rivers, he observed, "are particularly susceptible to this form of underground water pollution." In addition to earth pollution, small towns and communities disposed of their sewage in cesspools or abandoned wells. He tested a water well in a small town on the Smoky Hill River, then added an iron sulphate solution. Within forty-eight hours users could taste the iron. His test showed they were also drinking diluted sewage. A sugar refinery in Garden City piled up its pulp, which decomposed. Nearby wells "continued to throw off the vilest odors of sulfureted hydrogen gas and deposited in the troughs which conveyed the water to the factory a thick, heavy layer of organic matter." Many wells in small towns had barnyards and privies draining into them, becoming sources of typhoid fever, diarrhea, dysentery, and cholera. In addition, eggs of animal parasites worked their way into the intestines of imbibers.

Currently President Theodore Roosevelt's Country Life Commission was conducting its studies of agrarian life and, Crumbine observed, while the farm should be the healthiest place to live, the commission reported that their schools and houses "do not have the rudiments of sanitary arrangement." The study found that farmers were more concerned over their lack of economic power, school systems, churches, poor roads, and mail delivery than they were over sanitation. These items were visible and germs were not. Of the public water supplies in the state, 89 were ground water, 4 from springs, and 85 from wells. All were untreated and the results were 355 deaths in Kansas the previous year from typhoid. Crumbine dramatically called attention to the fact that the cost of care and loss of work wages from this statistic equaled $300 each and the value of human life he set at $5,000. Totaling this up meant a loss of $2,730,000 to the state and if one added this to deaths from other communicable diseases that year, "it swells the total to amounts which are almost beyond credulity."[65]

Crumbine noted in his paper that cities were making progress on water sanitation but farmers were not. He described the privy vault and the shallow well as "a most ingenious combination for the dissemination of typhoid":

> The innocent householder sallies forth and at an appropriate distance from his house digs two holes, one about thirty feet deep, the other about four. Into the shallower he throws his excreta, while upon the surface of the ground he flings abroad his household waste from the back stoop. The gentle rain from heaven washes these various products down into the soil and percolates gradually into the deeper hole. When the interesting solution has accumulated to a certain depth, it is taken up by the old oaken bucket or a modern pump, and drunk. Is it any wonder that in this progressive and highly civilized country 350,000 cases of typhoid occur every year, with a death penalty of ten percent?[66]

The energetic doctor needed a law to give him authority to act and he sought assistance from the school of engineering at the University of Kansas. Dean Marvin of that school had been serving as Sanitary Advisor to the board of health and, upon request, assigned Professor W.C. Hoad as the board's Sanitary Engineer. Marvin and Hoad then "prepared, and I secured from the legislature, an excellent water and sewerage law."[67]

J.J. Sippy, state epidemiologist, demonstrated how Crumbine and his health sleuths ran down their prey, the carriers of contagious diseases. An epidemic of typhoid fever broke out in a small town. Sippy used the required reportable statistics on the fever to put the information in parallel columns: date of onset of disease, water supply, sewage disposal, grocerman, screens on windows, etc. The cases appeared to have no connection until he discovered several came from a railroad shop. Then he found that many of the victims had eaten at a local hotel two weeks before being stricken. Yet none of these people worked at the railroad shops, although one local case had a traveling salesman friend who also came down with typhoid. Sippy soon learned that the railroad worker had taken his friend to his shop where several cases were later reported. The salesman had spread the disease wherever he went in town though Sippy never discovered where he originally caught the disease.[68]

The board of health, in Crumbine's campaign to clean up the water resources in Kansas, was greatly assisted by the two-year study of the U.S. Geological Survey that was made for the state for $1,500. The doctor also wanted to make a personal investigation to satisfy his curiosity. He was familiar with the old adage that running water purified itself every seven miles and, hoping it was valid, sought to verify this truism. Soon after the passage of the sewage law, he and M.A. Barber of the University of Kansas, who was state bacteriologist at the time, obtained a steel skiff one hot summer day and set sail on the Kaw River at Topeka, bound for Lawrence some twenty-eight miles downstream. They periodically took eighty-three samples of the water in small tubes every half-mile or so. The blazing sun was hot, the air muggy with humidity, and the river so low that the pair often found themselves stranded on a sandbar. They had to roll up their sleeves and trouser legs and get out and push the skiff to deeper water. Then they hit a long area of sandbars and were stranded every ten or fifteen minutes, so Barber left his sleeves and pants rolled up. Crumbine had to warn the professor, accustomed to the cloistered life of the classroom, that his arms and legs were sunburning. By nightfall they had covered several miles and decided to put in for the night at a farmhouse. The next morning the pair slowly arose by assisting each other to their feet and trying to walk out the stiffness together. The doctor applied medication for second-degree burns and asked the scholar if he was ready to quit. He replied, "I will proceed to Lawrence by boat if it takes two-and-a-half years" and off they went. The cruise went better the second day until they approached Lawrence and a gale blew them over a mill run, nearly capsizing the boat. Barber was confined to bed for several days with severe sunburn and Crumbine "looked like an egg fried on both sides." But they had secured their evidence. Tests showed the river did not purify itself of Topeka sewage in twenty-eight miles, let alone seven.[69]

Crumbine then investigated the Lawrence water plant that was operated by a private company from New York. He wrote to President C.F. Streeter of the condition in which he found the city's water supply, which failed to meet the board of health requirements. A "World reporter" called him over "Bell long distance," but he declined to make a public statement. When asked if he planned to attend a public session discussing the situation, he said he would if invited but certainly the board would be represented by the state sanitation engineer, Professor Hoad, and, of course, state bacteriologist Marshall Barber, who also lived there, was particularly interested in the problem. H.N. Parker, the hydrologist for the U.S. Geological Survey, made his headquarters in Lawrence but traveled to Topeka to meet with the board of health concerning Lawrence's water supply. The accumulated evidence showed the group that it was seriously contaminated by sewage. The city was especially concerned because the university was preparing to open its fall semester and "the water conditions" might "hurt the attendance." The furor was expected to assist the local campaign for a municipally owned water plant.[70]

The same newspaper reported that Crumbine and his agents had visited nineteen cities to investigate their water supplies and nine of the larger ones had sewage contamination. The initial tests of the nineteen cities were confirmed by a second visit and retesting. Crumbine never acted until he was positive of his evidence. Sixteen of the contaminated systems were municipally owned and three were private companies. "Two of the private plants were found to be in bad shape." All the towns were notified to complete filtration plants or their systems would be shut down. Crumbine refused to identify these cities "until the officers had one more chance to get the systems in better shape." Lawrence was one of the three privately owned and the newspaper concluded correctly that it was one of the two polluted systems. This was the era of the Progressive Movement when "gas and water Socialism" was becoming quite popular across the nation and many cities began operating their own systems, as did many in Kansas when their private plants were found to be unhealthful.[71]

The doctor found the Kaw River water unfit for drinking at Topeka. He discovered polluted water in the city mains and told citizens to boil it for drinking purposes and ordered officials to drill another well to meet the shortage created by cutting off the river water. An emergency chlorine treatment machine was also installed to clean up the water in the system. The city commissioner involved reported that they had to draw some water from the river recently because this was always necessary when they had to fight fires, In these emergencies, the city wells were insufficient for supplies. "A year and a half ago similar action was taken at Lawrence," a city newspaper reported, "and now Lawrence is said to have an adequate supply of reasonably pure water."[72]

In July 1910 Emporia endured an outbreak of typhoid fever, striking the Normal School there very hard. Crumbine and Hoad rushed to the city to investigate. They informed the mayor that the Neosho River, the source of the water supply, was the culprit and the city must install a filtration system. "The people of Emporia," editorialized William Allen White, "have faith in Doctor Crumbine, and when he says the Neosho River water is unfit for drinking purposes they accept it as true." By 1914 Kansas ranked fourth nationally in the number of towns with sewage treatment plants, an enviable record considering its late start in the battle over contaminated water and one Crumbine could point to with pride.[73]

Crumbine's one unrealized dream in purifying Kansas waters was to clean up the Missouri River. The situation in Kansas City, Kansas, was particularly serious as that city was the recipient of sewage from many upstream municipalities. The farther downstream it flowed, the worse the situation became. The doctor first appealed to the U.S. Public Health Service for help. The agency replied that the federal government had control over the interstate commerce of the waterway but sewage was not included as commerce. Sanitary controls there remained with the states involved that bordered on the river. The problem was that the discharged sewage and industrial wastes from Sioux City and St. Joseph refused to remain on the east side of the river, Crumbine noted. He called a conference of the chief health officers of Iowa, Nebraska, and Missouri to meet with him in Kansas City in 1915. They agreed upon a specific time for all Missouri River cities to cease discharging untreated sewage into the stream. Kansas immediately began regulating its cities located on the river and forced compliance but the other states, with less effective boards of health, proved to be helpless when their towns refused to accept the expenses involved in this type of control.[74]

He had better success with a similar problem on the Republican River, which came under his authority in Kansas. Concordia dumped its untreated sewage into the river and when it flooded it cut a new channel across a horseshoe bend. The sewage, still being deposited in the old channel, was now undiluted by a flowing stream and neighboring people complained vociferously. The city of Concordia refused to respond, claiming "an act of God" for which it could not be held responsible. Finally, the Kansas Supreme Court, while not denying the powers of Providence, believed that Kansans "still had the right to health" and compelled Concordia to abate the nuisance.[75]

The board of health's secretary enjoyed such success and popularity, and was so thoroughly trusted with purifying the state's food and water, that in 1909 the legislature gave him the additional responsibility for inspecting barber shops and enforcing state laws on weights and measurements. Barber shops constituted an obvious source for the spread of disease by using the same unsterilized clippers, razors, and towels for all customers. That June the board met and established rules for barbers. They must use at least one clean towel per customer and must sterilize all instruments. When shaving a man, they could use alum to stop any bleeding but must apply it with a clean towel, not styptic sticks. Crumbine also was charged with regulating hotels. Again, he instigated an educational program to pave the way and used "threats and finally rigid enforcement." Newspapers as far away as New York reported his uncompromising statement concerning two hotels that refused to comply with the rules with mere threats:

> I have closed one hotel in Clay Center and one at Jewel City for failure to comply with the law. The place at Jewel City was the only one in town but it made no difference. I play no favorites, and rather than have the law ignored, I would close down every hotel in the State.

The board also mandated clean sheets every day for beds. His inspectors soon found two types of violations. Under a headline proclaiming "A Crumbine Crusade for Clean Sheets Every Day on Hotel Beds in Kansas," a newspaper reported complaints were made that some managers removed the bottom sheet, which was badly wrinkled, and put the top sheet on the bottom, a process repeated every day and thus they could use sheets twice before washing them. Others managed to get three or four nights' use out of each by rubbing them between heated rollers in the morning to take out the wrinkles. They were no cleaner for the process but lack of washing did make the sheets last longer before wearing out. In 1911 the legislature ordered county health officials to perform these inspections. Crumbine believed this was ineffective and in 1913 persuaded the solons to create a separate hotel inspection board and removed this aspect of the work from the board of health.[76]

The doctor and his inspectors began confiscating outdated drugs used in mixing prescriptions. One day he watched a druggist compounding a prescription with old drugs. He also noticed that when the druggist needed a half-gram weight for his scales, he used a nail with the head cut off because his scale weight had been lost. Further inspections revealed use of similar aged drugs and bits of metal for weights. The druggists involved "howled to high heaven" but the law was enforced. On the other hand, the doctor brought home a peck of potatoes one day, weighed them, and found that he had received two pounds more than a peck. Investigations revealed that many grocer scales had not been tested or balanced for years. This discovery brought "a flood of lawsuits and much acrimonious debate" before grocers were able to obtain new scales and measuring devices and learned they must keep their scales adjusted.[77]

Crumbine received much publicity, some by his own generation, in enforcing legal weights and measures. "Every Kansas Store Scale to Be Tested," blared the headline of a story about how he saved the people of Kansas $1 million in 1909 alone:

| | |
|---|---|
| squeezing water out of oysters | $100,000 |
| stopping short weight flour sales | $500,000 |
| stopping short weight butter sales | $150,000 |
| forcing honest weights on drugs and other provisions | $150,000 |
| stopping sales of dirty potatoes | $100,000 |

His public support was enormous and by 1910 the board of health was receiving more mail than any other office in the capitol building. William Allen White enjoyed the colorful secretary, noting that "Dr. Crumbine is busier than a monkey with the itch."

Walt Mason, poet laureate of Kansas wrote,

When my dying eyelids close,
And the World is growing dim,
When I am turning up my toes
I may ask to hear a hymn,
And the people by my bed,
They will sing with streaming eyes,
While each humbly bows his head,
Boil the germs and swat the flies.[78]

# THREE

# CONFRONTING THE GREAT
# WHITE SCOURGE

Tuberculosis, whether correctly diagnosed as such or not, has been with mankind since the beginning of the written word. Throughout centuries when diagnosed with the disease, patients were placed in a sanitarium or sent to the country and put on a special milk-based diet with plenty of rest until they died of the affliction or from other complications. For the afflicted with financial means, travel to a "healthy" climate or region had always been an attractive escape. For "lungers" in America, this meant west of the Mississippi River and the high, dry climate of the southwest became their Mecca. Josiah Gregg, "a tubercular dyspeptic," made "an astonishing recovery after two weeks on the [Santa Fe] trail" and enjoyed a decade of prairie travel that resulted in his writing a two-volume *Commerce of the Prairies*. His reports led to an increase in health seekers traveling the Santa Fe trail until completion of the transcontinental railroads led to an accelerated amount of travel by these "lungers" to the more arid climes of the West.[1]

Dr. Samuel J. Crumbine witnessed hundreds and thousands of these victims migrating by train through Dodge City to their sanctuaries in the Southwest. The principal treatment at that time was the "fresh air" concept; move to a sanitarium in the West or find an outdoor job in the high and dry climates of the mountains or the Southwest. "Go west and breathe" was the slogan of one railroad in the late nineteenth century and many sought the public sympathy and support in Denver they had heard about "where there was no stigma yet attached to them as there was in the East." But by the turn of the twentieth century "the old attitudes of hospitality and compassion . . . were replaced by a terrible fear of the vast encroaching contagion" and they were no longer welcome in previously hospitable places. Thus, there was a growing apprehension among victims that others might learn of their affliction and shun them. Many of the travelers left their bacteria on trains in Kansas on their way west. This danger was all the more real because tuberculosis was not a reportable disease at the time and, until more was known about the scourge, the department of health "could not institute effective measures against it" in the Sunflower state.[2]

Once Crumbine realized the danger it represented for his state and was in a position to act, his first step was to secure a board of health requirement to report cases with the assurance of keeping the information confidential. The 3,000 practicing physicians under his jurisdiction received a form asking for a list of their tubercular cases, the source if known, and their prescribed treatment. The board of health (led by Crumbine) believed that with sanitary care and isolation, the disease could be checked from spreading further. The doctor's objective was twofold: inform doctors and patients of the proper care for the disease; and educate the public of its dangers. Most physicians did not know how to handle it, and the public and the patients' families were terrified of its spread. The board would forward to the reporting physician the meager literature that was available and instructions on what to do along with a package of prophylactic supplies. They also sent pamphlets on preventive measures to state high schools and colleges. This public arousal stimulated the interest of the state legislature sufficiently to make an appropriation of $1,000 to finance a traveling tuberculosis exhibit around the state.[3]

Crumbine found it increasingly obvious that many of the county commissioners across the state were creating problems for the department of health in neglecting to enforce statutes. Kansas law stipulated that commissioners were responsible for health conditions in their counties and required them to choose a physician, giving preference to one "adept in sanitary science," to be their health officer. But many county commissioners refused to take this costly step and remained their own county board of health and bore ultimate responsibility for those conditions. Commissioners in counties numerous enough to cause concern for the board of health took this duty too lightly. To save money, they often put the office of county health officer up for bid and chose the lowest bidder. This created an aura of indifference in the county, and sometimes outright antagonism, to the duties and work of the health official. The problem reached such proportions that in late 1909 Crumbine wrote a sharp letter of criticism to "the Honorable Board of County Commissioners, the County Board of Health," across the state reminding them of their statutory responsibilities in health and insisting upon their cooperation. He called their attention to the fact that the county health officer not only was responsible for supervising sanitary affairs of the county but also he was the local registrar of vital statistics, the supervisor and enforcer of the quarantine law, the inspector of slaughterhouses and meat markets, barber shops and hotels, public and private schools, jails, poor houses, and other public buildings, and especially to him is delegated the enforcement of the laws for tuberculosis control, which law is among the most important that has ever been placed upon the statute books.

To him, the position must not be treated lightly. He reported to the state board of health that this reprimand "has accomplished great good in many instances in eliminating contract or competitive bids, and in a number of instances increasing the salaries of county health officers, all the way from 50 to 500 percent."[4]

A great step in the worldwide fight against the White Death came in the fall of 1908 when 4,000 delegates from around the globe gathered in Washington, DC, for the International Congress on Tuberculosis. Secretary of State Elihu Root welcomed the officials, including the great Koch from Prussia and Albert Calmette from France who later worked on Bacilli Calmettte-Guerin (BCG), that became the standard vaccine for tuberculosis. Crumbine attended the event as a delegate of the Central Committee of the U.S. Public Health Service.

Robert Koch of Saxony pioneered in the germ theory and was best known for his battle against phthisis (Greek term of unknown origin). When he discovered the tubercular bacillus in 1882, phthisis was redefined as tuberculosis. He followed this discovery with a culture of tubercular bacillus that produced tuberculin, which he expected to be a therapy but that ultimately proved useful only as a diagnostic tool. He also discovered that it and other diseases could be communicated aerially. His prodigious research in microbiology was finally rewarded in 1905 with the Nobel Prize in Medicine. The means of early detection was at hand but the treatment of tuberculosis was still a long stay at a sanitarium.[5]

During the course of discussions at the DC gathering, Calmette and Koch engaged in a heated debate over the dangers of bovine tuberculosis. Koch insisted that this type could not exist in humans and Calmette countered that it was prevalent in his area but difficult to detect with the equipment currently available. Politics played a role in this exchange because he had hated Frenchmen ever since his participation in the Franco–Prussian War. Dr. Crumbine interceded with the observation that his old friend Professor Barber of the University of Kansas had perfected a device that permitted him to pick up and transplant a single bacterium from a microscopic field. The Prussian medical giant shouted "Impossible! I don't believe it! That cannot be done!" They telegraphed Barber to bring his device to the meeting immediately and demonstrate it. Koch was so delighted that he requested three of them to be sent to him. Crumbine came away from the conference determined to (1) establish a tubercular sanitarium in Kansas and (2) obtain a law requiring physicians to report cases of tuberculosis, as the survey of 1906 was voluntary, not mandatory. The latter goal would take him another two years to achieve.[6]

Crumbine was one of many health officers engaged in the fight to control tuber-culosis. As one authority has noted, "employing methods of persuasion that were well adapted to the new consumer society, anti-TB societies put together the first mass health education campaign in American history." These people, she added, "did more than any other single group to promulgate a new health code based on the gospel of germs." Science was their "touchstone" of how to cope with microbes and they combined this with usages of Protestant evangelicalism of publishing "catechisms" and calling health rules "commandments."[7]

Upon his return home, Crumbine called on Governor Edward Hoch, with the request that he summon a state conference on tuberculosis, with expenses to be paid by the delegates who volunteered to attend. The governor estimated that perhaps twenty people might attend under these circumstances and where would the doctor like to hold it? Crumbine thought probably twenty-five interested people might show up so they reserved Assembly Hall in the capitol building for December 3, 1908. The room proved to be much too small as the delegates occupied all the seats on the floor and the city newspaper reported "the visitor's gallery was packed with an interested, enthusiastic, and intelligent crowd." The governor adopted the proper spirit when he opened the meeting with the observation that "this is the greatest movement ever started in the state." He noted that Kansans were justifiably proud of the Twentieth Kansas Regiment then on duty in the Philippine Islands but observed that if all these men had died in battle, "the loss would only have been half as great as the annual loss from tuberculosis in this state." He startled the audience with the observation that more people died annually in the United States from tuberculosis than were killed in the Civil War. If an army invaded the state, he said, "we would tax every power of the people to repel" it but "here is an invader more calamitous!" He concluded that "never was there a subject of greater importance considered at any gathering in Kansas."[8]

Deaths from tuberculosis in the state were increasing at an alarming rate. J.W. Deacon, statistician for the board of health, presented the delegates with a chart he had prepared on the city of Topeka. Health reports indicated there were 480 deaths there from the scourge the previous year. This represented 12.62 percent of the municipal population. If this ratio were applied to the average state population over the previous ten years, this would represent 2,084 deaths annually. Accurate figures, of course, were not available until later when the mandatory reporting had been tallied. The scourge hit the black population in the capital city particularly hard as they accounted for nearly 25 percent of these Topeka statistics. A visit to "Tennessee Town" or "any other colored settlement in the city," Deacon pointed out, would reveal that "the hovels most of them live in are not conducive to good health." He also noted a concentration in the Santa Fe shops area, again a workingman's neighborhood where residents were too poor to clean up their unsanitary environment. The census of

1910 revealed that, statewide, blacks constituted 3.2 percent of the population, but 6.2 percent of the deaths that year were from tuberculosis. This ratio was lower than that for the country as a whole. At that time most of the nation's 9 million blacks lived in the rural South and their tuberculosis mortality rate was three times that of the white population. The delegates formed the Kansas Association for the Study and Prevention of Tuberculosis and elected Crumbine its president and Chancellor Frank Strong of the University of Kansas as vice-president.[9]

There was a close connection between fighting tuberculosis in man and in cattle, as infected cows could pass it through the human consumption of dairy products and in eating beef. In 1912 William H. Park and Charles Krumuride demonstrated that intestinal tuberculosis and "a large portion of tuberculosis in children stemmed from contaminated milk: thus there was a pressing need either to eliminate bovine tuberculosis or to pasteurize milk, or both." Serious eradication efforts did not begin, however, until the implementation of a federal/state program in 1917. This campaign in Kansas was hampered by the state legislature's reluctance to match federal funds. In 1917 approximately 5 percent of the cattle in the United States still had the disease. After a fifty-year effort at eradication, the percentage was reduced significantly to 0.08 in 1969. Historian Charles Wood wrote in 1980 that

> there is probably no disease of animals or man which is at present receiving more consideration from the practitioner, the sanitarian, and the economist than tuberculosis. Furthermore, it is one of the most prevalent diseases, and is responsible for more deaths among people and greater loss to stock owners than any other affliction.

The farmers and stockmen resisted the loss when their herds were infected, but at the same time tuberculosis killed more people "than all forms of cancer together today," the historian reported, and it was more important to destroy the animals than to expose people.[10]

As a part of the battle against tuberculosis, Crumbine immediately began work on cleansing the milk in Kansas. In the summer of 1908 he made this startling announcement:

> We are willing to assume the responsibility for the statement that it is our belief that from ten to fifteen percent of the dairy cows of this state are tubercular. Recent investigations by this department have revealed the fact that much of the milk on the market is unfit for use by reason of the enormous bacterial content occasioned in various ways, among which might be mentioned, first, dirty and filthy stables, which means dirty cows, much of which gets into the milk during the process of milking; and second, the improper care of the cans and other milking utensils; and third, the slow or improper cooling of the milk; and fourth, the age of the milk before marketing.

To eliminate this filth and the tubercular cow, Crumbine proposed a model law for cities to enact. Each seller would have to be licensed and each city would appoint a milk inspector who would check on sales of milk by any person suffering from an infectious disease or milk from diseased cows, or filthy cans. The inspector would be required to take milk samples and forward them to the dairy inspector at Kansas State Agricultural College for testing.[11]

There was a concurrent major national effort to persuade individual dairymen to test their milch cows as it was difficult to identify many small operators with a few head of cows selling milk to grocermen in small towns. By 1908 the tuberculin test for cows was so simple that "any intelligent owner of cattle may, if properly instructed, successfully test his cows," wrote a veterinarian for a popular farm journal, and he proceeded to give "proper instructions." The dairyman needed a fresh supply of tuberculin, a hypodermic syringe, hollow needles for injection, and "a strong clinical thermometer." Take the cow's temperature morning, noon, and night and carefully record the results. Late the following evening, inject two cubic centimeters of tuberculin in a fold of the neck skin or behind her shoulder. Take her temperature every two hours the next morning for four times and record them. If the temperature at noon is higher than that of 10:00 the previous evening, take another reading at 2:00 and 4:00 PM. If the rise is two or more degrees, the cow is infected. If the increase is $1^1/_2$ degrees, she is suspicious and should be tested again in three months. All the while, keep the cow in her stable and do not test if she is sick, excited, or during her calving period. Meanwhile she could have no cold water and if the cow weighed over 1,000 pounds, use an extra half centimeter of tuberculin. This procedure would save the owner the cost of a veterinarian visit.[12]

Rail carriers also presented Crumbine with public health hazards. At the turn of the century there were few rules regarding health precautions on railroads, except the commonly agreed need for fumigation. Railroads were concerned, of course, over the deaths and injuries they caused both for their workers and their passengers and developed medical organizations and built hospitals out of necessity. By the 1890s, car sanitation became a major concern and in a survey in 1899 "most were making modest efforts to improve ventilation and sanitation," with larger lines fumigating cars every six months with a gas containing formaldehyde. But the railroad companies fought the idea that dried sputum might be a source of diseases. It was not until 1905 that the Pullman company established the first department of sanitation for common carriers and the concept spread very slowly.[13]

Homes, schools, trains, and public buildings all provided common drinking cups as had been the tradition for centuries in Europe and America. This custom especially aroused Dr. Crumbine's ire. At the annual conference of the state health officers in 1906, unsanitary conditions on railroads were discussed during which someone raised the question of the common drinking cup. The meeting adopted rules for sanitary

Public Drinking Fountain [Kansas State Historical Society]

cleaning of coaches but did nothing about the cup, while all agreed it presented a significant health hazard. The next year Crumbine boarded a train to investigate an outbreak of smallpox. It was a hot dry day. At the water tank he met "an emaciated, pale man" drinking from the cup. Going forward to the next car, he saw several "lungers" coughing and spitting on the floor and in the next one there were two people by the water tank, "a cadaverous looking man" drinking from the cup chained to the tank and a little girl waiting for her turn for a drink. The doctor discovered he was no longer thirsty.[14]

A few weeks later Crumbine was on board a train out of Kansas City, enjoying a cigar in the smoking compartment and talking to two young men who had just sold several carloads of cattle. Then one of the men took a common drinking cup off the shelf and disappeared into the toilet. His friend kidded him when he left and then explained to Crumbine that he needed the glass to hold the mixture he had to use to treat himself for gonorrhea. The doctor was horrified when the man returned and replaced the glass without washing it and the two men went back to their berths. The conductor was the first person to come in for a drink. "Leaping" to his feet, Crumbine grabbed the glass and threw it out the open window, explaining to the man why he had done it. A few days later a Topeka physician casually mentioned that one of his young patients, "a woman of excellent character," had a "syphilitic chancre" on her lip, undoubtedly a result of the common cup she used on a train she rode a month earlier. At the next board of health meeting Crumbine carefully detailed his experiences. The members listened to his plea for a ruling against the common cup but decided they did not have the authority to issue one. If they did act, certainly the railroads would fight it.[15]

The scientific doctor decided he needed evidence for the board to rule against the common cup effectively to make certain that it would be sustained in a court action. He persuaded Professor Barber to take swabs of all drinking cups on trains coming into Union Station in Kansas City for a week. He took similar swabs of cups and glasses in the public schools of Wyandotte, Kansas. This collection, and the subsequent testing of the samples, took time but at last he had sufficient scientific proof of the danger. He then approached the general managers of the railroads operating in Kansas. They were quite aware of his concerns, activities, and reputation and, after his explanation, they agreed to comply with a board ruling he expected to obtain outlawing the cups on their trains, in schools, and in public buildings. The board of health issued his requested order, wisely excepting churches because of the sacrament of communion, to take effect from September 1909. Meanwhile, the doctor was promoting his campaign against the cup and meeting some resistance. One writer declared that he had always used the common cup and "nothing serious has ever happened to me." Another believed there might be a danger involved but it was not as great "as dying from thirst when you travel by train."[16]

The common communion cup of Protestant churches presented believers with a special problem (in the Roman Catholic church at the time only the priest partook of the wine). When physicians called for its abolition, fundamentalists countered with the argument that Jesus and His disciples used one cup at the Last Supper. Surely if He instituted this crucial sacrament He would protect its participants from danger. Reformers rejoined that many large congregations had already breached the unthinkable because the common cup made the service too lengthy. Most denominations eventually followed this plan and adopted communion sets with a tray and small individual glasses that could be sterilized between uses.[17]

It required much time and experience to destroy the traditional common cup. Trains traveling through Kansas complied with the ruling, then replaced the cup when they crossed the border into the next state. Even in Kansas it did not go smoothly. Schools failed to comply with the ruling until Crumbine asked the state superintendent of public instruction to intervene and issue an order to conform. Then the Kansas railroad commission advised the Missouri Pacific railroad that they, not the board of health, had total jurisdiction over rail lines, a rivalry the doctor had to adjudicate. When Crumbine finally decided he had conquered the menace of the common cup, a news reporter enjoyed informing him that one still existed at the water cooler on the second floor of the state building where the doctor had his office. Upon inquiry the building custodian agreed it was there and would remain because it was under his jurisdiction! This declaration required a quick visit to the governor's office to have the cup removed permanently. As Crumbine confessed, his campaign ultimately succeeded because his educational efforts had resulted in "a general sanitary awakening of the people to the danger of the common cup."[18]

His efforts to destroy the common cup, in the first state to do so, received a huge boost nationally when he was visited one day by a native Kansan. Hugh Moore, living in Boston, had been working on an idea with his brother-in-law, Lawrence Luellen. He came to the doctor's office with a primitive, cone-shaped pleated paper cup they were developing. After suggestions and improvements he returned much later to show him a machine-made one and thus was born what became known as the penny cup. Moore and Luellen began on a small scale, with their machines selling a drink of cool spring water at trolley car corners. In 1909, the year the Kansas board of health outlawed the common cup, they organized the Public Cup Vendor company to sell their machines and cups to railroads. The next year they reorganized into the Individual Drinking Cup Company in New York City, becoming the first to sell a two-piece paper rolled into a cone shape that they perfected and produced with a machine developed with the help of an engineer, Eugene H. Taylor. In 1909 Lafayette College biology professor Alvin Davison, studied the problem of the common drinking cups in the Easton, Pennsylvania, public schools and published "Death in School Drinking Cups" in *Technical World Magazine*. The Massachusetts board of health redistributed this gruesome article in November of that year and it boosted the national campaign tremendously to outlaw the common cup in schools and elsewhere in public.[19]

By 1912 the cup company had semiautomatic dispensers and began selling the product to drug stores and soda fountains as the Health Kup. The great influenza epidemic of 1918 boosted sales immensely, but it also stimulated competition, so the two executives renamed their product Dixie Cup in 1919 to set it off from their rivals. They moved their manufacturing facilities to Easton, Pennsylvania in 1921 and during the Roaring Twenties added the very popular Dixie Cup ice cream to their line. Moore reported to Doctor Crumbine in 1935 that his company had a monopoly on the idea at first but currently there were fifteen or twenty others making paper cups "of one kind or another" and he estimated their total annual production at 3,000,000,000. His successful company merged with the American Can Company in 1957 when Hugh Moore retired.[20]

Crumbine, as could be expected, had a poem for his crusade:

There are still a few,
Who swear
And tear their hair,
And get into a stew,
Because they can't sup

From the unwashed drinking cup.
You know
It had to go,
For Kansans wash their knives and forks
Before they are used again.
And why not the cup?
Great Scott!
This rot
About the inconvenience of not
Being allowed to swap
Spit
And germs
And filth and other things
With your fellow men,
Is a give-away when
You roar like that.
Won't you live longer
And be stronger
By being clean?
Well, I guess
Yes.[21]

Crumbine saw here another opportunity to use a catchy phrase in his efforts to educate the public about cleanliness and health. He had always had a passion against spitting and there was much scientific evidence that the sputum of consumptives carried the tubercule bacillus. He persuaded the state legislature to ban the widespread public habit in 1909. The law forbade people to

> spit, expectorate or deposit any sputum, saliva, mucus of any form ... on the floor, stairway, or upon any part of any theaters, public hall or building ... any railroad car or street car ... or upon any sidewalk abutting with a public street, alley or lane.

The statute also forbade the "dry sweeping" of railroad coaches in transit and required the presence of cuspidors or spittoons in smoking cars. The law required copies of the prohibition to be posted in conspicuous places.[22]

To promote his campaign, Crumbine came up with the phrase "Don't Spit on the Sidewalk." He persuaded a brick manufacturer in Topeka to stamp the slogan on every fourth brick and the Cherryville Vitrified Brick Company soon followed suit. Quickly the message was spread across the towns and villages of Kansas. Fifty years later the Tuberculosis and Health Association asked Kansans to send them one of the bricks. They quickly found that every Kansas county had one, as well

Common Drinking Cup [Kansas State Historical Society]

as several in neighboring states. In addition, presidents Hoover, Eisenhower, and Kennedy possessed one, as did the Smithsonian and Walter Reed Army Hospital. However meritorious in many other ways, his campaign had no effect on the spread of tuberculosis, although he and the medical field did not know this. It was not discovered until much later that "tuberculosis is spread almost exclusively by dried tubercule bacilli coughed into the air." This discovery led to a modern emphasis on ventilation for consumptive patients and to outdoor activities as the bacilli are easily killed by ultraviolet rays, even those in sunshine.[23]

In the middle of the twentieth century, years after Crumbine's work, investigators found that environment, washing patients' bedding and clothing, and room walls was not the answer to stopping the spread of the disease. Covering the mouth while coughing, good ventilation of patients' rooms, and sterilization of air with ultraviolet light was the key to infection control. In underdeveloped areas, dormitory conditions, or cases where overcrowding forced family members to sleep together in a badly ventilated room provided the optimum for spreading the disease.[24]

Mexican labor in Kansas proved to be a significant category of people for the spread of tuberculosis. They had always provided a primary source for the hard work of section hands on railroads and in the salt mines near Hutchinson. Their numbers also increased in Western Kansas in 1907 when they were encouraged to migrate to a sugar producing mill there and more came following the Mexican revolution in 1919. Small towns near these areas invariably had a "Little Mexico" arise on their outskirts where their families lived in poverty and filth.

The board of health found that Mexican railroad workers were "the greatest carriers of tuberculosis" in the state. John J. Sippy, state epidemiologist, noted that "they pile so many into one room, and lead such unclean lives that disease easily gets a foothold among them." He said that "we have found some cases where there were seven or eight Mexicans living in a one room and three of them had tuberculosis." Crumbine agreed that railroads had done much to try and clean up these camps but they needed to do much more. He asked them to employ visiting nurses for these workers for their own improvement and for the protection of Kansas citizens. "They bring these people into Kansas," he declared, "and it would only be fair for them to do everything in their power to protect the citizens of the state against the disease spreading proclivities of their employees."[25]

Doctor Sippy found an even greater problem among the Mexican workers of the Santa Fe and Rock Island railroads in Wichita, one of the major centers of these two large lines. He reported to Crumbine that "to look at the bare facts and figures does not do justice in the way of description." He discovered eleven people living in one boxcar, including a woman with tuberculosis and her four little children. The car was "dark, windowless and fetid, unventilated" and served as the center for cooking, dining, and sleeping. The woman died shortly after his visit, and when he returned, he found the children and the other inhabitants were scattered among different families and thus, obviously, spreading the disease. Sanitary conditions throughout the camp were "unspeakable," he wrote. The entire population used five toilets "of the common earth open-vault type, filthy beyond description. The water supply is from driven pipe wells with pumps (common pitcher type) and the yards around them reek with filth of every description."

Crumbine protested to the general manager of the Santa Fe that the state board of health was aware that these families had "a very low standard of living" but that other Mexicans living in the Wichita area "had decent houses and . . . water and sewage facilities" If provided the opportunity, he believed, the railroad workers "could do much better than they now are able to do." He laid the blame for these squalid conditions on the railroad management They could provide much better living facilities and would do so, he was certain, if they "were aware of the actual facts." The general manager of the Santa Fe promised improvements but the Rock Island lawyer defensively replied:

> The only way that living conditions may be materially improved is to force the Mexicans to change their way of living. I think you will agree with me that this is a rather difficult undertaking. The standard of living of these people is not up to the standard of this state, even though their present standard of living is far above what they were accustomed to in the native land.

The problem of unsanitary living for these transitory people continued and required constant vigilance and enforcement of the laws on the part of public health officials.[26]

The doctor listened to some pathetic stories during his campaign against the White Scourge, as it was sometimes known in rural areas. An Indian brought his son to his office one day. "They have put something in the eyes of my boy at Haskell where he has been to school. They say he has tuberculosis and cannot stay in school. Tell me about it." Crumbine could only try to explain to the father in lay terms what little he knew and he lamely recommended "outdoor living and careful treatment" for the youngster. In Western Kansas a widow with consumption lived with her two daughters. One of the girls caught the disease and died. The other girl wrote "my sister is dead. My brothers are afraid to come here. Mother is dying. In the name of Heaven cannot the State of Kansas help me some way and care for my mother?" A distraught Crumbine was forced to reply that he and the state were helpless in this type of situation until he could get a sanitarium.[27]

He discovered he could help a great deal through education. He persuaded the state legislature in 1909 to appropriate $2,000 for a traveling exhibit on the scourge. It was reported that the board of health was busy "for weeks" preparing the show. Crumbine drew "on all parts of the country for material, some things even being imported from Europe." Dr. S.C. Emley of the University of Kansas medical school was in charge of the production and Crumbine's son, Warren, directed the advertising. Emley also spoke to physicians and consulted on tuberculosis cases. Crumbine's exhibit included model sleeping rooms, tents, sleeping bags, and views of sanitary and unsanitary homes, "taken from actual places in Kansas." A model dairy was displayed and another exhibit featured a stereopticon flashing pictures on a large screen. He developed the story with a film on the fly and what the insect does to spread disease, including tuberculosis. The exhibit visited every county in the state and in small towns it distributed literature to school children that told the story of tuberculosis and how to combat it. He knew the value of teaching the public, especially the younger generation, what the scourge meant, how to prevent it, and how to help its victims. He also provided kits throughout the state for collecting specimens of sputum to be sent to Topeka for a free analysis of suspected tuberculosis. The previous fee for such a service "had the effect of preventing a very general acceptance of the opportunity of having such examinations made." This show marked the first time the state appropriated money for the prevention of disease, placing it in the forefront of the most significant hygienic movement of that generation.[28]

The Public Health Nurse program in Kansas was a direct offshoot of the mobile tuberculosis campaign. Laura Neiswenger, the first public health nurse in Kansas, was employed to accompany the traveling exhibit on a three-month basis as an experiment, this being unusual as her work in this capacity was disease prevention, rather than curing. The experience proved successful and she continued with the project so that by 1911 the Kansas Association for the Study and Prevention of Tuberculosis was employing five graduate nurses and one practical one. Following World War I the board of health created the Bureau of Public Health Nursing. When Crumbine's numerous activities forced him to relinquish his work on tuberculosis for other causes, Dr. Charles H. Lerrigo, a homeopath trained in England, became president of the Kansas Tuberculosis and Health Association. Author of a number of books, some of them fiction, Lerrigo became "a mighty force in the later stages of the tuberculosis drive," in eradicating the disease in Kansas. Among other activities, Lerrigo developed the highly effective traveling exhibit on tuberculosis that toured the state.[29]

Meanwhile the search for a better treatment of the White Scourge continued. One such experiment in Kansas was watched "with keen interest by the medical profession all over America." Experimenters established a sanitarium at Grover Station on the Santa Fe Railroad a few miles east of the capital, the Hoch-Wald Ranch (the German words meaning high forest). The director, Dr. Thomas J. Brunk of Topeka, based his treatment on the concept that consumptives improved in health when living in the high dry climate of the West but most of them eventually had to return home where they suffered a relapse. The nose constituted a major problem for these sufferers, he argued. Ninety-five percent of noses are abnormal in some way and this quirk increases the possibility of them harboring tubercular germs. Brunk and his colleagues at Hoch-Wald used a steel "snare" to pull obstructions out of the nose where those germs might find a foothold. One must "open the nasal passages and let the air flow into the lungs freely," they argued. This had to be combined with other treatment, including exercise and a diet emphasizing milk, eggs, meat, bread, and an ounce or two of wine daily. The patients lived in a tent in the summer that was partially boarded up on the sides, and were under the constant care of doctors and nurses. One must "remove them from the noise of any city" and make certain they receive fresh air, Brunk insisted. "The natural quiet and the general restfulness of the place" would effect a cure if the disease were caught soon enough. The search for a cure would continue for decades.[30]

The board of health supported the various efforts to care for these patients in Kansas. Crumbine always tried to put statistics into dollar costs, if possible, when he appealed for legislative support because Kansas solons tended to think in terms of costs and taxes, rather than benefits. By 1916 consumption was again on the increase, as were the numbers of victims leaving the state for treatment. It was estimated at that time that about 600 cases left the state annually and "five hundred dollars is a conservative estimate of what these cases will spend during a year of their absence," he said. This represented "a distinct loss to Kansas of $300,000 each year," and with proper equipment they could be treated in the state. $300,000 yearly would go far in securing the necessary equipment.[31]

The common roller towel also drew Crumbine's wrath. With his "tenacious energy ... and ... the abolishing of the roller towel and of causing the separation of water and ice in drinking water coolers," he started "a reform which has now become almost universal." An outbreak of smallpox occurred among traveling salesmen in June 1911. Investigation revealed they had all been guests of a certain hotel where the porter suffered from a skin disease. The man, he found, also was in charge of the washroom and the toilets. This episode prompted Crumbine and his inspectors to gather roller towels in restaurants and hotels in six Kansas towns and send them to the biological labs at the University of Kansas for analysis. The report came back that "all contained measurable amounts of human hair, numerous cells and shreds of outer layers of skin, numerous bacteria of various kinds, including staphylococcus and many yeast cells. Some of them had numerous bacilli coli, showing probable fecal contamination." With this evidence the board of health issued an order on June 12, 1911, forbidding the use of these towels in railroad cars, hotels, restaurants, schools, or public buildings in Kansas. Again another first in the nation for the Sunflower state.[32]

A sanitary alternative was becoming readily available from the Scott company. Two brothers founded this business in Philadelphia in 1879. Their main product for years was toilet tissue, but they were always searching for other items to manufacture from paper. During a flu epidemic in the Philadelphia schools in 1907, Arthur Hoyt Scott, a graduate of Swarthmore College, noticed the children sharing a common towel to blow their noses. This disturbing sight motivated him to develop the Scott Sani-Towel paper substitute that quickly found acceptance in washrooms across the nation.[33]

The *St. Louis Republic* warned its readers that "You Must Carry Your Own Towel, Brush, Comb and Drinking Cup when Traveling in Kansas." "Kansas is being sterilized, cleaned and fumigated from Garden City to Ft. Scott and from the Missouri River to the Colorado line," the story noted, "and no state in the world is having its health more zealously guarded." School children had been carrying their own drinking cups to school and now the board of health was also demanding they be given paper towels of their own for use in the washrooms. This was "just another phase in the warfare against the ubiquitous disease germs that somehow manage in the keen, bracing air of the Kansas plains. They will need to be splendid examples of the survival of the fittest in order to escape the vigilant warfare that is being directed by Doctor Crumbine." The story added that the Kansas board of health received more letters than any other governmental unit at that time because of its vigorous activities in improving public health.[34]

It was not until 1911 that Crumbine and his supporters persuaded the legislature to appropriate money for a state sanitarium. Senator J.A. Milligan, a medical doctor from Anderson County who also served on the state board of health, fought for the measure for several years before achieving success. Some members of the lower house, which the *Topeka Daily Capital* described in 1911 as having "opposed almost every appropriation for anything along new lines made strong talks in favor of this bill." The newspaper added that the favorable sentiment was "due largely to the educational campaign that has been waged by the state board of health," citing especially the traveling tuberculosis exhibit. The bill appropriated the considerable sum of $50,000, of which only $15,000 could be spent for constructing an administration building and the remainder for land, "inexpensive cottages," and for maintenance for two years. The senate approved the measure thirty-seven to two and the lower house ninety-two to eight.[35]

The governor appointed an advisory committee and the search was begun for a location somewhere in Western Kansas. They eventually agreed upon 240 acres in the Norton vicinity in Northwestern Kansas, but encountered "some difficulty" in purchasing the site. The next legislature repealed the 1911 appropriation and passed an identical measure that contained the proviso that the sanitarium would be located "in any county" where 160 acres was donated for the purpose. The businessmen of Norton then offered the requisite quarter section of land gratis and another 80 acres was purchased later to add to the institution. The cornerstone of the administration building was laid in June 1914 and a sixteen-bed unit was opened the following February with Dr. C.S. Kenney as superintendent.[36]

The town of Norton provided special train service for the opening and a crowd of some 4,000 heard speakers trumpet the historic event and witnessed the laying of the cornerstone some four miles east of Norton. Although Crumbine could not be present, other speakers included W.L. Brown, who was speaker of the house that approved the appropriation for the sanitarium, and Dr. Milligan, the state senator and author of the measure. Governor George Hodges reminded his listeners that the annual toll of the disease in Kansas exceeded the losses on the *Titanic*, only a slight exaggeration but a telling one as this recent tragic sinking was still on the minds of everyone. He added that the tubercular crisis was "a far greater one . . . because we know that 90 percent (of the victims) can be nursed back to health and strength."[37]

Dr. Kenney supervised the construction of Tent Colony # 1, consisting of four tents walled up three feet, with a roof, screens, and a solid floor, providing accommodations for ten each, or forty patients. He had to make an appeal for private contributions the following year. "More than 200 men and women" were dying from tuberculosis in Kansas because there was insufficient room and they "were begging" for admission to the state sanitarium. The law of 1913 was limited to maintenance expenses and they had sufficient funding for nurses, food, bedding, and supplies for more patients. They needed donors to make the tents available and the sum of $175-$200 would make it possible to handle two more patients each if private organizational support was forthcoming. Under the headline "Kansas a Beggar," the *Topeka Journal* lamented that the recent legislature and administration under Governor Arthur Capper cut the sanitarium's request for a $25,000 emergency appropriation "to the hurting point," while providing $310,000 for fighting the foot and mouth disease in Kansas cattle and horses, resulting in Dr. Kenney having to beg for help for sick people. The newspaper thought it "probable" that his plea would result in "a number of charitable organizations" coming to the rescue of the state sanitarium.[38]

At the same time the Kansas Tuberculosis Association began a campaign to raise $12,000 in the three larger cities of Kansas City, Kansas, Lawrence, and Topeka. Samuel P. Withrow of Cincinnati, who helped in a similar drive in Ohio, came to the Sunflower state to lend his assistance and expertise. Businesses, churches, and individuals were asked to buy twenty-four inch anti-tuberculosis pennants to be displayed in businesses and on automobiles. In addition, "chaperoned girls" would be on hand on the last day of the campaign to sell small stickpin pennants for 25 cents each. The funds raised would be equally divided between the Kansas Tuberculosis Association and the Public Health Nurses Association.[39]

Christmas seals also made an ongoing contribution to fight tuberculosis. In 1904 a Danish postal worker, Einar Holboell, initiated the idea of selling Christmas stamps for this purpose. The concept spread westward to the United States and by selling Christmas seals with the double-barred Lorraine cross, money was raised to help support the activities of the American Lung Association.[40]

The nation and Kansas were improving their methods of gathering vital statistics, including those on tuberculosis, soon after the turn of the century. In 1915, national figures released by the department of commerce showed that in the previous nine years the mortality rate for consumption dropped from 200.7 to 147.6 per 100,000, "the decline being continuous from year to year." The report emphasized that the rate was higher for blacks than for whites, mortality rates were higher for urban whites than for rural ones (because of the crowded, slum conditions in the large Eastern cities), and were abominably higher for states such as Colorado and California, which attracted consumptives from other states. The study happily noted that "with improved sanitation and with better understanding of the laws of health and the importance of pure air ... the 'White Plague' is rapidly becoming a less serious menace to health and happiness."[41]

Crumbine heartily endorsed the concept that people should sleep with their windows open. When the sleeping porch was invented, it seemed ideal for promoting this thesis. He recognized the old precept that a physician's advice would not be accepted if he disregarded it himself so he built one, "perhaps the first in Topeka," and found it to be a great relief on hot summer nights before the existence of air conditioning. The whistle of the Santa Fe train was the last thing he heard at night and the raucous sound of bluejays and a drumming woodpecker aroused him in the morning after a restful sleep.[42]

There were quacks, of course, who promoted their own "cure" just as there were peddlers of a "cure" for cancer at the time. A Berlin bacteriologist, Dr. Frederick Franz Friedmann and his brother, Dr. Arthur C.H. Friedmann, came to America early in 1913 to promote his "cure" of serum of "marine turtle germ scrum," inoculating patients before a group of doctors in Peoples Hospital in New York City. "Most of the physicians were not impressed" with his demonstration, he was told. His brother responded "with nervous explosiveness, to __ with them. In two months we'll be treating hundreds of patients and they'll be crawling around us begging for our serum." One witness reported that the German doctor brought his syringe wrapped in a piece of paper "and took scarcely no sterilizing precautions. . . . I don't think he knew where to find a vein" to inject the serum. The good doctor acknowledged it would take eight or nine months to determine if the patients needed another injection. "Think of that," exclaimed another doctor. "He will be able to tell, not if the patient is cured or on the way to a cure, but whether the patient needs another injection. Think of the enormous profits that can be rolled up by treating thousands of patients within the next few months." A month later the Surgeon-General of the United States named a board to investigate a culture of the German bacteria and would issue no opinion on the "cure" until he had received its report. Crumbine detested this type of quackery.[43]

At the turn of the century many organizations finally became concerned over the high incidence of tuberculosis in the Tri-State region but Samuel Crumbine "was one of the first persons to take an active interest in the health problems" of the area. When he and his colleagues surveyed the tubercular condition in Southeast Kansas, they found "an extraordinary situation." The Kansas counties of Crawford and Cherokee, Jasper in Missouri, and Ottawa County in Oklahoma, were known as the Tri-State region and miners in this area often worked in one of the other states but their occupation, wherever located, was fraught with mining diseases and with jurisdictional problems for health officials. Of crucial concern was the limitation on admissions to the Missouri state sanitarium in Mount Vernon.[44]

First Kansas officials tried persuading Cherokee County commissioners to provide for full-time health service. Failing in this they prepared large charts tabulating the number of cases and deaths from preventable diseases, especially tuberculosis, typhoid fever, and infant mortality in that area. Other charts illustrated the costs of these diseases to Kansas, including sickness, services of undertakers, loss of wages, and $5,000 for the value of each human life lost. In addition, they charted the number of widows, orphans, widowed parents, and broken homes. All this was presented to the people of the area in a mass meeting and in a massive publicity campaign. As a result of a groundswell of favorable public sentiment, the Cherokee County commissioners relented and agreed that a public health service was not only necessary, but would be a good financial investment as well.[45]

The Crawford County officials were not equally impressed so Crumbine tried an idea, "maybe a crazy one," he admitted, by writing his counterparts in Missouri and Oklahoma to join him in requesting the U.S. Public Health Service to create a Tri-State Sanitary District. In their letter the three secretaries noted that the mining region created a situation in which "there is constant and free interchange of persons and things which make it a particularly difficult problem in the control and suppression of communicable diseases." The U.S. Public Health Service honored their request and appointed Dr. Thomas Parran, Jr., as surgeon general of the district on September 17, 1917, with headquarters in Joplin, Missouri, some five months after America entered World War I. Parran became quite active and helpful in the Tri-State, conducting classes in the Kansas annual clinic for health officials and speaking throughout the region on health issues. He later headed the Division of Venereal Disease in the U.S. Public Health Service and eventually became surgeon general of the United States.[46]

The Cherokee County public health service did yeoman work in conducting studies of respiratory diseases among coal miners and their families. In 1913 the Federal Bureau of Mines assigned a sanitary engineer, Edwin Riggins, and Dr. A.J. Lanza of the U.S. Public Health Service to study the incidence of silicosis and tuberculosis in the Tri-State. It was noted that most of the miners were of native stock, two generations from farms in Arkansas or the Tennessee Mountain region and, at the time they took mining jobs, were usually fresh off Missouri farms. They were intelligent, industrious, married young, and raised large families. The Missouri sanitarium in Mount Vernon admitted only early cases of tuberculosis, with the result that few miners entered it because, when they finally sought help, they were in advanced stages beyond help. While investigators considered them more intelligent than the foreign miners they studied in other mining areas, the report concluded that they did not take care of themselves or their families, living generally in unsanitary conditions. Following completion of their survey, the experts made five recommendations to the mining operators, for abating rock dust and other sanitary proposals, including improved toilet systems, sanitary drinking water, and general cleanup around their rental homes and the mines.[47]

Economics proved the vital factor in their living conditions. Many of the miners received only two or three days work weekly in the best of times, none during the slack coal season in the summer. One contemporary reporter described their meager existence as "only rivaled by the worst of city slums." She found their houses to have bare floors, ragged beds, women and children barefoot and wearing rags. Inside the dwellings

> coal soot has blackened the walls and ceilings that never knew paint or varnish. Or ragged paper flutters from the walls. Rough pine floors with yawning cracks, worn knobby over projecting knots, discourage cleanliness in the best of house-wives among these miners. Through the broken roof and frail sides the rains ruin the few possessions of the miner's family and drip down on his wretched bed.

The "streets" had no sidewalks, trees, or grass. On wash days the children often missed school because they had to go naked until their one set of clothes dried. There was no amusement in the camp for children or adults—not even a five-cent movie. They drank polluted water, resulting sometimes in one-fifth of the inhabitants being sick with typhoid. A study by the state department of labor as late as 1926 found 3,500 of 5,000 houses in the Kansas region of the Tri-State as "unfit for habitation."[48]

Operators began opening up lead and zinc mining in the Pilcher, Oklahoma area in 1915. They built cheap houses for their workers on land leased from the Quapaw Indian reservation. Because miners could not own the land or their homes, they made little effort to improve their two- to three-room dwellings. Many houses were not connected to the few sewage systems available in the small towns. Drinking water was often hauled in open tanks and stored in barrels beside the house. Through the combined efforts of the U.S. Bureau of Mines, the Tri-State Association, and the Picher post of the American Legion, a cooperative health clinic was established in 1924. At the request of the companies, studies were made of the presence of silicosis and recommendations were soon forthcoming for annual physical examinations of the workers and an expansion of the clinic's operations. In 1928 the clinic examined over 9,000 people, including a few women and children, and found that over 21 percent of the men had silicosis in one of three stages, 3.41 percent had the disease complicated by early stages of tuberculosis, and 1.34 percent had the White Plague. With the ensuing decrease in demand for lead and zinc during the Great Depression, those in the first stage of silicosis were warned by clinic workers to find employment elsewhere; those in the second stage were no longer employed in the underground mines.[49]

In 1932, depressed economic conditions forced the closing of the Cherokee County clinic and conditions continued to worsen as the Great Depression unfolded. In 1939, a National Committee for People's Rights of New York City dispatched an investigator, Mildred Oliver, and a photographer, Sheldon Dick, to collect information in the Tri-State region. They surveyed eight towns on Oklahoma, two in Missouri, and Treece, Galena, and Empire in Kansas. Their report was illustrated with photos of huge piles of mining chat, ramshackle workers houses, interior views of rooms, usually with a sick miner in bed. Following publication of the report, newspapers across the nation began labeling the Tri-State "a health menace," "Pesthole of the Plains," and "Wasteland." Further studies showed that the children were affected by the high concentration of dust in the air and by living in the poorly constructed houses over extended periods of time quite similar to the underground miners who contracted tuberculosis or silicosis. Tubercular tests in 1936 of over 1,000 teachers and students showed 36.34 percent testing positive. This is one area where the state of Kansas and the national government failed their citizens terribly.[50]

Much of this occurred after Samuel Crumbine left the state. While he was fighting tuberculosis in Kansas, he did not neglect his campaign for pure food and drink products. He soon found, like Harvey Wiley on the national level, that advertisers and publishers used misleading or deceitful ads for their products. Crumbine lambasted these activities in a speech before the Association of American Dairy, Food and Drug officials in Maine. He noted that the national and state food and drug laws "had failed and would continue to fail to afford the fullest protection to the consumer" until statutes were supplemented by passage of false advertising laws. He did discern "a rapidly awakening ethical sense" on the part of publishers because many of them were beginning to censor the advertisements they were paid to print. He emphasized two types of advertising that harmed public health: the first was "fraudulent statements or devices that hurt the pocketbook of the purchaser" and the second type claimed to cure "cancer, Bright's disease, consumption, and other malignant and oftentimes incurable maladies." He also included in the latter category "those so-called Lost Manhood preparations." These problems would continue unabated until legal action was taken against misleading labels.[51]

Crumbine was particularly incensed by the "oxygenor" fraud that swept Kansas in 1915. Fakers were selling these contraptions for $25–$35 and guaranteeing they would bring health to the purchaser. It had sets of wires running out of a cylindrical tube at each end. Users were to place the cylinder on an open window sill, fasten the anklets around the ankles, grab the handholds, and sit before the window and wait. The oxygen would "impinge" on the tube and "chase itself around the tube" and "generate great waves of health-giving oxygen" that "would pass through the wires . . . and through the body in great oxygen health waves." A tomato can closed at both ends "would do just as well," snorted the skeptical doctor, "or at any rate no worse." He added that "I suppose it is healthy to sit in front of an open window."[52]

The Prof. H. Samuels Co. of Wichita was selling a particularly successful product at this time. The man, "rated as a millionaire," peddled a colorless liquid to be dropped in the eye that he promised would reach every part of the body "through the nerves" and would cure "practically every disease." From July 1 to December 31, 1913, he enjoyed a total of $9,775 in sales but early the next year he and his product were barred from use of the U.S. mail because his solution was found to be composed of salt and sugar "in ordinary Wichita hydrant water."[53]

At the height of his tubercular campaign Samuel Crumbine was reaching the zenith of his popularity and acquiring an enviable reputation in the medical world. Some supporters were pleased, many were worried, when the governor of Illinois wrote the governor of Kansas in 1913 asking to "borrow" Crumbine for a few months to set up "a pure food department like that of Kansas." Illinois experts considered Crumbine the nation's leading public health authority and there were many who hoped he would replaced Harvey Wiley on the national level. Governor George Hodges declined the request, even though the current democratic-controlled legislature had just completed a partisan investigation of the secretary in order to remove Crumbine from office. The American Medical Association assigned a Providence doctor to investigate the operations of state boards of health. "I stopped off in Kansas," the investigator wrote, "to learn, not to investigate. Dr. Crumbine's work is too well known in the East to require anything but emulation." When Crumbine was elected to his second four-year term as secretary of the board of health, the *Boston Evening Transcript* celebrated the event by editorializing

> When a man not only performs the routine duties of an important office, but revolutionizes for public benefit old systems and practices, the country likes to know about him. . . . He had a keen professional eye for the causes of diseases and he acted promptly upon his discoveries. . . . Believing the people of Kansas would be willing to take the simple means necessary for protection against typhoid, malarial fever, and other germ diseases if properly instructed and warned [,] he prevailed upon the State printing committee to have printed five hundred copies a month of a health bulletin. It contains suggestions for preventing practically all the contagious and dangerous diseases incident to the State, with discussion of the pure food laws and the regulations of the department. The bulletin has a circulation of five thousand a month and possesses great instructive value.

J.W. Kerr, assistant surgeon general, made an investigation of Crumbine's work in Kansas in 1914 and reported that it was "one of the few really active states in health work."[54]

Crumbine and the state board of health, along with the U.S. Public Health Service, made water, sewage, and sanitation surveys of Wilson County under his direction in 1915 that cost $4,500. Wilson was selected for the study both because it was considered an average county and because it had encountered numerous cases of typhoid fever in recent months, caused by poor sanitation. This work was capped by a huge Sanitation Day in Fredonia, as one newspaper expressed it, "a new stunt in public health work." It was, the *Topeka Daily Capital* explained, "a combination of a homecoming week, a circus day, a farmers' week, and a Chautauqua." And it became a stunt only Samuel J. Crumbine could create. Schools in the area were dismissed and people from miles around came to see the parade. The governor, the state's two U.S. senators, many congressmen, Dr. L.L. Surgeon in charge of the rural sanitation work of the U.S. Public Health Service, and countless public health officials applauded the brass bands and twenty-six floats of one-mile length. Led by a grand marshal, mounted city marshals, and a platoon of Company E of the state militia, one float carried fifteen pretty girls with the banner "Better Cooks, Better Food, Better Health." Another float featured an enormous fly ridden by a skeleton and dozens of dolls, representing babies, lay at its feet. This was followed by an undertaker's hearse, then a float with a septic tank that had been adapted for rural use. A boy pumped water on another float with the label "Unsanitary Well. How About Yours?" Boys dressed in black robes had ropes tied around their necks, held by "Typhoid, the Lord High Executioner." Merchants sponsored floats for a sanitary baker, a sanitary grocer, etc. Ten thousand people cheered Dr. Crumbine when he called for a full-time health officer and the popular Governor Arthur Capper spoke for improved public health conditions. "We have reason to be proud of the place that Kansas has taken in the fight against preventable disease," the governor exulted.

> The secretary of our state board of health is not only himself a figure of national importance and international reputation, but many of the reforms he has instituted, many of the precautionaries he has promoted to safeguard the public health have—after a period of opposition and sometimes of ridicule—been adopted by all the more progressive states of the nation. Kansas has led the way in several health movements of vital importance.

Kansas had led the way because of Crumbine's emphasis on educating the public, which he was achieving in Fredonia that day.[55]

Samuel Crumbine was exceedingly, and justly, proud of his bulletin. He was quite pleased one day in 1911 when he received "the most encouraging letter" concerning it from Professor William T. Sedgwick of the Massachusetts Institute of Technology. The noted professor informed him that in a recent bulletin he "found . . . a statement so full of common sense and so unusual in its judiciousness that I felt impelled to drop you at least a line to say how good it seemed to me." The lines pertained to a food report concerning samples his inspectors found in a railroad work camp. The MIT professor noted that in America "second grade food" was not, contrary to popular opinion, "unwholesome . . . and people may be able to live comfortably, cheaply, and even happily." Americans, however, were reluctant to eat "broken grains of rice, beans or peas" that are "just as nutritious and wholesome as the whole grains of these stable foods." Some time later the doctor was in Sedgwick's office and noted a number of his bulletins on a desk. "Well you don't know it, Crumbine," he was informed "but I often find some useful source material for my classes in your bulletins [*sic*], especially your water and sewage reports." Using the facilities of the Lawrence Experiment Station of the Massachusetts Board of Health, Sedgwick was a pioneer in applying bacteriology to sanitary sciences and offered one of the nation's first courses in sanitation and public health at MIT. As noted earlier, he and Hiram Wells perfected the open slow sand filter to produce safe water.[56]

Crumbine, though, was not without his enemies, ever ready to pounce on a slipup. The editor of one of the Wichita newspapers wrote an editorial that "exhausts the syntax of sarcasm and deposits the results upon the mangled remains of Crumbine." Among other items, the editor resented his rule against the storage of undrawn poultry. "Why," exclaimed the writer, the Arctic explorers found walruses frozen in the ice, which have doubtless been there hundreds of years and just as fresh as the day they died." Another editor responded to this "rabid and unwarranted" attack by calling attention to the fact that the ruling came from the board of health, not just the secretary. The rule was not made "simply to make trouble for somebody" but came as a result of experience and investigation. The writer wondered if "the pure food regulations were pinching somewhere in the region of Sedgwick County."[57]

The national split in the Republican party in 1912, as a result of the Progressive Movement, also created a sharp division in the party in Kansas and this always was good news to the minority Democrats. As a result, the Democrats captured control of the governor's office in that election, as well as control of the state legislature for the first time in state history. Some of the victors decided their day in court had arrived and the well-known Republican doctor would be their victim. Aided by John Kleinhans within the department of health and led by Mike Frey, a Democrat from Junction City whose food preserving firm had been labeled "filthy" by the board of health, a combination of new political leadership, continuing critics of the board of health, and food and drug adulterers pounced on the diminutive doctor. The Kansas State Bottlers Association met in Salina and elected a delegation to go to Topeka "to help the fight being started" to remove Crumbine from his job. "They claim he has too much power and has put in force too many 'fool' rulings," they insisted, and W.H. Hazelton of Topeka was selected as their secretary to draft resolutions against him.

"Ole Doc Crumbine is to be investigated on various fool charges, and he chortles with glee over it," editorialized William Allen White of Emporia. "Nevertheless,"

"My little man, don't you think you are making too much noise for a peaceable community like ours?"

Crumbine Cartoon [Courtesy of the Clendening History of Medicine Library, University of Kansas Medical Center]

he continued, "the proposition to investigate him is insulting and only a fathead would be responsible for it." The critics hoped to find sufficient fault to be able to reorganize the board of health and staff it with "sensible" businessmen who understood and sympathized with the problems of the wholesale food and drug companies. A number of bills were introduced to change the board of health accordingly. The chief one provided for a board of health of seven physicians and three businessmen and the secretary could not be a member of the board, all of which could make possible Crumbine's removal from his office. Fortunately, three congressmen who were also physicians "made very plain to the members of the legislature the meaning of the proposed legislation" and "the vast majority of the legislature promptly killed the proposed reorganization scheme." The board's enemies, however, "were in such a powerful position" that the House Ways and Means committee "crippled" the board's budget for the next biennium.[58]

When this effort to eliminate the doctor failed, state representative Frey of Geary County introduced a resolution in the legislature calling for an investigating committee, which was named on February 27, 1913. Frey was a traveling salesman for a Topeka drug company that had given the food and drug division "a great deal of trouble" after the Kansas law was enacted. In addition, Frey's brother operated a restaurant and a Crumbine agent had arrested him after repeated warnings to correct "the filthy conditions" of his establishment. The resolution charged the committee to examine a number of issues including the waste of money on useless supplies, junkets to the East Coast for investigations, and the claim that Crumbine was drawing more salary than what was entitled to him, because he was also serving as dean of the state's medical school at the time. Support for the popular doctor quickly materialized from the press, pulpit, medical societies, citizens, and "a surprising number of grocers and druggists." *The Merchants Journal* editorialized that there was sufficient evidence to convict the doctor "of good management." William Allen White responded "that's the worst of politics. No matter how highly a man distinguishes himself for efficiency and devotion to the public service, he must expect attacks from pinhead politicians who want to attract a little attention. Crumbine has done more for the good fame of Kansas than all the one-horse politicians the state ever grew." On the eve of the doctor's appearance before the committee, one newspaper editor wrote

Investigatin' Crumbine
(With apologies to Kipling's "Dannie Deaver")

"What are the blow-flies buzzin' for"
    said Files on Parade.
"They think they're turnin' Crumbine
    out," the Color Sergeant said.
"What makes them seem to bloat and
    gloat?" said Files on Parade.
"They think they've got 'is bloomin'
    goat," the Color Sergeant said.
They're investigatin' Crumbine, you
    can hear the Dead March play;
The Committee in the State House, it
    investigates today,
They want to take his glasses off an'
    tear his eyes away

They're investigatin' Crumbine in the
    mornin'!"

What makes that beer-tank breathe
    so 'ard," said Files on Parade.
"'E' "s getting next to Doc old pard,"
    the Color Sergeant said.
"What makes that dope-fiend man
    fall down," said Files on Parade
"His joy's gone to his woozy crown,"
    the Color Sergeant said.
They're investigatin' Crumbine, turn-
    in' of 'im inside out;
They're bound to know his infamy
    'an just what he's about;
And I 'ope they catch it proper when
    they hear the people shout.
They're investigatin' Crumbine in the
    mornin'.

"What makes that old tin dipper
    play?" said Files on Parade.
"It goes to work agin today," the
    Color Sergeant said.
"What makes those oyster dealers
    sigh?" said Files on Parade.
"The oyster trade's been very dry,"
    the Color Sergeant said.
They're investigatin' Crumbine as they
    feel in duty bound,
They want to take his works apart
    and see the wheels go 'round,
The mourners are invited an the cof-
    fin's on the ground
They're investigatin' Crumbine in the
    mornin'.

"'I' 'd always 'eard that 'e was straight"
    said Files on Parade.
"'E wouldn't let 'em underweight,"
    the Color Sergeant said.
"'E didn't want to let me spit," said
    Files on Parade.
"And now he'll get the wust of it," the

Color Sergeant said.
"The're investigatin' Crumbine, you
    must mark 'im to his place;
They're familiar with canning an'
    They want to "can" his face
Let's 'ope they won't do nothin' that'll
    Bring the state disgrace
    Investigatin' Crumbine in the
    mornin'.
                    A Westerner[59]


One by one Crumbine countered the charges against him. His junket to Portland, Maine, where he had been elected president of the American Association of Food, Drug, and Dairy officers, had received prior legislative approval. Frey's charge that he had purchased and littered his office with a good deal of useless material amounting to $3,000, such as tin sputum cups, napkins, and waste bags was correct but they were to fill the prophylactic packets being mailed out to victims of tuberculosis, as required by law. The charge that the doctor was paid twice faded. He drew $4,000 yearly as dean of the medical school, but he had declined his salary of $2,500 for serving as secretary of the board of health during this period and it was never drawn. After taking much testimony similar to the above, the members finally came to the meat of their grievances against him. "Dr. Crumbine," roared the chief inquisitor, "on this bill from your office we find an item for a dictaphone. Can you explain sir, how you came to buy a talking machine for your home with the state's money?" The little man, his face impassive, responded quietly by explaining the function of a dictaphone and how, by purchasing one, he had saved the state the expense of hiring another stenographer at $900 annually. Unabashed, Congressman Taylor Riddle of Marion County returned to the attack. "Dr. Crumbine, we of the committee and all the other gentlemen of the legislature, have to shave with an old-fashioned straight back, or pay our money to the barber. Can you explain, sir, why you spent fifty dollars of the state's money for a shaving set?" Not at all nonplussed, with a straight face, the witness responded that the shaving kit was an instrument used to shave the costly dictaphone records so they could be used repeatedly. The inquisitor uttered a weak "oh," and this ended the investigation into Crumbine's dishonesty and incompetence.[60]

Congressmen Frey of Geary County and Riddle filed a minority report, refusing to exonerate Crumbine as the majority had done. Both houses voted almost unanimously to accept the majority report, although it was agreed that the dean of the medical school should also serve as secretary of the board of health but that the official's total salary should not exceed $4,000 annually, which was currently the situation. Otherwise, Democrats supported Republicans on the point that the investigative farce should end. William Allen White happily noted that all the other bills aimed at crippling the board of health that session "have been killed" and that "strong administration men laugh at the rumors of his removal." In fact, Crumbine ran unopposed for secretary two years later and was reelected for another four-year term. As a journal editor noted several years previously when Crumbine was being seriously touted by many for his obvious qualifications for the governor's office, he succeeded because "he has managed the affairs of his office independent of any political influence or the meddlesome activities of pure food cranks and it is doubtful if his sphere of usefulness could be increased by giving him the highest office in the state." Following the legislative session the board of health accepted food inspector John Kleinhans' resignation, noting that this action should not "be construed as excusing or condoning in the slightest degree his unjust, ungrateful and treacherous actions affecting the honor and efficiency of this Board" in supporting the investigation of its secretary.[61]

# FOUR

## IMPROVING CHILD HEALTH

Kansans found it difficult to survive the usual infant and childhood afflictions on the frontier. Officials kept inadequate records in the late nineteenth century, but the extant ones show that in 1875 almost 50 percent of the burials that year were of infants and children; in 1890 in Leavenworth, 134 of 233 burials were for infants and children under five years of age. A report two years earlier listed eight children in that city as having died of "teething," which indicates the inadequate medical reporting of the period. Infectious diseases constituted the greatest causes of these deaths. The prevalent diseases of scarlet fever, a streptococcus bacterial infection that was widespread, and smallpox and cholera were especially dreaded. Even measles took its toll as people found vaccinating against any of these diseases at that time to be very haphazard, especially in remote areas.[1]

Physicians contributed to part of the mortality rate because they tended to treat sick children the same way they would adults. In 1880 the American Medical Association established a "Section on the Diseases of Children," and the specialty of pediatrics developed soon thereafter, "but through the nineteenth century most of the medical care of children took place in the home." Modern doctors used the relatively new stethoscope but most on the frontier were inadequately equipped, in instruments, in knowledge, and in therapy. Some of their emetics and cathartics, and especially bloodletting, were downright harmful to sick children who were weakened, diarrhetic, and dehydrated by the time the parents finally took them to a doctor. Smallpox vaccinations had been common for decades and diphtheria antitoxin was coming into use, as was one for typhoid fever in Kansas after 1915. Crumbine's campaign for safer water and better sewage systems helped reduce deaths from these diseases dramatically, as did his educational campaign for healthier living. Abysmal knowledge of sanitation led many a pioneer mother to expose her children to infectious diseases and inadequate facilities and scarce material for diapers often led to drying dirty ones and then scraping them clean and airing them. Yet conditions slowly improved. As one authority expressed it, any community "that placed a high value on child life could not long overlook the problem of infant mortality and its causes." Improvements evolved and life expectancy increased. As urban areas built sewage and water plants and developed public services, health improved. Early in the twentieth century "public health measures, better nutrition, improved personal hygiene, and enhanced medical knowledge" led Samuel Crumbine and the state board of health to promote better infant and child care.[2]

Concern over the health care of infants and young children increased dramatically during the Progressive Movement. Efforts to protect them first centered on the concept that they should not be exploited by parents or employers, that they should not suffer from cruelty. Gradually that expanded exponentially until it included the right to life itself. Progressives eventually came to view reduction of infant mortality as representing "the same type of basic requisite for achieving an advanced level of civilization as outlawing child labor." Critics charged, though, that American policy focused rather narrowly on fighting infant mortality by emphasizing medical education and technology rather than a more comprehensive one of maternal support systems. This approach also was criticized for its unequal access to health care, leaving the poor at greater risk.[3]

From 1880 on the focus changed from concern over infant environment to that of how they were fed because of the high mortality rate from digestive and nutritional disorders. Then at the turn of the twentieth century reformers began concentrating on the problem of motherhood and the abilities of mothers to bear and rear healthy babies. It was at this juncture that Samuel Crumbine and his board of health took an increasing interest in child health reform. These concerns escalated attention across the nation, in Kansas, and in Crumbine's mind as he struggled to improve the condition of infants, especially among the poor and the rural, because their plight was by far the most serious in baby mortality. It was in this area that Crumbine's fame drew national attention and led to the last great phase of his career in promoting better public health.[4]

The board of health had authorized Crumbine to buy and distribute antitoxin for treatment of the poor periodically, but in 1916 he had depleted his appropriation for this purpose by June and some diphtheria epidemics were spreading in Southeast Kansas. He approached Governor Arthur Capper, requesting $250 from his emergency fund. Sorry, the governor told him, the fund was exhausted. A *Kansas City Star* reporter met him as he emerged from the chief executive's office. He knew something was wrong from the look on the doctor's face and quizzed him. That evening the news was splashed across the state "State Board of Health Unable to Furnish Antitoxin As Diphtheria Rages in Southeastern Kansas." Newspapers began asking "will the poor children be permitted to die while the state waits for the next appropriation?" When William Allen White read of this crisis, he asked ten good friends to send $25 to the board of health, which they did. When Crumbine reported his windfall to the governor, Capper curiously responded that he should return White's money and he would find "several hundred to tide you over." It is remarkable how adverse publicity can sometimes motivate politicians to find solutions to financial problems they otherwise would prefer to ignore.[5]

There were rascals who sought to take financial advantage of the diphtheria scare. The *Topeka Daily Capital* warned that Crumbine "has a knife out for all patent medicine vendors who claim to have a cure for diphtheria." Among other steps, he warned wholesale druggists in Kansas to watch for these swindlers as "there is no absolute cure and anyone who advertises is an imposter and violates food and drug laws." He noted that the department of health had "dozens of letters" from parents who tried these "cures," then went to their doctor for antitoxin and found it was too late to save the child.[6]

Crumbine also encountered the problem of skepticism on the part of some members of his profession. The anti-vaccinationist movement had many adherents at this time, among the public and also with a few in the medical profession. They believed that compulsory vaccination violated the liberties of the individual and that civilization should adhere to nature's laws of cleanliness. Sanitarians should remove the foul conditions that produce the disease, such as the polluted water systems that should be cleansed, they argued.[7]

Governor George Hodges wrote Crumbine that a child in Topeka had died from diphtheria and he was disturbed over the attending physician's attitude. The doctor declared that she did not believe in using antitoxin for the disease because "it is just as bad and that it kills as many persons as it cures." The governor asked Crumbine to investigate the case and "take such action for the protection of the public health as may seem necessary."

Crumbine detailed Dr. John Sippy, current state epidemiologist, to investigate and he quizzed Dr. M.A. Swift thoroughly. Swift was a homeopath with a degree from the State University of Iowa who had been practicing medicine since 1882. She had diagnosed the little girl as having tonsillitis and treated her accordingly. A short time later the child began "choking badly" and she then correctly identified diphtheria, but refused to administer an antidote. When Sippy queried Dr. Swift about the fact that the antitoxin was harmless when injected in a healthy person, she responded she had no personal experience with it but believed it produced "paralysis and affects the heart(,) producing death." Sippy concluded that the girl's death resulted from "ignorance," rather than neglect by Dr. Swift, adding that it was "lamentably true that we have far too many of this class of physicians, who are not well informed."[8]

Then there were doctors who, through ignorance, did much harm. A Woodson County doctor attempted to help his patients during an outbreak of smallpox but accidentally inoculated the community with a live virus instead of the less virulent form of vaccine and caused "a terrible epidemic."[9]

Despite opposition from anti-vaccinationists and outdated doctors, Crumbine and his board decided to experiment with the immunization of the school children of the entire county of Waubunsee. Meetings were held, the necessary public education was undertaken, and then he completed the first countywide immunization program in Kansas. The following year recorded the last death from diphtheria in Waubunsee County. The success here led to similar programs being conducted in other counties and states.[10]

Dr. Crumbine wrote that the time was fast approaching "when every case of diphtheria will be an indictment against the intelligence of the parent" because they were being made aware of courses of action for prevention of the disease, and if they did not take advantage of it the fault lay with them. Then he added, "nor will it be many years before every death from diphtheria will be referred to a coroner's jury for investigation to fix charges." At the same time he announced plans of the State and Provincial Health Officers Association, to which he was elected president in June 1913, to try to immunize all the pre-school and school children of the United States and Canada at the beginning of the fall term in 1916.[11]

Through Crumbine's persistent efforts, the state legislature finally helped children by insisting that their existence be recorded. The Vital Statistics law of 1911 required all births and deaths in Kansas be reported by the local county health official. Crumbine informed the public that death notices would assist in locating centers of disease and they cooperated. Kansas was added to the federal Registration Area for Deaths, indicating that mortality records were significant, and justifying Crumbine's demand for them, if such were needed. As for birth registrations, state registrar William J.V. Deacon pointed out that Kansans were paying 25 cents to $5 to register their animals, thus why should they not want to spend a quarter to register a son or daughter? "Who knows what contingency might arise." he asked, that would "make it desperately difficult for her to prove herself your child?" Inheriting from her parents, for instance, might be a challenge this would resolve. Everyone needed to have their birth, marriage, and death recorded officially and this would now be achieved in Kansas.[12]

Coinciding with this effort to require official statistics, came Crumbine's determination to study rural mortality rates. Reform of infant mortality rates began as a problem of urban areas but his state was primarily a rural one and this issue was of great concern to him. Under his auspices, the United States Department of Labor dispatched Elizabeth Moore and Frances Valentine to Kansas to obtain "the first statistics on rural mortality ever undertaken by the United States government." On the doctor's recommendation, they selected Ford County to begin their study. They planned a house-to-house survey of the county in which a baby had been born since October 1, 1914. The specialists, who were cognizant of rates differing from area to area, previously had studied nine cities and they wanted to ascertain how rural people compared to their urban counterparts.[13]

Child health reform was beginning to concern specialists everywhere during this era. Dr. S. Josephine Baker became the driving force behind New York City's public health campaign against high infant mortality rates after the turn of the century. By 1908 she had lobbied successfully to convince the city's board of health to create a child hygiene division with her as its head. Designing a program of maternity education, she developed "several methods of baby-saving that were copied by health departments throughout the country." Among other techniques, she used trained nurses to visit mothers, examine their babies, and instruct them in proper child care. The infant mortality rate had long troubled Crumbine and he decided to work for a similar bureau for Kansas. First, though he needed to mobilize his forces.[14]

He made certain that Kansas mothers became aware of Baker's great work in reducing infant mortality rates in New York City. When concerned parents formed the Kansas branch of the Mothers and Parent–Teachers Association in Topeka, a child development committee was established under its aegis. This group then resolved to petition the next legislature to create a similar division under the umbrella of the state department of health. Soon thereafter, with publicity assistance from Crumbine, a State Good Citizenship League met in Emporia and resolved to join this movement, as did the State Federation of Women's Clubs meeting in Wichita at that time, a very powerful organization for reform in Kansas.[15]

Crumbine proceeded to draft the necessary legislation, which the legislature adopted during its 1915 session. The measure directed the board of health to create a Division of Child Hygiene whose duties "shall include the issuance of educational literature on the care of the baby and the hygiene of the child, the study of the causes of infant mortality and the application of preventative measures for the prevention and suppression of the diseases in infancy and early childhood."[16]

The House Committee of the Whole unanimously recommended passage of the bill. H. Lewellen Jones of Meade was the lone voice of protest when he tried to place control of the new bureau under the board of health, not its secretary. "The perennial fight against Crumbine," reported the *Topeka Daily Capital*, "appeared for just a moment, but got nowhere." Robert Stone of Topeka, speaker of the lower house, promised the legislative members that "this new bureau is going to get an appropriation from this legislature sufficient to enable Doctor Crumbine to carry out the provisions of the bill. The few thousand dollars required are as nothing compared to the saving of the lives of the babies of Kansas that are lost every year from preventable diseases." Everyone appeared supportive of motherhood and babies, for the moment! This was the second child health division in the nation, following that in New York.[17]

Crumbine's child health campaign was preceded by, and accompanied with, his usual public relations effort of educating. When the International Congress on Hygiene and Demography met, he publicized their announcement on infant hygiene. The congress stressed the importance of infant mortality statistics and noted that Sweden and Norway had the lowest rates in the world because their mothers led the world in percentage of breast feeding. Some of the speakers emphasized that half the current American infant mortality rate was preventable and Dr. William H. Davis of Boston read a paper that concluded that baby deaths would decline 60 percent if none were fed from a bottle. Others urged keeping babies away from dogs, cats, and other house pets because "the fur from these animals gathers up disease germs as a broom gathers up dust."[18]

"Flies Kill Babies, Dr. Crumbine Says," blared a headline announcing the doctor's summer campaign in 1915—"To Cut Heavy Deaths in Kansas." Last year, the story reported, 3,601 babies under two years of age died of various causes, representing 20 percent of the state's deaths.

> That's too many babies dying for Kansas, said Dr. Crumbine. Nearly all these deaths from digestive diseases can and should be stopped, and the board of health is going to wage a campaign for the babies this summer. During the hot weather the babies often have to wear too much clothing and too hot clothing. Sometimes the mothers are not just as careful about the food as they should be, and they let flies get into the baby's milk. Flies cause more deaths of babies than anything else. They spread poison and disease in their food. Give the baby just as few clothes as the law allows and see that the baby has the purest sweetest, and most carefully guarded food that can be provided, and don't be afraid of water.

Summer diarrhea was the major cause of baby deaths at the time, especially in urban areas. The story announced that the board was preparing a special issue of its bulletin with instructions for physicians on clothing and feeding babies, noting that a pamphlet on feeding and caring for infants had already been sent "to every mother in Kansas," but doctors also needed instructions on this important health problem.[19]

The German Max von Pettenkofer was the first to calculate the cost of sanitary reform versus the savings it produced and his concept was utilized readily by Crumbine and his staff. "When the average funeral costs $60 and a baby's life can be saved for $15, save the babies," was the phrase coined by Crumbine in 1916, a graphic slogan taken up by Kansas club women in an effort to persuade the state legislature to appropriate $15,000 annually for child hygiene. With this sum, the doctor believed, 1,000 Kansas babies could be saved annually. "Put the question on a straight commercial basis," he said. "A thousand babies would make a thousand families happy and the expense of $15,000 would in reality be a net saving of $5,000" because of burial costs of infants lost. The club women eagerly endorsed his plan to use the money to gather vital statistics weekly rather than monthly, and to send a corps of nurses into Kansas homes to assist mothers and their babies. With shocking statistics such as this, and support for his ideas, the doctor persuaded the legislature that a department of child hygiene would be a good investment for the state.[20]

This story was followed by a lengthy news article in the capital's leading newspaper entitled "Common Sense Rules in Care of the Baby." The report emphasized the importance of breast feeding for the health of the baby until it was at least six months old. Regularity in time, clean nipples, and a maximum of twenty minutes per feeding were recommended, as well as proper rest and a diet for the mother, consisting of less meat than usual, more milk, and avoidance of fresh sour fruits. All this was good advice, assuming the mother did not have to work to help support the family, as did so many mothers of poor families.[21]

To garner more publicity, Crumbine and the department of health sponsored a Better Babies contest at the State Free Fair in Topeka in 1914. This was a popular national competition but a stunt that to the modern mind appears much like the judging of livestock at the same function. On the other hand, this was a period of a "cult of motherhood" where middle-class women were "flocking to well-baby classes, organizing baby health shows, and purchasing Holt's *The Care and Feeding of Children* in such numbers as to make it a bestseller." They wanted to learn how to be the best mother possible. The magazine, *Woman's Home Companion*, sponsored "best baby" shows and the National Federation of Women's Clubs were successful in having a "national baby week" proclaimed.[22]

Crumbine's forces erected a large tent as a center and both graduate nurses and practicing physicians specializing in dentistry, eye, ear, nose, and throat diseases were on hand to assist mothers and to judge the 460 babies enrolled in the contest. Billed as "one of the greatest drawing cards of the fair," speakers included Crumbine, J.J. Sippy, and J.E. Hunt, head of the baby hospital at the University of Kansas Medical Center. Louise Bullens, a nurse from Topeka, held a roundtable for mothers, instructing them in proper baby care. Each child received a thorough examination before the contest to insure against the spread of infectious diseases. Mothers, of course, are convinced their baby is perfect and some received a jolt from the results of the inspection. The judges had a rehearsal for their judging and some mothers asked for their babies to be examined in this preliminary round to demonstrate how well theirs would score. One woman was "shocked" when the doctor discovered "adenoids" because she "had not the remotest idea that her baby was imperfect."[23]

The new division of child hygiene was launched on July 1, 1915, under the supervision of Samuel Crumbine, who chose Dr. Lydia Allen DeVilbiss of New York City to administer it. She had been directing better baby contests for magazines with large national circulations for several years and was recognized as "one of the best known and most capable authorities" on child health in the nation. Currently DeVilbiss was in charge of the educational and child health division of the New York Board of Health, but Crumbine convinced her to move to Kansas and use her experience to establish his new bureau. "The united pleas of club women and labor organizations of the state" convinced her to take a cut in salary to accept the challenge in the Sunflower state. In announcing her acceptance of the job, Crumbine said that "most of the babies who died under two years of age have only the carelessness of the mothers to blame for this." Dr. DeVilbiss was "coming to Kansas to conduct an educational campaign to save the lives of the little folks," he said. "Her job is to see that every baby has a chance." Despite repeated assurances of adequate funding, the legislature had cut Crumbine's request for $15,000 annually for the division to $5,000. Whenever a baby was born in Kansas, the department of health received a report of it and Dr. DeVilbiss announced that she "would see that every baby had a chance" at life by having physicians and nurses trained in child hygiene available for assistance in the home.[24]

Upon her arrival in Kansas on July 2, 1915, DeVilbiss was reported "Enthusiastic Over Outlook" for her bureau, with an agenda "this long," stretching her arms as far apart as possible. She had "gone over the ground with Dr. Crumbine and have found out just what things Kansas already has along the lines of child welfare." The expert "expressed herself agreeably surprised when told of the recent establishment of the small debts court," one of the products of the Progressive Movement, and was pleased to learn that Kansas had pioneered in this idea. "It shows an advanced state of public opinion," she stated, "when such laws as this are enacted." She promised to begin issuing a bulletin from the division periodically and pledged to work with—and through—the federated women's clubs, parent–teachers organizations, and existing child welfare agencies.[25]

She learned rapidly and, like her counselor Samuel Crumbine, Lydia Vilbiss soon became a center of energy in planning, executing, and educating. Besides editing bulletins, she gave numerous public speeches and prepared "The Kansas Mother's Book," which became so popular it went through numerous printings. She supervised the appointment of Juvenile Health officers in the public schools and sent instruction forms for teachers to use in reporting on the health of their students.[26]

A leading newspaper reported that she "seems to have the art of getting publicity," much like her mentor. Not all editors were pleased, however, with her selection. The *Atchison Globe* took pleasure in referring to her as "the skinny old maid trying to teach Kansas mothers how to rear children." The *Salina Journal*, on the other hand, responded that she actually was "buxom" and observed that "many Kansas editors are kicking up an awful ruckus because Kansas has employed a woman to see that the babies have a better chance." The *Topeka Daily Capital* reported that "the woman in charge of this new bureau has already qualified (as a child expert) because the whining of the shocked men in Kansas does not perturb her."[27]

Like Crumbine, DeVilbiss gave sound, commonsense advice to mothers that included the admonition that babies do not know right from wrong, so harsh punishment has no place in their rearing. Instead, regularity and habits were important in baby development, she warned. Babies are born without them "and what habits he shall develop and whether they are good or bad habits depends usually on the mother or those who are responsible for their care." Nervous impulses from the senses pass to the brain, making pathways, and repetition travels over the same path leading to habits. Make certain those impulses were good ones so proper habits would form. Babies should have abundant fresh air and sunlight and the right to cry as that is part of their physical exercise. She cautioned mothers against rocking the baby too strenuously, jumping them up and down on her knee, shaking the bed, or constantly keeping the infant in motion.[28]

Her Little Mothers League was highly successful, an idea she brought with her from New York City. S. Josephine Baker initiated this program in New York City to attack the problem of immigrant families using the oldest daughter, often a child herself, to take care of infants. Her idea was to teach them to nurture their young siblings and, in the process, not only improve this care but also expecting the girls to make an impression on their mothers in the raising of children. The idea caught on and by 1915 some 45 cities had almost 50,000 young ladies involved. Girls were enrolled with membership cards and graduated with certificates. They attended meetings and lectures on proper care of babies and had "hands on" experience with dolls or oftentimes with live infants. In the process the girls learned a great deal about personal hygiene and would, as a result, have healthy bodies and become better future mothers.[29]

The goal of DeVilbiss was eventually to reduce infant mortality by 50 percent. Five thousand babies under age two died annually in Kansas. "If a tornado were to wipe out a city like Wellington, Galena, Concordia, or Junction City," she said in her first bulletin, "the entire state would be instantly aroused," but the numbers were similar. "And the greatest tragedy of all," she added, was that "these 5,000 babies are born only to sicken and die needlessly." A majority of them would survive if their mother had "known how to care for them." Her objective was to teach that proper nurture and save at least half of the losses.[30]

Because the baby clinic at the state fair in 1914 had proven so popular, DeVilbiss planned a repeat the next fall, but she learned from the previous year's experience. When the fair planners fretted about replacing the baby contest, which Crumbine wanted done because of its competitive nature, DeVilbiss developed a child hygiene exhibit that promised to be "one of the greatest educational parts of the fair." The *Topeka Daily Capital* headlined the clinic as "First of Its Kind to Be Held West of Mississippi." Lillian Davis, superintendent of the Public Health Nursing Association in Topeka, pledged "plenty of nurses on hand" to examine babies while mothers were visiting the fair exhibits. A large tent placed "in a cool spot" had cots available and, with all the arrangements completed, all babies who were brought there would "have all the care they need."[31]

More important, DeVilbiss set up a program to grade babies on their strengths and weaknesses. The accompanying certificate would contain information on how to correct defects that were discovered, such as adenoids or imperfect teeth which, if remedied in time, would improve their health. Her approach was to have ultimately an organization in every town in Kansas that would sponsor a "Baby Week" where babies could have a thorough examination free, both physically and mentally, with a score card. Those children passing with a score of 90 or more would receive a Grade A certificate. Those with Grade B certificates would have the defects and remedies listed for parental remedial action. Her intention was to "obviate the heartaches and petty jealousies" attendant to baby contests with points and prizes that had occurred the previous year. No one but the parents and the division of child hygiene would know the child's score. Teeth scored eight points, and eye, ear, nose, and throat were twelve each, with mental scores up to twenty. Attention span, irritability, and digestion also counted.[32]

The "baby week" in Topeka that fall produced good scores by infants in the capital city. "Kansas Babies Surely Quoted Far Above Par" read the headline of one newspaper. Some of the more prominent citizens brought their youngsters for examination and, among other results, this pricked the bubble that the poor man's child was healthier and better developed than the rich man's and it "is in great danger of bursting." Interestingly, given the strong beliefs of Dr. DeVilbiss on physical punishment, Dr. C.H. Van Horn of Topeka was a featured speaker at the meeting at the city auditorium during the fair. He believed in "the limited and controlled method of corporal punishment of children." He advocated the use of the paddle "conscientiously and properly" to solve many "household juvenile problems." He insisted that "child training in the home has as great effect upon preserving health as upon instilling into the child proper morals and thrift."[33]

DeVilbiss soon initiated another program begun by Dr. Baker in New York City, the idea of a portable school of motherhood, an affair that she could move from town to town. Courses on feeding and clothing infants would be presented that would replace the old method of learning by trial and error. "This was too costly a method," she announced, because the death rate was higher among first-born babies "on whom the mothers are experimenting." The mothers often went to dry-goods stores and purchased a pattern to make baby clothes, for instance, that were "fluffy ruffles, be-ribboned and be-feathered." Instead, she said, "every child has the right to beautiful and comfortable clothing." She emphasized that

> we have read of the sacrifices to the god Moloch. Children were cast into his bowels, a fiery furnace, as a propitiation to him for sin. We are also familiar with the stories of how children were thrown to the crocodiles along the Ganges, children in China were left in towers to die, weak children in ancient Sparta were left out in the open to die from exposure. Yet in the wealthy state of Kansas, civilized and cultured, there are offered 4,000 children, ten each day of the year on the altar of sacrifice—sacrificed to the god of greed and ignorance.

The previous year in Chicago, Dr. Harry J. Haiselden captured national headlines and heated debates with his refusals to operate on newborn defective babies. Surely DeVilbiss was aware of this potent debate over eugenics when she made her statement about infanticide practices of these societies. She was learning quickly from Crumbine the methods of propaganda in swaying public opinion.[34]

Acting upon the suggestion of Crumbine, DeVilbiss established a system of surveying children and their medical needs when their parents were financially unable to provide the necessary care. She sent application forms to county health officers concerning dependent, crippled, or defective children and the legislature was persuaded to make provision for state aid to them. As a result, a boy who badly burned the ends of his fingers and had two of them grow together, received an operation to relieve the problem. Another boy with crippled legs was placed under the care of a surgeon who straightened them. In other instances babies who were becoming blind because of inadequate treatment had their eyesight restored. These outcomes, DeVilbiss noted, "cannot be measured in dollars and cents." Requests for help in planning these programs poured in and she traveled widely to other states to give them assistance in establishing similar programs. Crumbine also was in constant demand as a speaker on child health.[35]

This involved a huge mailing program and Crumbine was rapidly depleting the department of health's budget for the year. He explained his problem to friends in the U.S. Public Health Service and they responded by appointing him a "collaborating epidemiologist." This appointment carried with it the franking privilege to mail correspondence connected with this work. Physicians would report child health problems to him with franked envelopes he gave them and the division of child health, in turn, would frank bulletins entitled "The Care of the Baby" to mothers whom doctors had reported. He received an initial supply of 25,000 of each of these bulletins and envelopes. One newspaper headlined this as "Dr. J.J. Crumbine Now Stork's Advanced Agent" and noted that this franking privilege saved the state of Kansas $3,000 annually. Actually, this permitted the department of health to use its meager funds for other beneficial purposes.[36]

J.W.V. Deacon, state registrar of vital statistics, picked up on the theme of ignorance, by announcing that "thirteen hundred short coffins that should not have been necessary were used last year in Kansas," because of ignorance or carelessness. Half of the 2,598 infant deaths in the state in 1915 could have been prevented but for "dirt, destitution, and disease." He happily noted that the number of lives of babies that were wasted because of improper food was on the decrease. Sixty-eight counties and registration cities in the state enjoyed a waning of the mortality rates, although forty-three counties showed an increase over the previous year.[37]

When the famous Theodore Dreiser became editor of *The Delineator*, he joined the campaign of saving babies and educating mothers. His publisher hired nurses and doctors to examine babies and visit homes. In 1917, *The Delineator* reported on its campaign for better statistical reporting and for stimulating public interest in reducing infant mortality numbers. Under the title "Save the Seventh Baby," taken from the current statistic that one American baby in seven died before its first birthday, the journal published advice columns and dispatched nurses throughout the country to communities of 10,000 to 40,000 population to work with local organizations on surveying infant mortality and making recommendations to try to raise the health consciousness of the public. It also made available a laboratory chemist to analyze milk supplies and sent a traveling exhibit to tour the country. The magazine's doctor wrote a summary of the findings, telling people how to save the lives of their babies by improving their water and sewage systems, by upgrading the quality of baby milk, by reporting vital statistics more accurately, by increasing the medical knowledge of the mothers, and by establishing clinical services. It was easy to prove that establishing a health nurse would save any community money. Samuel Crumbine wrote the editor to congratulate the journal's attempt at "a quickening of the public consciousness to a keener realization of the waste in our high infant mortality, a considerable portion of which we now know to be entirely preventable."[38]

That same year Crumbine's special campaign against deaths from typhoid fever began to produce real results. His demands for improved water and sewage systems were proving effective. In addition, the survey in Sumner County in 1914 helped. The study "was hooted at by some of the wise ones when it started," but the resulting recommendations that were carried out resulted in a drop from seven typhoid deaths in that county to zero in one year. A few weeks ago, Crumbine advertised, overall the federal census showed Kansas "to have the lowest death rate of any state in the registration area of the United States and also graded the work of the vital statistics registration department as the nearest perfect of any state in the Union." These were accomplishments in which he took special pride.[39]

DeVilbiss' division of child hygiene established a new contest in 1916. An inter-county competition was held to determine the healthiest county in the state. The one with the best record on junior health officers, absence of child labor, effectiveness of county health office and medical society, sanitary conditions of churches and community clubs, child hygiene activities of women's clubs and organizations, activities of county commissioners, and pure food and drug inspections, would receive an annual Capper Trophy.[40]

In 1915 the National Tuberculosis Association sponsored the Modern Health Crusaders program and DeVilbiss quickly picked up on this idea and promoted it in Kansas. Participants were encouraged to bathe regularly, wash their hands before meals, and brush their teeth twice daily. When these were completed, the children would chart them and progressively qualify as "pages," "squires," and "knights." In addition, the Metropolitan Life Insurance Company organized a Health and Happiness League in which its members pledged not to use a common drinking cup, not to spit in public places, not to litter streets, and "to destroy every house-fly [they] possibly [could]."[41]

In 1910 Crumbine faced an epidemic of infantile paralysis or poliomelytis of unknown proportions. Ninety such cases were reported to him in 1909 but the following year the number jumped to an alarming 200 along with a 24.6 percent case fatality rate. As he noted to a physician friend in New York, "the disease was quite unknown in Kansas at that time" and doctors "were more or less confused as to diagnosis and treatment." Crumbine requested the University of Kansas Medical Center to assign Professor A.L. Skoog to assist him in surveying the epidemic area. He reported the results one year later. First, they discovered that there had been "a very hot and dry summer" especially in the two counties that were hardest hit. Secondly, they found that "many horses and cattle died in the epidemic area." Dr. Skoog thought that the latter might have a significant connection with the human epidemic but they "had neither the time nor the funds" to pursue this line of research further. This plague continued to bedevil the child health bureau during its existence, some years becoming worse than others without rhyme or reason.[42]

The Northeast "suffered one of the most devastating polio epidemics ever recorded" in 1916. The case rate was 28.5, or more than three times the national rate in the previous seven years, in the most blighted area. In New York City a case fatality rate of 27 percent was reported and a case worker noted that mothers would not allow

Healthiest County Award [Kansas State Historical Society]

their children on the streets and closed all the windows to prevent the "disease" from entering the house. Crumbine faced a similar crisis in Kansas at the same time.[43]

Representing the Kansas board of health, Crumbine met with Dr. F.H. Matthews, president of the Missouri board of health, to plan for a united front in fighting the potential epidemic that was "sweeping the nation." Parents of young children were terrified of the disease and at that time Crumbine could only advise them to keep their youngsters away from homes where there was an acute illness or from persons who recently arrived from New York City. "Don't begin doping the children," he counseled, "but make certain their food and water are pure and keep them away from crowds of strangers." Otherwise, there were no known medicines or preventive measures to be administered. Jonas Salk would not develop his vaccine until 1955. A week after the first case, the doctor received a report of a case in Salina, the sixth such in the state. Still, he noted, the death rate from tuberculosis was 95 percent and, while he did not want to minimize the dangers from polio, he wished "the people could become as fully aroused to the dangers of tuberculosis as they are of infantile paralysis."[44]

The state legislature that met in 1919, following the end of World War I, was dominated as usual by agrarian representatives but proved to be particularly conservative and parsimonious. The war period witnessed an inflationary rate of 100 percent and the postwar era sparked a reactionary impulse across the nation. The *Topeka Daily Capital* concluded that this legislature especially had "a grouch against the wimmin folk." The two most prominent women in the state government faced difficulties with those solons. The antilabor legislature that established the Kansas Industrial Court to determine arbitrarily labor–management issues, nearly succeeded in revising the state department of labor into a state of incompetency and eliminating the position of Linna Bresette, secretary of the industrial welfare commission. More importantly, the legislature refused to give Dr. DeVilbiss a much deserved raise in salary. Of the seven states that then had divisions of child hygiene, Kansas paid its director the lowest, yet had the lowest infant mortality rate in the nation reported two years earlier in 1917. Those states paid salaries of $4,000–$6,000, while DeVilbiss received $2,500 for similar responsibilities. No legislator proposed an increase for "the official who every working day in the year is busy sending mothers information that helps them save their babies," complained one newspaper, "or is compiling information that enables health authorities to solve problems in child welfare." She initiated the prenatal service that was quickly adopted by California, Massachusetts, and Wisconsin. More than a dozen states used her "Kansas Mothers' Book," yet the state paid its livestock commissioner $3,500 annually, which was "considerably more than what the head of the division of child hygiene received." Even the Marion County health officer and the health officer of Manhattan received a higher salary than DeVilbiss. One legislator begged his colleagues to pay "as much for little children to come unto her who has in hand the welfare of the children as we are preparing to pay for little pigs to come unto him who is livestock sanitary inspector," to no avail. Pigs were important to these agrarian representatives.[45]

Crumbine mounted a campaign to seek greater public support for his work and his subordinates. During the legislative session he planted a story in the state's leading newspaper emphasizing the success of the division of child hygiene. Through "an intensive campaign to educate mothers in the care of their children" over the last two years they managed to save the lives of over 500 babies, "exclusive of epidemic influenza," it said. The account noted that "hundreds of friendly letters of appreciation from mothers are received weekly, thanking the child hygiene division for 'the real service being given.'" The division's $7,500 annual appropriation for helping the state's 600,000 children actually cost one-sixteenth of a cent per child. But the legislature was in a cost-cutting, not cost-increasing mood, at least for little ones.[46]

The senate Ways and Means committee, in a fit of economizing, cut the requested appropriation for the state livestock commission from $25,000 to $15,000 and the child hygiene request from $12,500 back to the current $7,500. The senator from Emporia presented strong arguments against cutting the livestock commission appropriation because of the fear of a hog cholera epidemic and successfully persuaded a majority to rescind the reduction. The senator from Topeka sought to restore the slash in the child hygiene request also, but was unsuccessful. "That is just the trouble," groused the solon, "the legislature commences on the children when it becomes economical." Saving pigs again won out over saving babies.[47]

Dr. DeVilbiss had finally had enough. All state employees deserved a significant increase in salary to offset the wartime inflation rate of 100 percent, but her salary was scandalously low even before American entry into the war, without augmentation. "She has turned the eyes of every state in the union towards Kansas to see what Kansas folks are doing for their children," reported another Crumbine story in a newspaper. But enough was enough. When the legislature of 1919 adjourned without rewarding her properly for her great work, she announced "I can't afford to stay any longer." She spent that summer in Chautauqua in the East and in the fall of 1919 she joined New York University "in special work."[48]

DeVilbiss was replaced by Dr. Florence B. Sherbon. She lasted two years on the job before she surrendered and began a teaching career at the University of Kansas. In an interview upon her departure from office, she admitted regret at leaving Dr. Crumbine and the department of health but she could not continue another two years on state financing that averaged 1.5 cents per child annually. The division of child hygiene received the same $7,500 annually that it had received since its founding, yet wartime inflation had cut this amount in half. While she did not begrudge the handsome funding for calves and pigs in Kansas, she said, the law required the division to visit all children's homes and maternity homes twice annually but this was impossible without adequate support. Even these license fees for inspection went into the state treasury instead of the division. As a result, Kansas was losing "practically as many mothers and babies during childbirth as it did a decade previously." Dr. Crumbine "is better appreciated outside the state than he is in it," she concluded, proving the Scriptural adage that a prophet is without honor in his own country. She found her situation hopeless and she admitted that "one gets weary of trying to make bricks without straw."[49]

The Warren Car [Kansas State Historical Society]

The "Warren car" proved to be the most publicized, and effective, campaign of the division of child hygiene, but it too faced sparse financial support from the legislature. In 1916 the Pullman company donated a railcar that Crumbine and Charles H. Lerrigo, his successor as president of the Kansas Tuberculosis and Health Association, converted into a public health exhibit to tour the state in promoting the current drive against tuberculosis and for improved child health. It was named Warren after the Crumbine son. Warren graduated from Washburn College in 1913 and two years later he married Beulah Searle of Geneva, Ohio, whom he met while they were in college. The couple held a joint wedding reception with the twenty-fifth wedding anniversary of his parents. Katherine was a member of the Topeka Federation of Women, the Morning Music Club, the Westside Reading Club, and the Forestry Club. The ladies of these organizations, plus Samuel's medical colleagues, made certain this was a major social event for the capital city. The young couple left soon after for Shanghai where the groom managed the Amos Bird Company, a large egg-packing house. In February 1916 he died of double pneumonia, a devastating loss to the Crumbines. Beulah also contracted pneumonia, but she fortunately recovered and returned to America.[50]

The Warren car became a successful educating exhibit and the railroads carried it free of charge. It visited all towns in Kansas of 500 or more population and stayed from one day to two weeks, depending on the size of the area. After it visited every town on the Union Pacific it was switched to the Missouri Pacific and the two lines and their branches combined covered most of Kansas. It ultimately toured the state for five years with displays on infant and child care. One observer described its effectiveness as suggesting "the method and directness of a circus organization." They sent advanced publicity to city officials, club women, school superintendents, and newspapers. When it arrived in town the telephone operator gave the rural folks a line ring. One section used wooden dolls to carry messages of importance on fresh air, exercise, correct food and clothing. Another popular one featured model school lunches. It was especially effective with young ones. Children, with their receptive and impressionable minds, visited the car in the mornings in groups of classes and parents with infants and preschoolers came in the afternoons. Mothers could have one of the public health nurses examine their babies and receive advice and literature on child care, all without traveling to their doctor and this service was free. Operators reported the following interests of visitors in rank order: (1) diet, (2) sanitation, (3) tuberculosis, (4) communicable diseases, (5) shoes for women. All of this cost Kansas citizens one-sixth of a cent annually per capita, compared to 25 cents they spent yearly on livestock and agricultural purposes. Even this minute amount proved to be too expensive for the niggardly state legislature and the car was retired on July 1, 1921. Meanwhile, other states eagerly copied the idea and during the legislative session that refused further appropriations to keep it in operation, the division of child health received an invitation to bring the car to Des Moines to lobby, successfully, for a similar exhibit in the farm state of Iowa.[51]

During the debate over the appropriations in 1921, one legislator offered to donate $2,000 of the $3,000 requested for the Warren car, but the majority insisted on economizing. The importance of the division and its educational efforts with the car, meant by that time that the average Kansas child could expect to live five years longer than those from other states. "Such a record for Kansas," the eminent public health authority Dr. Haven Emerson wrote Crumbine at the time, "reflects the work of the state board of health and is an answer to the talk of cutting down on the appropriation—which means lessening our work—for the state board of health."[52]

During the year that the Kansas legislature decided the state's children did not need such lavish funding, the national Congress concluded that this work was important enough to deserve national support and enacted a grants-in-aid program in 1921 to assist states in funding. Following passage of the pure food and drug law in 1906, members of Congress were increasingly swept up in the Progressive Movement and enacted a number of measures to help working people. In 1903 it created the Department of Commerce and Labor and a decade later separated the two so that laborers would have a cabinet-level department working for their interests. In 1910 Congress established the Postal Savings system, which provided working people with an outlet for depositing their meager savings at interest, small sums that banks would not accept.

In 1911 Congress passed the Weeks Act, which was designed to assist states in forest fire prevention. This program had immense ramifications for future growth of federal power, launching it into activities previously considered the exclusive realm of the states. As new areas of need for governmental assistance opened up, and states could not always finance these expensive new requirements, the national government began its first dollar-matching concept with the Weeks Act that granted money to states with conditions attached to the spending of those funds. (Some federal agencies had adopted this principle earlier to support their work, such as the National Bureau of Health in the late nineteenth century.) Toward the end of the Progressive Era Congress extended this type of aid to states in the construction of highways, for agricultural extension programs, and for assisting disabled veterans of World War I. By the time the latter was enacted, World War I had ended the Progressive Movement, but the grants-in-aid concept had succeeded so well that the national government utilized it increasingly for the remainder of the twentieth century. By this means Progressives sought to encourage states to support socially beneficial activities they could not fund without financial assistance.

In the second decade of the twentieth century, the American Association for Labor Legislation (AALL) assisted Progressive reform by pressing for a medical insurance program for laborers that would include lost wages compensation, death, and medical benefits, including maternity assistance. The women of the working poor usually had to work in order for the family to survive but either lost this income during the childbirth period and risked exhausting meager savings or else had to return to work far sooner than was good for her or her baby. The upper house of the New York legislature approved the plan but none of the states passed legislation to establish a sickness program. There was just too much opposition to the idea from commercial insurance companies and employer associations. Reformers turned, instead, to the concept of grants-in-aid to meet the challenge.[53]

Jeanette Rankin, congresswoman from Montana, introduced this legislation in the sixty-fifth and sixty-sixth congresses and Senator Joe Robinson, Democrat from Arkansas, sponsored a similar bill. Their measures were based on the report in 1917 by Julia Lathrop of the Children's Bureau on the need for this legislation. But it was not until 1921 when a Democratic senator from Texas and a Republican congressman from Iowa sponsored it that Congress approved the "Act for the Promotion of the Welfare and Hygiene of Maternity and Infancy," or the Sheppard–Towner Act. Infant and maternal welfare activists, such as Josephine Baker and Philip Van Ingen testified in support of the bill. They argued that 80 percent of American women were without prenatal care and, as a result, America's neonatal and maternal mortality rates were higher than any other industrialized nation. Led by the powerful American Medical Association, opponents of the measure argued that it would grant control over medical matters to lay people, provide an opening wedge for socialized medicine, and, most important, that it invaded states' rights. The American Medical Association would oppose the concept during the program's lifetime, arguing that it was "senseless and unjustified because the existing state programs were not substantial enough to justify" giving them money for this work. Supporters, including the American Child Hygiene Association and the Child Health Organization, countered that spending $4,000,000 annually on saving babies and mothers was fiscally responsible, especially when the nation was spending twenty times that amount to improve and protect its livestock. But the most vocal and effective support came from the nation's mothers and their publications, spearheaded by the Parent–Teachers Association, the Women's Christian Temperance Union, and the National Consumers' League. They "joined in an organized lobbying effort that was described by many in Washington as the most intensive campaign to influence the vote on a single bill they had ever seen."[54]

The annual appropriation was reduced to $1,240,000 and the states had absolute control over these funds. It provided for a direct grant of $5,000 for each participating state and $1,000,000 in matching funds provided by the states. Governor Henry J. Allen indicated participation by Kansas, as required by the legislation, to demonstrate that the state accepted its provisions approval, pending legislative approval. The act was administered by the Federal Board of Maternal and Infant Hygiene and the cooperating states tended to concentrate their money in rural areas where neglect for these concerns traditionally had been the greatest. Many states used their money to match county appropriations to promote public health nursing. Wherever it was spent, the funds provided a great boost for maternal and infant care, an area sadly in need of national attention.[55]

This assistance permitted the Kansas state board of health to expand its current programs of education and study of maternity and infant mortality. Previously, the division had one clerk and one supervising nurse for 130 public health nurses scattered across the state. The additional funding would permit them to hire four more badly needed nurses. In the summer of 1921, Kansas received $8,991.51 in federal funding, a sizeable sum, part of which the state had to match. Many attacked the unusual program, including numerous Kansas politicians, on the basis that it was an unconstitutional invasion of state affairs. One house of the Kansas state legislature refused to accept the grant, as did the state legislatures of Massachusetts, New York, Rhode Island, and Louisiana and the Sunflower state never participated beyond the initial funds given to each state. The Commonwealth of Massachusetts challenged the law's constitutionality and the case went to the Supreme Court in *Massachusetts v. Mellon*. The justices held that this was a political question and thus not justiciable and the court therefore had no jurisdiction over the issue. In addition, the opinion pointed out that if a state did not desire to participate, the law did not mandate it to do so. If Kansas wished to reject the funding, the legislature could do so, and it did. President Calvin Coolidge allowed the law to lapse in 1929, but it was revived on a larger scale with the Social Security Act of 1935. Franklin Roosevelt's Committee on Economic Security called Grace Abbott, who succeeded Julia Lathrop as head of the Children's Bureau, to testify on the health needs of infants and her testimony was crucial to passage of the law. In addition to social security programs, titles V and VI of the act provided millions of dollars for maternal and child care and for public health.[56]

As if Samuel Crumbine did not have enough to keep him busy at this time, with his fights for pure food and water, and against typhoid, diphtheria, tuberculosis, and high infant mortality rates, all at the same time, supporters at the University of Kansas asked him in 1910 to become dean of its medical school. This was a crucial position for the future of Kansas health because its medical school was at a significant crossroad and whether or not it continued to exist was largely a political issue.

Medical schools were in overabundance in America at the turn of the twentieth century but good ones were rare. Under the proprietary system of the nineteenth century, they proliferated because doctors who usually owned the school and taught there, wanted the tuition money that accompanied teaching classes to supplement their income from medical practice. The various philosophies or schools of therapeutics clashed with each other and there was no referee in the struggles for dominance. Normally, the only state controls were simple requirements for a degree from an "accredited" school of medicine to receive a license to practice, but there was little in the form of standards or agents for determining accreditation for training in medicine. In fact, usually there were no requirements of literacy or anything else for admission to these proprietary schools, except proof of ability to pay tuition and often this was permitted to accumulate until graduation. At that point, of course, it was a question of paying overdue tuition, or not receiving a degree. This chaotic system resulted in widespread vying for students with tuition money and the loosing of incompetent doctors upon the rightly suspicious public. The American Medical Association had long sought strict standards for accreditation and licensing but the various medical philosophies were too powerful politically for them to make progress very rapidly in upgrading the profession. The medical school at Johns Hopkins was a significant exception because when it opened its doors in 1893 it required both a college degree for admission and a four-year program of study before graduation, the most strict standards in the United States at that time. Other schools slowly began raising their standards in response. A turning point came for these schools with the Flexner Report in 1910.

The Carnegie Foundation for the Advancement of Teaching chose Abraham Flexner to investigate medical education in America. He had a bachelor's degree from Johns Hopkins and he persuaded his brother Simon to take a medical degree there where he became a protégé of William Welch and later served as president of the Rockefeller Institute for Medical Research. Beginning with Tulane University in

1908, Abraham visited every medical school in the United States. Thinking he might be surveying for the Carnegie Foundation with grants in mind, the schools opened their doors wide to him, especially showing their weaknesses with the prospect that Carnegie funding would help them make improvements. His report in 1910 castigated many of them severely and embarrassingly for their staffs who cared more about tuition money than teaching, libraries with few or nonexistent medical books and resources, and totally inadequate laboratories. He described the dissecting room at the Kansas Medical College at Topeka, a department of Washburn College, for instance, as "incredibly filthy." The room contained, "in addition to necessary tables, a badly hacked cadaver, and was simultaneously used as a chicken yard." The room was not utilized until cold weather arrived and, meanwhile, a medical professor who had his office there, stored a coop of live chickens.[57]

Flexner's report and the work of the American Medical Association, had several consequences. One was the demise of numerous totally inadequate medical schools: in 1906 there were 162 medical schools in America; by 1915 the number had declined to 95. Secondly, the better schools that survived adopted standards closer to those at Johns Hopkins. As Robert P. Hudson notes, however, Flexner's report served as a "catalyst to an already evolving process" of these schools making improvements in their medical education and to supplement grants from the Rockefeller Foundation. Third, the public "responded by opening its pocketbook" to improve their medical institutions. All except Kansas, where the agrarian-dominated legislature viewed all medical doctors with skepticism or belligerence. Doctors were needed, according to many of the rural solons, only for treating wounds and setting broken bones and this trade could be learned easily by experience. Finally, the board of regents of the University of Kansas decided they must find a dean for the medical school to provide political leadership to establish the school on a sound academic basis.[58]

When the legislature created the University of Kansas in 1866, plans for a future medical school were envisioned but at first only the basic sciences of chemistry, biology, and physiology were offered. This was expanded to a one-year program in 1880 when courses in human physiology, materia medica, and comparative anatomy were added. As with many agricultural states in the Great Plains at the time, especially because they were "area" states or had artificially drawn boundaries, their poor economic base made it difficult to fund expensive scientific studies. Kansas, like its neighbors, made agreements with other states for their students to complete their medical education in four-year schools elsewhere. KU students normally were accepted at the Ohio Medical College in Cincinnati, or Rush Medical School in Chicago. During this early period, though, Kansas did not suffer from a dearth of physicians, qualified or otherwise, because of the current proliferation of proprietary schools. Indeed, an authority on Kansas medical history observed that in 1883 the state had 729 allopaths,

515 eclectics, and 104 homeopaths, or more eclectics than there were at the time in all of New England.[59]

The rivalries of the three major schools of medical thought continued and deepened, with each forming its own fraternity. By the turn of the twentieth century all were ready to accept state regulation—if each could determine the standards. The State Board of Medical Examination and Registration required doctors to have a degree from "a legally chartered medical school in good standing as determined by the board." Of course, all the various medical societies accredited their own schools. The law required all three major types of medical doctors to be represented on the board with no one branch having a majority, although patronage-hungry governors sometimes found this stipulation difficult to observe. These medical schisms also amplified the political divisions over the question of where the state medical school should be established. The larger cities of Topeka, Wichita, Manhattan, and Kansas City "all claimed to deserve a medical school more than Lawrence."[60]

In 1894 Dr. Simeon Bishop Bell, a Kansas pioneer doctor and land speculator, offered to donate land and money, valued at $75,000, to the state to establish a medical school in Rosedale, a suburb south of Kansas City, Kansas, where he had property holdings. This was a considerable sum at the time but he wanted to honor his wife, Eleanor Taylor Bell in this manner. Political and local interests forced the state to defer accepting his offer of a gift until 1905, when increasing medical costs that necessitated locating the school in a large metropolitan area for an adequate supply of patients persuaded the legislature to accept his donation. After Bell offered an additional $25,000 that year, the legislature decreed Rosedale as the location of the state medical school and authorized construction of a hospital there, completed in 1906. Chancellor Frank Strong of the University of Kansas optimistically announced that the time had arrived "to establish the best medical school between Chicago and San Francisco" in Rosedale, but the school encountered problems from the beginning.

Basically the first two years of course work were completed in Lawrence and students took their two years of clinical work in Rosedale. After the state of Missouri failed to establish another medical school in addition to the one in St. Louis, Chancellor Strong persuaded the three proprietary schools—the Kansas City Medical College, the Medico-Chirurgical College in Kansas City, Missouri, and the College of Physicians and Surgeons in Kansas City, Kansas—to affiliate with the Rosedale hospital. The Medico-Chirurgical school in Missouri had the best teaching staff. In addition, Kansas City, Missouri furnished the majority of the patients at Rosedale. As a result, the other medical schools in Kansas, and their cities, resented the fact that most of the faculty of the new Rosedale school were Missouri residents. In addition, Kansas City, Kansas was four hundred miles from the western border of Kansas and these citizens certainly felt ignored in terms of state medical training. This was the unusual and perilous situation Flexner reported in 1910: a state medical school divided between two cities, political pressures from other Kansas cities who hoped to acquire the state medical school eventually through default, and a parsimonious, rural-dominated legislature unwilling to fund the state's medical education adequately, regardless of its location.[61]

Dean George Howard Hoxie faced serious problems in making his school function under these circumstances. The one hundred member faculty, most of them inherited from the Medico-Chirurgical College and the Kansas City Medical College, produced a marvelous student–faculty ratio for the ninety-six students the first year, but were resented in many quarters for being Missouri residents and receiving Kansas dollars in salaries. Chancellor Strong persuaded Hoxie to resolve this problem by making the clinical courses elective and ultimately this would eliminate the less able professors by "some variant of the law of survival of the fittest." While this approach eventually worked, it caused further resentment in the Kansas City, Kansas medical community because the most capable professors lived in Missouri.[62]

In addition, physical problems existed, such as the Eleanor Taylor Bell hospital being located on a steep hill, three blocks from the nearest streetcar line. The school offered clinical teaching in two Kansas locations and at St. Margaret's Hospital in Missouri. With no direct transportation connections and in the days before widespread use of automobiles, students had to take a streetcar to downtown Kansas City, Missouri, where the best teaching faculty were located, transfer to a Kansas line, then walk the three blocks to the Bell hospital for clinical work. In addition, the school dispensary operated on Independence Avenue, location of the old chirurgical school, and students received much practical experience from it but, again, this was resented by the Kansans. The medical program soon outgrew the space provided and in 1913 the state built another hospital at a cost of $50,000. Patients arriving there had to navigate the one hundred feet up Goat Hill, so-called because a herd of the animals inhabited the steep slope. These drawbacks contributed to the biennial decisions the legislature faced on whether to continue to invest in Rosedale or move the medical school to Topeka, the location of the proprietary Kansas Medical College, but also the one that Flexner had graded poorly. Many of the "short grass politicians" wanted to locate the school in Manhattan, home of the Kansas State Agricultural College, because they looked upon medicine as a trade and not a profession and the "ag" school seemed the proper location for it, while citizens of Wichita wanted it built in their community. Much of the dissension centered around Hoxie's assistant dean, Mervin T. Sudler, a Johns Hopkins graduate who insisted on high standards for admission and graduation of students, which was widely resented. In 1911 the legislature had even cut the medical school's budget "to a pitiful $35,000." Hoxie later referred to his term of service as dean as "a bad dream."[63]

A letter from the American Medical Association's accreditation committee to Chancellor Strong in 1912 strengthened the Rosedale chances of retaining the school.

Before issuing its final report, the committee wanted to notify the school in advance of its favorable impressions, but also of the weaknesses it would report. It criticized the bifurcation of the school and was especially critical of the staff at Lawrence, because only two of them had medical training, an undesirable situation. Professor Lewis Lindsay Dyche, for instance, was a one-time polar explorer who taught anatomy. The Rosedale facility received more favorable treatment. The major criticism there was the lack of sufficient bed facilities that could easily be corrected and this fault was improved with the addition of St. Margaret's Hospital in Kansas City, Kansas, a short time later. The school retained its accreditation for the time being.[64]

These conditions indicated the medical school badly needed some political clout in the legislature and, when Hoxie resigned in 1909, the regents chose Samuel Crumbine to replace him. The doctor's ties to the University of Kansas had been increased and strengthened during his years as secretary of the board of health. Early in his tenure he began utilizing specialists in chemistry, such as E.H.S. Bailey and sanitary engineer W.C. Hoad as scientific experts. In 1909 Crumbine was appointed as lecturer on pure food and drug regulations and sanitation at the university. The following year the regents authorized a department of Hygiene and Public Health in the medical school to cooperate with the state board of health. Most importantly, the struggling school of medicine needed a political force in Topeka, someone highly regarded by the legislature, and Crumbine fit that description better than anyone else they could have chosen.[65]

Chancellor Strong first consulted the Kansas Medical Society, which appointed a committee to discuss the medical school situation with him. He called on Samuel Crumbine for advice. He uncovered differing views but one doctor expressed the opinion of many when he told the House of Delegates session of the Kansas Medical Society in 1910 that, "if they want the cooperation of this society they had better get rid of the Missouri men and get Kansas men.... It must be demonstrated whether it is a Kansas School or a Missouri School." In pondering his options, Chancellor Strong thought, Who would command greater respect than Samuel Crumbine? Who could better heal the breach between the doctors and the University? Who in the state would not support the idea of tying the medical school to "the popular State Board of Health"?[66]

One day William Allen White, a regent for the University of Kansas, strode into Crumbine's office and announced he had good news. "Are you regents going to give me that public health laboratory we need?," responded the doctor. "Maybe later! Now the good news is that the board has elected you Dean of the School of Medicine and I've been delegated to tell you." Crumbine mumbled something about not having any particular qualifications for the position but White reminded him that it would enable him "to use the experts of the School of Medicine in a much broader and more useful way than you have been able to as yet," and this suggestion had its desired effect.[67]

Crumbine yielded to the entreaties and his appointment was "widely applauded." Typical of the many favorable newspaper editorials was that of the *Hutchinson News*, which declared that "no man in Kansas possesses all the necessary qualities equal to Dr. Crumbine." The *Kansas City Star*, a Missouri newspaper, not surprisingly concluded that the medical school of Kansas should remain in Kansas City. The editor was elated at the selection of Crumbine, saying

> the elevation of Dr. S.J. Crumbine to be the executive head of the medical school of the University of Kansas is a commendable move in the direction of bringing the work of the university and the state health department into a more effective cooperation. Doctor Crumbine has thoroughly established his efficiency as secretary of the Health Board of Kansas. He has applied the practical ideas to the methods and operation of the department that have made it a factor in the life of the state.

As events developed, Crumbine was rarely present at the Rosedale campus. It was never intended that he would be the literal administrator of the school of medicine but would be the friend, supporter, and chief lobbyist for it in Topeka.[68]

With the complete agreement and support of both men, Associate Dean Sudler continued to administer the school of medicine as he had been doing since Hoxie's resignation in 1909. Sudler, who had a surgical practice in Lawrence and Kansas City but still managed to spend four days weekly at Rosedale, undertook the immense task of making the bifurcated school function. One of his first moves proved to be very unpopular. He named Dr. George E. Coghill, a member of the University of Kansas faculty but not a physician, in charge of admissions and the latter established high standards. Many doctors in Kansas, "especially those whose sons and daughters failed to meet academic requirements," were critical of this choice. In addition, supporters began a campaign, unsuccessfully, to enlarge the Rosedale hospital and acquire appropriations sufficient to pay the faculty adequately if they were in vital positions and in danger of being recruited away by other states. One of the Flexner criticisms, for example, was that the professor of pathology had to have an outside income to make a living. When Simeon Bell learned on his deathbed of a strong movement to relocate the school in Topeka, the ninety-three year old doctor movingly wrote the legislature:

> Knowing that I am nearing the other side, I earnestly ask that the legislature of 1913 finally and for all time so settle the question of the location of the Medical School that I may, with an unshaken faith in the people of my state, die in peace. And as my last request I ask that the appropriation for the medical school this year be granted.

The dying man's plea was in vain as the legislature proved stingy with its appropriation. Again in 1915, Chancellor Strong asked the legislature if the school of medicine should be continued. Of course, the reply came back, but operate it without an increase in appropriations. A majority wanted the school but did not want to fund it properly. When they approved a new hospital in 1915, Governor Arthur Capper vetoed the measure. The school graduated ten physicians the previous year "at the expense of $30,000 above all fees and tuition," he noted. "Certainly Kansas cannot afford to pay from the state treasury $3,000 each for the education of new physicians." It was not until the city of Rosedale matched the $33,000 raised by the medical school's faculty, graduates, and friends that the legislature appropriated $435,000 for a new physical plant in 1921 and the issue of permanent location was finally settled. The new school was located at 39th and Rainbow, one mile south of the early Rosedale location. In 1924 Rosedale was annexed by Kansas City, Kansas and this materially strengthened the medical school's political position to be in the largest city in the state. This occurred after Crumbine resigned as nominal dean of the school.[69]

Although only titular dean and busy though he was with his various public health duties, Samuel Crumbine played a significant role in strengthening the ties between the medical school and the state board of health and during the legislative sessions proved his worth. He lectured to senior medical students once a week. Most important, he used his new position to assist the newly emerging field of public health work.

As with most pioneering efforts in public health, the East Coast was experimenting with providing training for state officials. By 1906, for example, the University of Pennsylvania was offering courses in public health and Harvard University was co-operating with Massachusetts Institute of Technology in offering a special school for health officers. The Rockefeller Foundation became interested in promoting the concept of a specialized school for this purpose. In a series of meetings from 1913 to 1916, Wickcliffe Rose of the Foundation, Abraham Flexner, and William Henry Welch, professor of pathology at the Johns Hopkins University Medical School, developed the overweening priorities of such a school: it should be completely independent but should have a close connection with "a good general teaching hospital. After visiting proposed sites in Boston, New York, and Philadelphia, the group recommended a grant to Johns Hopkins University. The Rockefeller Foundation awarded funds to the university on June 12, 1916, to develop a School of Hygiene and Public Health. This school, in turn, offered leadership in this field and stimulated other states to develop programs in course offerings for their public health officials.[70]

Crumbine kept abreast of these developments and established the first postgraduate course for county health officials in the nation in 1911 by bringing them to the Kansas City medical campus for a week of free instruction. He had been successful in educating the public about various health issues, so why not instruct these officials and public health nurses in the latest developments in their areas of expertise? This became an annual affair and his influence on public health would soon expand to every corner of the state and beyond. After becoming dean, he used this position in various ways to promote postgraduate courses for health officials. He increased the school to a two-week session with the U.S. Surgeon General sending a delegation of experts to lecture, in addition to the Kansas faculty. In 1914 the medical school appointed him Professor of Preventative Medicine. At that time he conferred with Chancellor Strong, an ardent supporter, about expanding the department of health's annual program to involve the school of medicine more completely. Strong "not only consented, but declared with enthusiasm, the facilities of the university would be at the disposal of the school, wherever they could be of help." The following program included features that would attract the practicing physician, in addition to the county health officials, with lectures by Professor Andrew L. Skoog of the medical school and William C. Hoad of the engineering school. An incredible number of fifty physicians attended the school and it became a pioneer in efforts to improve public health conditions in other states.[71]

In 1915 a separate public health program was offered for nurses, "one of the most successful and daring projects we every [sic] undertook," reported Crumbine. He anticipated eight or ten graduate nurses, hoping they could then serve as public health nurses for the Kansas Society for the Study and Prevention of Tuberculosis following completion of the course. When forty-five had registered before the opening date, he related, "we were greatly surprised and really astonished." and they had to move it to larger accommodations. The final enrollment was much larger. The instructors did not receive remuneration but he "paid railroad and hotel bills out of Board of Health funds" for the attendees This was not repeated as its original purpose had been fulfilled and to do so, he noted, would require "an equipped building and a staff of teachers, that only a legislature could provide." The current frugal legislature, as usual, wanted to economize.[72]

The annual public health school continued and expanded until World War I when many Kansas physicians went to war and others were swamped with cases from the great influenza epidemic of those years or died from it. Crumbine was forced to bring in what experts he could muster for the school and even sent public health nurses to communities without doctors to try and meet the medical shortage. Then, too, he recalled, "there were certain ambitious Kansas City physicians who never were satisfied with anything that Dr. Sudler or I ever did, in formulating policies for the School of Medicine and making appointments for the School of Public Health." But Chancellor Strong was determined to continue and improve the school, so Crumbine structured the program "to fit the available instructors and any acute state problem that at time confronted us." This type of approach proved unsuccessful and was discontinued.[73]

Crumbine's last regular school for public health officers in 1922 was a smashing success with 478 doctors, nurses, and public health officials in attendance. This number included 259 Kansans, 177 from Missouri, and others from as far away as Connecticut, New York, and Washington, DC. The state board of health continued these public health schools after 1923 intermittently until adverse economic conditions in the 1930s brought an end to them. After 1936 the board offered district institutes, conferences, and refresher courses for physicians but without support or participation from the school of medicine. One problem concerned the paucity of hotels and eating establishments in the Rosedale area. This, combined with the problems arising out of World War I, Crumbine's resignation as dean of the medical school, and finally the election of Jonathan Davis as governor and Crumbine's decision to leave Kansas, spelled the end of the school except for limited and sporadic sponsorship by the department of health and the U.S. Public Health Service. These sessions were held in Topeka, until the Great Depression ended the concept.[74]

Meanwhile, Crumbine was becoming increasingly committed to his child health program to help crippled children and the doctor also involved the medical school in this work. A nurse discovered a boy so badly crippled he had to crawl into the classroom. She found his grandparents who took care of him but refused to take him to a surgeon for consultation. When she queried them about this they said they did not want to hurt him with an operation, but actually they were using him to garner income by playing a violin on the streets and begging. A judge ordered the operation and the surgeon straightened his twisted legs. Out of this incident came the Capper Foundation for Crippled Children in 1920 to help such unfortunates and in 1926 the Kansas Society for Crippled Children was established to continue this work. In addition, the legislature enacted three laws designed to alleviate this problem. First, the child of any indigent poor person in Kansas with a physical deformity could go to the Eleanor Bell Hospital for free treatment. The second broadened the definition to include any indigent or poor person regardless of residence, and the third included patients of obstetricians who were public charges.[75]

With numerous similar instances being brought to his attention, Crumbine came up with the idea in early 1918 that something must be done for the children with these disabilities who were undiscovered, to prevent them from growing up mentally or physically deficient because of neglect on the part of their parents." He assigned Lydia DeVilbiss to make a survey to locate these unfortunates and she sent application blanks to local health departments to be returned to the hygiene division. The state would provide care for these hapless youngsters, but first they had to be located. As dean of the medical school, Crumbine established a special surgical ward at the Rosedale hospital and all state health officials were required to report all indigent children who had correctable deformities. Dr. Mervin Sudler proceeded to take away the source of family income from many of these unlucky children by operating on them free. When physically normal, they could no longer beg successfully. If another specialist was needed, the state paid the expenses. "Immediate attention" would be given to these reports, Crumbine reported, because in many cases they "must be treated at once." The problem of mental deficiencies was particularly touchy as parents were afraid their children would not be treated kindly or properly. This was "an injustice to the child" he argued, because at some point he or she would be "thrown upon the community" when the parents died "and trouble always arises." The results, he added, "are worth all the trouble and cannot be measured in dollars and cents."[76]

Crumbine continued as secretary of the board of health while he was dean of the medical school, but drew no salary as secretary. His enemies continued to lurk over his shoulder and in 1919 he tried and failed to get Dr. J.J Sippy, state epidemiologist, a well-deserved raise. One newspaper described Sippy as "one of the most widely known and efficient state officials." His work over an eight-year period had "built up the department of communicable diseases until Kansas advanced her standing among other states of the country." But the legislature of 1919 "advanced the whiskered argument that someone is always ready to take a state job" and raised his salary a mere $300 to compensate for the current 100 percent inflation rate of the war period. Sippy immediately accepted the position as state epidemiologist of Montana with a $1,200 increase in salary, just as Crumbine feared would happen. The frugality of this legislature was costly to Kansas. It resulted in the departure of Sippy and DeVilbiss and the resignation of Crumbine from the medical school.[77]

The same legislature set all state employees' salaries that year at a certain level, including Crumbine's at a miserly $4,000. But one of his foes inserted the phrase that the board of health secretary "shall hold no other office or position in any other department of state for which he may receive compensation." While Crumbine drew no income from the board of health, the word "may" precluded him from continuing his deanship. His position was the only one in state government, incidentally, that was singled out in this manner in the appropriation bill. Crumbine resigned as dean and it was accepted with an "appreciation of the valued service rendered by Dr. S.J. Crumbine." By that time the Kansas School of Medicine was on its way to success and his political services were not that crucial. Also, at that point America's involvement in World War I was completed except for the formalities of treaty-making.[78]

# FIVE

## FIGHTING THE GREAT WAR
## AT HOME

Unlike the aftermath of Pearl Harbor over two decades later, it was a divided America that entered World War I in April 1917. The Senate approved the war resolution 82 to 6 and the House of Representatives 373 to 50 on the basis that German U-Boats failed to respect American neutrality on the high seas, a situation very similar to that one hundred years previously that precipitated the War of 1812. This division over participation in the Great War was even greater in Midwestern areas, such as Kansas, where freedom of the seas held less priority than it did on the Atlantic seaboard. From this divergence of opinion, President Woodrow Wilson decided that American minds, as well as the economy, must be mobilized to support the war effort.

To this end he established the Committee on Public Information, headed by George Creel, a Denver journalist. The Creel committee subsequently made the conflict a "Great Crusade" (to make the world safe for democracy) by flooding the country with propaganda that taught citizens to hate the Kaiser, and anything German. Under this barrage, Kansans soon changed their views on opposition to the war, even to the point of believing foolish rumors of spies and sabotage abounding everywhere. Anything different, such as the Industrial Workers of the World (IWW) and their socialistic ideas, were viewed as dangerous and should be suppressed. Everything, even civil liberties, must be sacrificed to win the Great Crusade. The war closely touched the lives of Kansans, with the draft and with the location of Fort Riley near the center of the state, a major post in the military effort to defeat the Hun. In June 1917 the Army decided to build Camp Funston, a huge training facility on the Fort Riley reservation, and this greatly increased the significance of the Sunflower State as an important military center.[1]

Soon after the declaration of war, the French sent a delegation to America to plead for immediate assistance. Besides munitions of war, they said they needed military personnel and 5,000 medical staff were their first priority. Physicians were thus among the first in Kansas to be mobilized for military service and soon many communities were without the services of a physician. This, in turn, pressured the University of Kansas School of Medicine to produce more graduates. Summer classes were held in 1917 for the first time in the school's history and the shortage of doctors led one small town in Kansas to offer an automobile and house rent free for a year as an inducement to secure the services of a physician. All these developments quickly involved medical school dean Crumbine and his state board of health. Soon after Congress enacted the conscription law he was named as the medical member of the Kansas Draft Appeal Board. The board could excuse men of draft age if they were in employment essential to the war, such as farming. The members soon were swamped with requests for deferment for critical jobs that led many on the board to believe the appeals were hampering the goal to raise an army "to make the world safe for democracy." Dean Crumbine estimated that 40 percent of the effective physicians available would be required for "war demands." Not only would all able-bodied men between ages twenty-one and thirty-one be absorbed but the military might have to resort to conscription for some doctors between ages thirty-one and fifty-three. Early volunteers had provided only one-fourth of the required number. This situation, he observed, meant that the nation "must take better care than ever of health problems" because aged physicians, even those retired, would have to care for the civilians because of the critical shortage. The problem, he noted, was that currently "it requires about seven years to turn out a person equipped to practice medicine."[2]

To help keep more students in medical training, Surgeon General William C. Gorgas announced a plan for all second-, third-, and fourth-year students to enlist in the medical reserve corps. These men were within the age eligibility limits for conscription. At that time there were 125 medical students at KU and about forty were eligible for the draft. If they passed their medical examination, Gorgas strongly suggested, they would be allowed to complete their medical education, provided they remained in the reserves, to help ease the critical doctor shortage when they graduated. This and other war duties began to absorb Crumbine's time and he was forced to resign from the appeal board.[3]

Doctors serving on medical advisory boards were exempt from conscription. In August 1918 Governor Arthur Capper began receiving protests that too many young doctors were doing everything possible to be appointed to one of these boards. Six young doctors in Salina volunteered for military duty, for example, and soon twelve others moved there from nearby small towns "to profiteer on the patients of the soldier-doctors," one complainer wrote, and some of them were seeking appointment as medical advisers. T.C. Coffman of Wichita wrote Capper that there were currently two vacancies on the Sedgwick County board and he insisted that the governor appoint only doctors over forty-five years of age to the board so that younger doctors could be available "to serve their country as they should be willing to do." He considered the young ones to be "slackers," a term bandied about a great deal at the time to disparage those who attempted to evade military service, whether legitimate or not. At the same time the Kansas Council of National Defense laid plans for making certain all state physicians were enrolled in either the medical officers reserve corps or the volunteer medical service corps. An executive committee of state military personnel and medical doctors, including Samuel Crumbine, was established to send out questionnaires to physicians to determine their classifications and assign them to the volunteer medical service corps if necessary.[4]

The continuing problem of tuberculosis in Kansas reared its ugly head when young men were rejected for the armed forces because they had consumption. The board of health sent a public nurse to interview these fellows in mid-1918 to try to persuade them to go to the state sanitarium for treatment. Financial problems complicated this effort because, while the state board of administration provided tent houses for the victims, there was an accompanying $1 per day maintenance fee connected with the service. Crumbine requested Governor Capper to summon a meeting of the county boards of commissioners, or at least their chairmen, to meet with the state board of health at its annual gathering to request them to provide this maintenance fee for their citizens. As usual, many counties complied with the request while other penurious ones declined.[5]

One poor consumptive, Leslie J. Foster of Carbondale, just could not seem to keep out of the Army. When he registered for the draft in June 1917 he waived exemption and was inducted that October. He was shipped from Camp Funston to Camp Kearney, California, where he was diagnosed as having tuberculosis and was summarily discharged as unfit for military duty. In August 1918 the Lyndon draft board placed him in Class 1 and again inducted him. He was ordered to Jefferson Barracks in St. Louis but the doctors there "sent him back in a hurry." Foster signed an affidavit that the Lyndon draft board knew he had been certified by Dr. J.J. Sippy, secretary of the Kansas Tuberculosis Association, as tubercular and had applied for admission to the state hospital at Newton. Some draft boards were overzealous and "continued to send men with hernias, bad teeth, and flat feet to cantonments." This practice, of course, raised the numbers of men found unfit for military service during the Great Crusade, figures that caused great alarm in the minds of many Americans.[6]

Kansans also were worried lest their boys be exposed to the dangers of alcohol while serving in the Babylon of France. Not to worry, though, because General John "Black Jack" Pershing banned "strong liquor" to his men in France and was "considering prohibiting all alcoholic liquors." Governor Capper enthusiastically applauded this action, assuring the general that "it has gladdened the hearts of Kansans to learn you have taken precautions to ensure the sobriety and high moral standards of the American troops under your command." But it was the high rate of incidence of venereal disease among troops that presented Crumbine with his greatest moral and legal issue of the war. The Great Crusade "helped lift the veil of silence about venereal disease," one authority states and it became a major concern for General Pershing in France.[7]

Many Progressives believed that the war provided a great opportunity to complete their domestic agenda with an attack on social vices and diseases and to reform the outdated Victorian code on sexual conduct. During the Progressive Era they investigated every major city for vice and often tended to emphasize the spectacular in their reports. Their emphasis on the largely mythical "white slavery" practice, for instance, led to the enactment of the Mann Act, which made it illegal to transport a woman across state lines for "immoral purposes." They tended to underline not only the moral side of prostitution but also its medical aspects. One result was the successful drive for sex education in public schools and a study in 1922 found that 46.6 percent of the nation's secondary schools had some instruction in sex hygiene to stress the dangers of social diseases. During this time two schools of thought had emerged for combating the evils of prostitution, which contributed heavily to venereal diseases. The first, and most popular in Europe, was state control and inspection, or reglementation. This was never popular with American Progressives who rejected this approach and stressed repression and demands for physicians to report venereal disease to public health authorities. The highly popular Broadway production of Eugene Brieux's play, *Damaged Goods*, dealt frankly with the theme of venereal disease and was considered a successful attack on the Victorian sexual reticence code.[8]

They viewed American entry into the conflict as providing a means to "rid the nation of vice, immorality, and disease." Their subsequent efforts during the hostilities provided "one of the most fully articulated ventures in social engineering in American history." They faced the opposition of the strong military tradition that soldiers required sex in order to be good fighting men and doubts of military officialdom that change could be feasible. In previous wars the soldiers were volunteers, but in the Great Crusade the men were conscripted and the draft tended to take men from the lower socioeconomic levels of American society. Reformers resolved to provide "a healthy environment" for them in their training camps and in France. They had the experience of the recent border war with Mexico as a model for their purposes.[9]

During the Mexican expedition that Pershing led in 1916–1917 the problem of troops being exposed to venereal disease was met with the establishment of a guarded, fenced area where the prostitutes were kept. Affectionately known as the Remount Station, soldiers were examined when they entered and given a tube of prophylactic ointment when they departed. This approach appeared to succeed because none of the men were reported contracting a disease. With the American Expeditionary Force (AEF) in France, however, this would not work as there were 2,000,000 men involved compared to 11,000 in the earlier campaign and they were civilian, not professional, soldiers. "If word leaked out that the American commander was running whorehouses for their sons," in France, it was noted, families would cause an uproar.[10]

By 1917 the British had nearly two divisions hospitalized with venereal disease, with an average confinement of seven weeks. The British solution to the dangers was to lecture to their men and distribute pamphlets on the subject. The French, on the other hand, realistically acknowledged that their men would find women regardless of official policy, so they licensed and "controlled" prostitution in what was labeled "reglementation." The women had to be inspected once a week and, if infected, had their license suspended and were hospitalized for treatment. The whores, however, were servicing dozens of men daily, with one in a bordello being observed as handling forty to fifty clients in twenty-four hours, and they often transmitted diseases with equal frequency before their weekly checkup. The result of this approach was 1,000,000 French cases of gonorrhea or syphilis from August 1914 to the summer of 1917 when American forces began arriving at the front. The Germans followed a similar policy, even to the extent of sending around trucks with private cabins. Learning of these varying policies and their results, Pershing decided upon an unheard-of program in wartime—abstinence.[11]

"Sexual Continence is the plain duty of the AEF," he announced, "both for the vigorous conduct of the war and for the clean health of the American people after the war." "Sexual intercourse is not necessary for good health," he added, "and complete continence is wholly possible." Immediately after the first American soldiers arrived in France, Pershing issued General Order #6. This required "scare talks" to be given to the men and a medical examination fortnightly for all. Every command would operate a prophylactic station and anyone exposed to venereal disease had to report there within three hours of contact. This approach had problems: it did not include a ban on drinking nor on visiting prostitutes, as long as the three-hour requirement was met. In addition, the prophylaxis included an ointment to prevent syphilis and an injection into the urethra to prevent gonorrhea, not a pleasant experience that led many men to ignore the rule and "take their chances." Also, many soldiers did not mind being infected and sent to hospitals in the rear where they had clean beds and good food.[12]

This plan obviously was not working so in September Pershing issued Order #34 that established small infirmaries at the front for treatment. The order also directed commanders to provide "wholesome entertainment for the men during off duty hours." Later the AEF established leave areas in the south of France for men with a week's pass. The month after he issued #34, however, the venereal disease rate rose 500 percent at the port city of St. Nazaire. Investigation showed the docks were congested and men, already cooped up during the voyage, were "restless when they disembarked and headed straight for the Cognac and the girls." MPs stacked the drunken men on trucks and dumped them unceremoniously at their units with no visit to the prophylactic stations. There were just too many to handle.[13]

Upon being told of the situation, Pershing immediately issued the harsh General Order # 77 in December 1917. Houses of prostitution and saloons were "placed absolutely off limits." Any man returning to his unit intoxicated was presumed guilty of having had sexual relations and given a prophylaxis. No ship could dock in Europe without an advanced report of venereal disease of its passengers and infected crewmen were not allowed ashore. Commanders had to file written reports of venereal disease incidence while in port towns and these were entered in their personnel records for use in determining future efficiency. This was drastic, but effective, as commanders quickly discovered that Pershing was serious and the results were soon apparent: the Americans had by far the lowest rate of social disease incidence among the Allied armies. In September 1918, one man per thousand in the AEF was hospitalized for venereal disease. "No other army in Europe approached that record." About 5.6 percent of the draftees had a venereal disease and the rate of admission for infections at home was 134 per thousand; the rate in France steadily declined with an average of 35 for the war. Although men entered the Army with venereal disease, Pershing was determined that none should leave with it. On the home front, military and civilian health officers, including the U.S. Public Health Service, decided on a policy equally as rigid and Samuel Crumbine willingly enforced it where possible.[14]

After several years of considering options, in 1912 Congress expanded the United States Marine Hospital Service into the U.S. Public Health Service. In addition to publishing health information for the public, it also began investigating typhoid and other epidemics and assisted the Rockefeller Foundation in its fights against hookworm and pellagra in the Southern states. During World War I its work expanded, especially when it created a Division of Venereal Disease. The division received an appropriation of $200,000, plus an additional $2,000,000 to assist states in their work on social diseases on a matching fund basis.[15]

Eleven days after the declaration of war, the Commission on Training Camp Activities (CTCA) was created with Raymond B. Fosdick as its head. CTCA began a two-pronged attack on venereal disease "with elements of uplift and distraction and coercion and repression." Recreational centers were established but prophylaxis services also were made available. CTCA produced a full-length dramatic film entitled *Fit to Win*, a graphic story of venereal disease, and also supported locking up arrested women often without due process of law. The organization was actively involved in encouraging state efforts to control social diseases, a problem that became a crisis in critical military areas, such as Kansas.[16]

When Congress held hearings on the Selective Service Act in May 1917, they heard testimony on the vice problems of the Mexican border conflict. As a result, they added Sections 12 and 13 to the law, forbidding liquor and prostitution in areas "proximate" to training camps. Secretary of War, Newton Baker, subsequently explained these provisions in a letter to the state governors and established the Civilian Committee to Combat Venereal Disease in December of that year. The committee was aggressive in trying to enforce these laws and in promoting positive approaches for providing "a wholesome environment" in the "proximate" areas. The Y.M.C.A. was the most active of volunteer groups in this effort, in many ways playing the part in World War I that the USO (United Services Organization) played in World War II.[17]

Governor Capper appointed Crumbine to the State Council of National Defense. Prevention of the spread of disease constituted one of the council's main concerns and the members called on parents and physicians to report the knowledge of any communicable diseases. They further asked all health officials to trace these diseases to their origins and quarantine those involved, including surveillance of any persons who came into contact with the source during the incubation period. The Army aided Kansans in this work by attaching Lt. Charles D. Shelton to the state board of health. At first he encountered a lack of cooperation from citizens, so the lieutenant and the board appealed to the commander of Camp Funston, General Leonard Wood of Spanish–American War fame, who subsequently refused to allow furloughs to soldiers who wanted to travel to the recalcitrant counties. "Considerable publicity" was given to this policy and it produced immediate cooperation from county health officers.[18]

The military also charged Crumbine and his board of health with the sanitary control of a five-mile cantonment zone around Fort Leavenworth and the Fort Riley-Camp Funston areas. This was a complicated responsibility because thousands of people and thousands more soldiers lived there or entered the zones daily for their vocations or other legitimate reasons. Drs. J.G. Wilson and Charles E. Banks of the U.S. Public Health Service were placed in charge of Leavenworth county and city and the Riley–Geary county zones respectively. Trained sanitarians were recruited and the board of health staff worked diligently in inspecting restaurants, hotels, food and drug stores, outdoor toilets, and other places for possible unsanitary conditions.[19]

As great numbers of men from diverse regions of the country were suddenly housed together they communicated an assortment of diseases to each other. Five months after the declaration of war, cases of meningitis, the most feared of the prevailing diseases, were reported declining at Camp Funston, "at a rapid rate." Pneumonia, which has caused the greatest number of deaths thus far," also was on the wane. Measles were prevalent there but had caused no deaths. Communicable diseases constituted a serious enough problem to require an "isolation camp" to be built between Camp Funston and Fort Riley. Crumbine's chief concern in this category, however, was the control of venereal disease.[20]

Dr. Franklin Martin of the general medical board of the Council of National Defense stressed the importance of this problem in a telegram to Governor Arthur Capper. In the twelve weeks ending December 17, 1917, almost 22,000 new cases of V.D. were reported from thirty-one cantonments across the nation, he wired. This not only meant loss of time but also the money to maintain these men while they were being treated, and this sum amounted to more than the maintenance of Fort Dix alone. In addition, he warned, there was the possibility of the men suffering a relapse once they arrived in France, which would disappoint General Pershing and no one wanted to do that. Dr. Martin stressed the need for Governor Capper and the state Council of National Defense "to cooperate with Dr. Crumbine . . . in every way possible to eliminate sources of venereal disease." Capper took this as a direct order.[21]

When the state board of health held its second quarterly meeting in 1917, on November 2, Crumbine introduced a series of rules and regulations on venereal disease for the members to consider. The board subsequently adopted them "for the control and suppression of gonorrhea and syphilis within extra cantonment zones." They authorized the deputy health officer in these military zones to ascertain the existence of these diseases and their sources. They further were instructed to examine, isolate, and treat these infected people. The quarantines would remain in effect until they were no longer infectious. A cure was defined as two successive smears within forty-eight hours of gonococcus infection or until all lesions of skin or mucous membranes of syphilis were completely healed. The files of these officers were closed to the public and they were forbidden to issue certificates of freedom from venereal disease because these certificates could be, and often were, used by women for purposes of solicitation. At this meeting Crumbine described the state plan for social hygiene that he had developed and the governor had approved.[22]

Wherever any significant numbers of military personnel gathered, members of the world's oldest profession soon followed. Even before the declaration of war, officials tried to prepare for the inevitable influx of women into military areas. Congress assisted these authorities by designating five-mile radius zones around military installations and authorizing naval and army officials to control vice in the civilian zones surrounding the bases. In March 1917, under the headline "Vice Driven From Every Army Camp District in U.S.," CTCA chairman, Raymond B. Fosdick, declared that there was "not a single red light district existing today within an effective radius of any army cantonment or naval base where any considerable number of soldiers or sailors are in training." Nationally, twenty-five districts of these five-mile zones, he announced, had enforced "absolute repression" of vice as Congress had intended. "Varying degrees of public ignorance and prejudice" had hampered this effort, he conceded, because of "the failure to realize the destructive influence" of vice in the civilian areas "upon the military efficiency" of soldiers and sailors. This proved to be a highly optimistic report.[23]

This apparently efficient military control broke down quickly with accelerated mobilization and rapid growth of training camps. Ogden, a tiny community between Fort Riley and Manhattan, mushroomed into a tent city of 2,500 souls within two months. The area had housing facilities for a few hundred people but no sewer services and sanitary controls were hopelessly inadequate for the population plus an additional 1,000 workers passing through the vicinity daily. After receiving an alert and making an investigation, Crumbine met with the governor to warn the chief executive that the region faced a critical typhoid epidemic because of the dearth of sanitary facilities. One case had already been reported. A "clean up" program costing $12,000 was required immediately, he insisted. The city of Manhattan agreed to provide one-third the amount, although it had no financial obligation to do so, and the Red Cross office in Washington, DC agreed to fund one-third. George O'Malley, chairman of the Riley County commissioners, proved adamant against appropriating the remaining third and defiantly demanded the resignation of Riley County health officer, Dr. J.C. Montgomery who had reported the deficiency originally, and whom Crumbine described as "one of the most efficient health officers in the state." A quick visit of Crumbine with the governor resulted in the fiat "Make Ogden Sanitary" and a "veiled threat" from Capper that if O'Malley continued to remain obstinate, his resignation would be requested and Ogden would be quarantined. No city wanted that death sentence. This suggestion prove sufficient to convince the Riley County commissioners to act, but it did not resolve the problem of the numerous prostitutes who had flocked to Ogden to ply their trade. They remained.[24]

As the huge construction project at Camp Funston began to materialize and the drafted men arrived for training so, too, did the girls. It soon became apparent to Crumbine that Kansas City was a major source for this vice invading the Fort Riley area. Two months after the declaration of war he wrote the secretary of the Kansas City chamber of commerce to warn him to "clean up the alleged hives of vice" or the city would face quarantine. He said:

> As executive officer of the Kansas state board of health, I believe I am in a position to know, and certainly in a position to appreciate the menace that Kansas City has been to the lives and health of the people of Kansas. It can be said without fear of successful contradiction, for the records will bear us out, that approximately 50 percent of the infection from venereal disease reported at Camp Funston and Fort Leavenworth, and practically the same percentage reported from the civil population of the eastern

one-third of our state is contracted in Kansas City.... For years we have been able to trace, in fan-like radiation, infectious diseases coming from Kansas City to be scattered over our state. A city as great and important as Kansas City that treats its department of health as a political football and that changes its health officers three times in twelve months may not be expected to be greatly interested in the health and safety of its citizens or, at all events, cannot expect to achieve results in disease control.

This ridiculous situation, he warned, must change or the city would be quarantined.[25]

Following Crumbine's report, the war department wrote the governors of Kansas and Missouri requesting them to send representatives to Topeka to discuss the infectious disease problem facing the 30,000–40,000 young men expected to arrive at Camp Funston that fall. Raymond B. Fosdick, also Aide to Secretary of War Newton D. Baker, explained that "it won't do merely to pile the thousands of young men in the camp and provide nothing for them to do out [side] of the long working hours." He declared the purpose of the meeting to be planning for "proper surroundings" for the "doughboys" in terms of wholesome recreation. Kansas, a prohibition state, would not have the booze problem faced in other states but work of a "positive" nature also needed to be done to provide the proper recreational facilities in the surrounding communities of the cantonments for men on leave, especially those accustomed to the ready availability of alcohol. The governors' delegates would be apprized of military plans and Junction City and Manhattan would need to cooperate with F.D. Barnes, a recreational and social worker from New York City who would serve as area coordinator for military recreation.[26]

Junction City was a small community of some 6,000 people. Ogden was a "tent city," and the nearby college town of Manhattan was totally unprepared for the influx of soldiers on leave from the largest camp in the United States. "Rapid progress," though, was soon reported on recreational facilities. The citizens of Junction City raised $15,000 to construct a new community building for concerts by regimental bands and local orchestras, community sings, games for soldiers, and Saturday night dances. A member of the community service council opened a fifty-room hotel in the vicinity with rooms costing $1 per night to accommodate the temporary surge in population, playgrounds were developed for school children, and a city playground for soldiers offered an athletic field, a baseball diamond, and a swimming pool. Efforts to help Negro soldiers were concentrated in the "tent city" where money was raised to construct a community house. Despite efforts of fraternal and church societies in Manhattan, however, that town accomplished little along these lines and a census showed that on one weekend 246 people were unable to obtain rooms on visiting day at Camp Funston. But Manhattan was making an effort. The city government voted $15,000 in bonds and the Rotary clubs raised $20,000 to build a permanent community building, although this did not materialize until very late in the war.[27]

Still the prostitutes came. "Government Breaks Up 'Slave Ring' at Riley" blared a headline. Three women from Kansas City and a soldier stationed at Fort Riley were arrested and charged with violating the "white slavery" law, or Mann Act, of 1910. Soldier Joseph Moran had accompanied the three women from Kansas City, Missouri, and thus the Mann Act had been violated by crossing a state line for "immoral purposes." Mrs. Mattie Powers, age 23, paid for the tickets for the other two girls who were "not more than nineteen." These women were infecting the troops and, as the problem ballooned out of control there and elsewhere, the question became one of what to do with them. Besides the obvious punishment for violating state and federal laws, they needed to be treated before being released or they would continue to spread venereal disease.[28]

Crumbine faced this crisis with his usual common sense aplomb. "Why not adopt the same procedures and regulations that we would use to control serious communicable diseases," he asked rhetorically. "There is a war on and we must not pussyfoot any longer in dealing with this ancient and sinister pestilence." Recruiting police and sheriffs for their campaign, public health officials began rounding up suspects. If they had suspicions about a woman, she had to submit to an examination. If infected, she was quarantined. Jails were soon overflowing with "soiled doves." Many were deported but soon returned, some two or three times, before finally being sentenced and taken out of circulation. The question soon arose of where to treat them during quarantine.[29]

Crumbine consulted with the state board of control and the attorney general and received permission to quarantine them at the State Industrial Farm for Women, an adjunct of the state prison at Lansing. Prison Warden J.K. Codding was warned to be prepared to handle "the horde of lewd women now in the vicinity of Fort Riley." A delegation from Junction City informed the governor that "from two to fifteen dissolute women" were arrested there every day. This facility soon proved inadequate, as the doctor noted, because "our collection of 'wild women' was increasing so rapidly" that they had to find additional facilities. In addition, there was the problem of feeding the women as there were no funds available for this. The state legislature had authorized the state board of administration to hold these women in the camp until they were released and voted $25,000 for this purpose. But the funds would not be available until the following year, which left the current problem unresolved. Crumbine discovered a solution when he approached the state board of control for help. Lumber was cut and sawn on the prison farm and shacks were built and tents erected for housing them. The infected women were subsequently treated and released, with the warning to stay away from military camps or face a jail sentence. That November the board of health adopted even more stringent regulations. They created an extra cantonment zone around Fort Leavenworth and Camp Funston and a deputy state health official in each zone was empowered to inspect all persons suspected of engaging in "evil practices" and, if infected, to quarantine them immediately and send them to the women's camp with no process of appeal. The state's leading newspaper declared that Kansas thus became the first state in the nation to arrest and arbitrarily detain and treat women with social diseases.[30]

This was part of the frenzy of the Great Crusade to win the war regardless of the damage done to civil liberties. During this period zealous officials did great harm to the civil liberties of the 1st Amendment, leading to the creation of the American Civil Liberties Bureau, later renamed the American Civil Liberties Union. President Wilson pointed the way with the Creel Committee, Congress followed with the Espionage Act of 1917 and the Sedition Act of 1918 that enforced conformity in very broad terminology, and federal district judges aggressively enforced these measures. Socialist Kate Richards O'Hare, for example, was sentenced to five years in prison for a speech she delivered in North Dakota that she had delivered many times previously "with impunity." This was not a good time for people who had broken the law to fall into the clutches of those responsible for prosecuting the war effort.[31]

The plague of venereal disease became so acute nationally that Crumbine was called to Washington to receive his third major assignment of the war, an appointment to attack the problem on a regional basis that resolved his problem of jurisdiction over infectious diseases. With hundreds of prostitutes in quarantine and no sign that progress was being made to control them, he journeyed to Camp Funston in connection with his new assignment to consult with Leonard Wood. The general assured him that, as he was also a physician, he understood the problem, and he agreed with Crumbine on the need for action. He said "the state board of health can't work in the dark [and] one must know the location of the enemy, before a successful attack can be launched." Wood ordered his chief medical officer to report to Crumbine as to the source of all new cases of V.D. As Crumbine expected, the trail again led to Kansas City, Missouri, which was beyond his current jurisdiction.[32]

"While brooding over this hopeless situation," Crumbine recalled, Surgeon General William Gorgas of the war department called him and Dr. Watson S. Rankin, state health officer of North Carolina, to meet with him in Washington. Gorgas had asked the U.S. Public Health Service to organize the states for a V.D. control program. Receiving no response from that organization, he decided to proceed with his own plan. He ordered Rankin to combine six southern states and Crumbine to do likewise in seven midwestern states with large military installations, for V.D. control. Crumbine agreed, but called attention to his dilemma with the two Kansas cities. Major Victor C. Vaughn, chief of the Division of Communicable Diseases, offered to add Kansas City, Missouri, to Crumbine's jurisdiction and quarantine the city. "No," Crumbine responded, "let's give them another opportunity to clean up. I'll stop and see the mayor on my way home." It proved to be "the most amazing trip [he] ever took as a health officer."[33]

When he asked the mayor of Kansas City to arrest, quarantine, and treat infected women, the response was "sorry," but they were under the jurisdiction of the Metropolitan Board of Police Commissioners, appointed by the governor, so he had no jurisdiction over them. When the doctor asked the police commission for cooperation, he received the answer that when a prostitute was arrested, the city court let her off with a small fine or suspended sentence and she was soon back working the streets. "Why not see the man who owns the city courts?" was the next suggestion. Straight to Boss Tom Pendergast went the determined doctor and the political boss appeared to be expecting him. Crumbine related his purpose in calling on him and Pendergast responded, "I think the city courts will do what I ask them." "I will give you just one week," Crumbine ordered, for the city courts to hold all those arrested for street walking and have them examined and treated. When freed they were to be given "a stiff jail sentence and kept out of circulation as long as the law will allow." "You won't have to wait a week, doctor," the boss answered. "If the courts aren't doing what you wish by this time tomorrow, let me know." Boss Pendergast would do anything to avoid having his city quarantined and his orders were obeyed. In a short time the infection rates in Kansas camps dropped.[34]

In mid-1918 the Army Medical Corps announced the statistics on its successful drive to curb social diseases. With 700,000 men mobilized in France, one new case per thousand was being announced weekly, compared to the lowest prewar rate that was double this figure. Five-sixths of the number of cases reported among troops still in America was contracted before induction. Venereal disease had claimed more victims than any other communicable disease and it accounted for more men being withdrawn from active service than did injuries or illnesses. Only about one hundred men were discharged for being physically unfit as all other cases had been cured. But in March 1918 the Kansas board of health went even further in authorizing any local or county health official to make examinations of any person whom they suspected of being a prostitute and "to use every means at their disposal in suppressing the traffic."[35]

These procedures for controlling social disease seemed to some people to be high-handed tactics on Crumbine's part. When three male procurers were quarantined at Lansing for infections, they brought suit for a Writ of Habeas Corpus against Crumbine and the board of health for having them incarcerated. One of them, George Buckner, was found to have chronic gonorrhea and the Topeka health officer had ordered him sent to the state penitentiary at Lansing for treatment. The men sent there for treatment, the judicial opinion noted, were "generally speaking, a bad lot." Buckner and fellow appellants assailed this board of health authority as a delegation of legislative power to executives and insisted that one cannot be sent to the state prison for having a disease. In broad language, though, the Kansas supreme court upheld the powers of the board of health's authority to quarantine for the protection of the public's health. The justices agreed, however, that the health officer in Topeka should not have used the term penitentiary in his order, but should have said the men were not being interned in the prison and the board of health was merely using its facilities for necessary treatment of diseases, all of which was within their jurisdiction.[36]

A curious situation developed when the "soiled doves" were thrown together with hardened female prisoners serving time in the Industrial Farm for Women for committing capital offenses or other felonies: the latter loathed the prostitutes and also feared associating with diseased women, forcing the authorities to provide separate eating, bathing, and laundry facilities for them. The infected prostitutes, in addition to doing their own laundry, which they were not accustomed to, had to work on the farm while recovering. As a result, Crumbine observed, "their physical and mental condition improved to an extent little short of miraculous." It was amazing what good food, hard physical work, and plenty of sleep did for them. But when released they invariably returned to their profession and started the cycle all over again. It might be of great help, the doctor reasoned, to know some of the history of the women and their future aspirations in order to try and alter this vicious cycle.[37]

Crumbine engaged Mrs. Darlene Doubleday Newby, an experienced social worker, to attempt to engage the confidence of these women and to record what information she could obtain from them. But how should she approach the task? Again, Crumbine had a flash of inspiration. He convinced Mrs. Newby to be quarantined and she was sent to the farm with the next group of infected women. The Matron, Mrs. Julia Perry, was the only one who knew Mrs. Newby's identity and the latter was to be given only work that involved typing. At the end of two weeks she was released and she submitted her report to the doctor. Most of the girls listed waitress as their occupation because this allowed them to advertise and it also precluded conviction for vagrancy while they plied their trade, although almost none of them had any knowledge of cooking. Most of them came from impoverished homes and had completed only the sixth grade at best. Death of a parent or the breakup of the home launched their career. Some had gone to high school and had held good jobs but followed soldiers to camp and eventually turned to prostitution and became infected. A few were war brides who remained at the camp when the husbands were shipped overseas. If lost souls need friends, these girls easily qualified and Mrs. Perry tried to provide both a role model and counseling.[38]

The young, wayward girls, comprising perhaps 20 percent that could be designated as "normal," might respond to a plan for reform so Mrs. Perry placed them in the most favorable environment possible, providing them work within their capabilities and of a nature that might help them find employment when released. She called her farm the "Land of Beginning Again" where courses were offered in typing, shorthand, and domestic sciences to help them begin a new life if they could manage to break with the old. One of these girls later reported that three months at the farm "brought her to her senses." Being thrown in with hardened prostitutes made her realize that she could become one of "these pitiful creatures" unless she reformed. When released, she reentered high school and, after she graduated that June she reported, she planned on attending college. But such a girl was rare at the farm. Large numbers were described as "listless and stupid-looking," misfits in public schools who found themselves in normal times eventually in the county courthouse "looking for the Commissioner of the Poor." Some were classified as having "psychopathic personalities" who, like the young waywards, might be tractable and make progress toward reform. Most, though, returned to their miserable profession.[39]

Mrs. Newby continued her work with these women for two years and reported on over 400 who had been quarantined in the state farm. She summarized her findings as:

> In the study of home conditions cases are roughly designated and divided as follows: Home conditions bad, 69 percent; home conditions fair, 25 percent; home conditions good, 6 percent. Of the women studied, 50 percent covered less than seven grades in school; 9 percent had some high school work; 1 percent entered college. Of those married, 62 percent did so before 16; 59 percent bore children.

As Crumbine observed, "how strange that it took a world war to shock us into discussing such problems, hitherto taboo in polite society." In the first eighteen months of the program, 497 women were sent to the farm; 410 were committed for treatment of venereal disease and 87 as prisoners convicted of vagrancy or prostitution. Few of them tried to escape, for which Crumbine gave credit to the management skills of Mrs. Perry.[40]

Surgeon General Gorgas placed Crumbine in charge of formulating plans for the control of venereal diseases in six other states. He visited first with the governor of each state, then with the head of its council of national defense, and finally with the leading state health official to assure cooperation of the leaders in each state in developing its program. He met with resistance in only one state where the governor and other state officials warned him he would have to secure the support of the Bishop to succeed. This he found complicated by the fact that a local official who was a member of the Bishop's church owned several houses of prostitution. The Bishop received him courteously but insisted he had his own methods of teaching morality. Crumbine tried to explain that he was interested in the health of soldiers, not their morality, but the Bishop appeared to believe the doctor was trying to interfere in church matters. The doctor finally resorted to an old lawyer's trick of requiring a yes or no answer. When "I . . . report to the War Department . . . may I say that you will cooperate with the federal government in this important phase of national defense?"

After a moment of hesitation the Bishop responded, "That I will. Of course I will. I want our country to win this war as much as any man. Certainly I'll cooperate. Of course I'll do all I can for your program." Following Crumbine's report to the governor, the state's council of national defense voted $5,000 for the program and the state that he believed might be most doubtful was the first to act with a campaign for control of venereal disease and public education in social hygiene. Amazingly, control of venereal disease was comparable in the military and civilian areas under Crumbine's jurisdiction to that of Pershing in France.[41]

In 1918 Congress enacted the Chamberlin–Kahn Act, which appropriated $1 million dollars to help the states in combating venereal disease. Crumbine was able to put these funds to good use until the state legislature decided Kansas could do without this program after the war on the basis that admitting the facts about social disease made many people uncomfortable.[42]

General Merritt W. Ireland replaced William Gorgas as Surgeon General when the Spanish–American hero retired just prior to the Armistice. In his first public pronouncement in his new office, Ireland declared that "the extraordinary success of the American Army in the war is built on the good health of the soldier." "We have got to thank the thousands of doctors and the thousands of nurses for the Army's superior health," and, he added, "the American Army has the best health record or [*sic*] any army in the world." The 25,000 Army doctors "patriotically" abandoned their practice in the states "to keep our soldiers well."[43]

Ireland later became more specific, noting that "Kansas stood first of all the states for having the largest number of men physically fit for military service in the war." Out of over 4 million men examined nationally, the Kansas percentage was thirty-five defects per hundred, compared to sixty-four for Rhode Island. He believed Kansas ranked first because it was an agricultural state and because of its high percentage of native-born population. Cities furnished 51 percent of the defective men and in all classes more than one in five was "physically unfit to perform any type of military service either at home or abroad." The Army statistic that 30 percent of the draftable men were physically unfit to serve because of defects that could have been remedied when they were young, helped gain support for the work of the department of health's division of child hygiene. Much credit had to be paid to the state's department of health.[44]

In 1913 the American Medical Association chose Charles V. Chapin to conduct a comprehensive study of the state boards of health. While Crumbine had much work to do yet at that time to bring his board to the top of the list, Kansas was well in the forefront by the beginning of the war. Chapin listed New York, Massachusetts, and Pennsylvania in the first rank, with Minnesota, New Jersey, Indiana, Kansas, and Vermont in the second. Kansas received extra credit here for "fighting nostrums." Kansas ranked eighteenth of the forty-eight for per capita spending on public health, not bad considering the frugal legislature that Crumbine had to face every biennium. The state was given special citation for having "kept out of political entanglement" and for the close relationship between the department of health and the state university. The report noted that "excellent work is being done for the protection of water supplies and for solving problems of sewage disposal." As with most states, Kansas needed to improve its local health administration, Chapin added. Crumbine was working on that problem when America entered the war.[45]

Samuel Crumbine used reported statistics to conclude that "Kansas is almost a health resort," compared to other states. "For years," he observed, "the typhoid death rate in Kansas has really been somewhat of a disgrace" because it is a preventable disease. "It seemed we just couldn't cut it down." He credited improved sanitary conditions, typhoid vaccinations, "and the rigorous preaching of common sense health rules to young mothers" for the decline in typhoid and enteritis death rates. In the last two years after the war the death rate for enteritis among children under two years of age had been cut in half. Also, "Dr. Crumbine admits freely, Kansas naturally is a healthy state." The census of 1920 confirmed the doctor's rather chauvinistic statement when it was reported that life expectancy for white males in Kansas was 59.73 years and that for white females was 60.89. Wisconsin was second highest in the nation with 58.77 years and 60.70 respectively.[46]

Just before the war ended Crumbine had to deal with one of the most extensive plagues in history. In the winter of 1917 reports began filtering into America that the Spanish influenza was hitting Europe. By spring it reached the Atlantic coast and it rolled across the country in three waves, two in 1918 and the third in the winter of 1919–1920, laying low millions of Americans. It could not have come at a worst time because 25,000 doctors and even more nurses were serving in the military forces. In addition, it had been twenty-five years since an influenza crisis had struck the United States and current medical people were unfamiliar with its causes or symptoms. Little could be done to stop the spread in any case because, as Gerald Grob points out, scientists "have yet to understand why it proved so deadly" and "virtually all preventive and interventionist measures proved futile." Thousands of soldiers were crowded together in the Kansas cantonments, and Crumbine's board of health had just been denied an emergency fund to combat epidemics by a parsimonious legislature.[47]

The U.S. Public Health Service greatly expanded its work during this pandemic. A great demand for physicians quickly surfaced but too many doctors were in military service to meet the crisis. Fortunately, many medical people who were ineligible for Army work had organized the Voluntary Medical Service and almost 2,000 of these physicians responded to the call. The service also helped mobilize trained and untrained nurses for the emergency and Congress appropriated $1,000,000 to help them fight influenza.[48]

In September 1918 the *Topeka Daily Capital* reported that influenza had killed sixteen people in Boston in six hours. This was a major port of embarkation for the AEF to go to France. Ten of the dead were sailors and in the fourteen naval stations in that district 2,331 cases were reported. The plague spread to the naval prison at Portsmouth, New Hampshire and about 2,000 soldiers were reported ill at Fort Devens in the Northeast. Influenza was not a reportable disease in civilian life so authorities did not have the correct or complete information to predict how it was spreading, but medical officers believed "they had the situation well in hand." Not so, as the following day the newspaper reported seventy deaths from influenza, and pneumonia that often accompanied or succeeded it, in New England within the previous twenty-four hours. At Camp Devens there were now 3,500 cases, "mainly among Negro soldiers." Unsubstantiated rumors quickly circulated that the germs were introduced into the country by enemy agents who were landed on American shores by German submarines.[49]

One week later the headline read "Spanish Influenza Epidemic Spreads Thruout Nation." In anticipation of this development, Surgeon General Rupert Blue of the U.S. Public Health Service had immediately wired Crumbine when the cases first began to spread that the outbreaks would have a significant impact on war production and he requested the doctor keep him apprized of the situation in Kansas. Crumbine responded that he would be happy to comply with the request but it would be difficult. Both the average physician and layman, he noted, "are inclined to call any acute coryza as 'influenza' or 'grippe,'" and his reports would be "in all probability, very inaccurate." It would be helpful if Blue would forward "authentic information concerning the symtomatology" of the diseases in Boston and also about its bacteriology."[50]

The disease was reaching epidemic proportions in some areas and spreading rapidly to the Pacific Coast. Health officials called an emergency meeting in Washington, DC, where Surgeon General Blue reported cases appearing in twenty-six states. It was epidemic in New England, reported in most eastern states and Minnesota and Iowa, and spreading to new Army camps every day. For the first time Camp Devens was no longer the leader; that designation fell to Hoboken. Camp Funston now reported 135 cases. Some communities were considering the drastic step of forbidding public gatherings.[51]

Once the plague appeared in Camp Funston it spread rapidly through Kansas. Crumbine was soon swamped with calls for help and he had little or none to send. Western Kansas, with its sparse population, was especially hard hit and some counties were without a doctor. Fortunately, Congress approved an emergency fund and, out of the Kansas share, he was able to send eight physicians from Eastern Kansas and Western Missouri to their rescue. Some cases were dreadful. A nurse reported to him that she received a call from a sick rancher about a neighbor. She hurried to the neighbor's ranch and found that the father, mother, two children, and hired hand were terribly ill. The cattle herded into the corral the previous day were wailing horribly and this had roused the neighbor to call the nurse. They had not had feed or water for over a day and neither had the family. The frantic bawling of the cattle had possibly saved some of those lives.[52]

The scourge hit Forts Leavenworth and Riley, Camp Funston, the University of Kansas, and Kansas State Agricultural College quite hard. In the Funston–Riley cantonment influenza and its complicating companion, pneumonia, reached a toll of eighty-six dead in one day. The University had no hospital facilities and the small city hospital was overflowing. Chancellor Frank Strong begged Crumbine for assistance but the doctor was helpless. At the time a barrack for housing students in military training was partially completed with a roof over it, but nothing else—no doors, no windows. In desperation the doctor appealed to General Leonard Wood for beds and medical supplies to use in the uncompleted barracks. Crumbine knew they were available at Funston because over 50 percent of the soldiers there had left for France. The general, however, was forced to refuse because of military regulations. A week went by with the hearses carrying off the bodies of the young people before Crumbine placed another frantic call:

> General, it so happens that you are the only person who can help us, for there are no other supplies available here or in Kansas City, so we are counting on you to save the lives of these fine boys and girls and the parents of these young people are counting on you too. . . . It is impossible to wait longer.

How could this appeal be resisted? General Wood decided to risk his career and promised "an express-car load of equipment and supplies on the evening train, for I am convinced, from our experience here, that the situation demands prompt attention and action." Three days later Wood reported that headquarters in Chicago had refused to approve the loan and he feared a court-martial. Crumbine immediately called Kansas Senator Charles Curtis who pushed through the Senate a joint resolution approving Wood's action. The House of Representatives endorsed it the following morning and it not only legalized the general's good deed but it authorized the use of federal supplies throughout the ongoing influenza epidemic.[53]

When the epidemic first struck, Crumbine issued a pamphlet on it and requested anyone with medical training to volunteer for an assignment. On October 3 reports indicated a decrease in cases in Army camps but it spread rapidly from Funston to the cities of Leavenworth, Atchison, Topeka, Wichita, and Hays. Five days later Crumbine banned all visitors from state institutions, including colleges. On the ninth of October most theaters, churches, schools, and meeting places were closed. University classes were suspended and fraternity dorms at Kansas State Agricultural College were used as hospitals. By the fifteenth there were 12,000 cases reported in the state. Whole families were stricken and stories were told of children crying at the side of their dead parents. In military camps scenes had become "indescribable." One account told of "men attempting to evade confinement with the dead and dying, [who] lay gasping with the disease in their regular quarters and soon found death all around them, even there." Tiers of rough pine coffins began to block the loading docks of railroad stations at the camps.[54]

Stern measures had to be taken. Crumbine telegraphed Dr. C.W. Robinson, Atchison County health officer, that he had consulted state Attorney General S.M. Brewster who approved closing the crossings at the Kansas–Missouri border when needed. Acting on this authority, Brewster closed the bridge against "excursions" from the saloon town of East Atchison on the Missouri side of the river. At the same time the state board of health advised against holding public sales or any outdoor amusements where crowds might gather. A week later the plague struck the capital city severely enough that city health officer Dr. H.L. Clark forbade all public gatherings of twenty or more people, including a "patriotic meeting" that a state senator was to address, and he closed the public schools. In addition, all houses containing a case of influenza must be carded as such.[55]

The state board of health issued the following notice and advertised a free pamphlet on influenza:

**Influenza Spanish Influenza "The Flu"**
The disease that is now epidemic in Kansas is highly catching and is spread by contact with the sick or "carrier" cases.
Influenza is a crowd disease. Therefore avoid crowds as much as possible. The State-wide closing order was made as the only way to prevent the progress of the disease by prohibiting crowds.
Influenza probably spreads mostly by inhaling the germ-laden droplets that are sprayed in the air by the careless cough or sneeze. People should cover their cough or sneeze in order to prevent the spread of the disease. The habit of spitting on the floor or sidewalk is to be condemned as another way in which disease is spread.
Shun the common drinking cup, the roller towel, for they may spread disease.
Keep out in the open air as much as possible, and sleep with your windows open.
Wash your hands before eating.
There are no preventatives except God's pure air, good nutritious food, cleanliness of body and keeping the body sewers open.
AVOID CROWDS, and again we say AVOID CROWDS!
Cover your cough and smother your sneeze, For the Kaiser laughs when you spread disease.[56]

Acting for the board of health Crumbine wrote the governor of the need for a general closing order because "strict measures now" might check the spread of influenza and reduce its virulence. Governor Arthur Capper responded by immediately ordering all schools, churches, theaters, and public assembling places in the state closed for one week, possibly to be extended. At that point the epidemic had spread to seventy-four counties and 1,000 new cases had developed in the previous twenty-four hours. "The history of the disease," Crumbine explained, "shows that its virulence depends to a considerable extent upon the rapidity of transmission." The people must not assemble in crowds. Theaters, he warned, were the worst places because they usually were converted old store buildings without ventilation. With each announcement of new cases, Crumbine reminded the people that the actual figures were even more terrifying because many doctors were too busy attending the sick to make reports. One Hill City physician reported seeing his home once every twenty-four hours. Starting before daybreak, he slept while a driver took him on his rounds, returning early the next morning for a hot breakfast and a change of clothing, to start another day. Several doctors also, of course, succumbed to the plague.[57]

By October 19 Crumbine saw a small decline in the epidemic. He permitted farm sales, as they were open air affairs, on the conditions that no food or drink were served and if only prospective customers attended. He noted that Crawford County was still suffering greatly and he hoped to send more needed medical assistance there soon. At the mining community of Crowberg, it was reported that a church deacon and an evangelist were arrested for holding a meeting and there was "unrest" at several other communities. Despite this public disquiet, health officers of fifty towns and cities were unanimous in recommending the governor extend the closing ban and Capper agreed that another week of protection for the public would "far outweigh all business or political conditions." Crumbine further advised all people to wear gauze masks on the streets and in "businesses employing any considerable number of people." Streetcars had to operate with open windows, regardless of the outside temperature.[58]

Captain Frank Shaw, commandant of the Student Army Training Corps (SATC) at Washburn College tried to cover up an epidemic in his unit by telling the men they merely had colds and filing a report affirming this. The story broke when one man about to be inducted into the SATC, died of influenza and another was reported close to death. When queried about the situation, Crumbine responded that the unit had not reported any cases but that he had received informal reports that the boys were suffering from colds and now his office would investigate the situation. At the same time a delegation of parents called on Governor Capper, demanding to know why their sons could not return home for treatment if they were not suffering from influenza as Washington authorities had led them to believe. Governor Capper assured them he would investigate the matter and the unit was quarantined.[59]

While there was a steady decline in the number of cases in late October, Crumbine warned the public that the disease would "not be driven out under four or five weeks" and he visited Lawrence to determine when the University might be reopened. People were chafing under the continuance of the closing rules but were warned there must be no relaxation of precautions because that would only "bring the epidemic back with renewed vigor, as had been the case in Kansas City." Slowly town after town lifted its closing ban but in early November Crumbine felt compelled to send an additional appeal to teachers. He reminded them that motion picture theaters had been fumigated and all schools had been "scrubbed." If children came to school with only a "very inoffensive sniffle, sending the youngster home may not only save the child's life, but the lives of other people." Slowly, though, normal life returned to Kansas.[60]

Almost immediately a resurgence struck. In late November 1918 an outbreak occurred in Topeka but Crumbine and the board of health decided to wait before issuing another unpopular closing order. By the end of the month, though, they banned all nonessential meetings, closed churches, and ordered stores and pool halls to allow only a small number of customers inside, allowing an average of 100 square feet per person and they had to close at 4:30 PM. Lawrence suffered more cases than it had in the first outbreak and again closed schools. On December 10 Kansas City, which had prematurely lifted its closing ban, broke all its mortality records with thirty-six deaths from influenza, eleven from pneumonia, and eighteen from other causes. By December 21 the epidemic had crested, but Crumbine publicly declared that hundreds of Kansans had committed suicide by remaining on their jobs long after the disease had gained a firm foothold on them. An outbreak again in 1919–1920 was less severe than the first two had been.[61]

After the crises ended, Crumbine tallied the cost to Kansas. Over 5,000 lost their lives, or the same number of Kansans killed in the war. About 250,000 people were stricken and the economic loss was dreadful. Some 12,000 teachers were idled for two months. Businesses lost $1 million daily for sixty days. Agriculture suffered as the epidemic hit during a harvesting time. The *State Journal* carried a story of J.J. Sippy, state epidemiologist, who summarized the effects of the awesome plague:

> Nothing to compare it with has ever occurred in this state. Every line of business endeavor has been compelled to absorb tremendous losses—losses which in many instances cannot be overcome readily. . . . I doubt if more than sixty percent of the cases were reported to the state board. . . . Never before in the history of the state were the doctors called upon for such tireless service. Never did the nursing corps of a state give more faithful, tireless, devoted and heroic service than during the days when the epidemic raged in every section of the state.

Sippy placed a value of $4,100 on each human life, making a total loss of $22,742,700 for over 5,000 people who died of the influenza. The average doctor bill for the 250,000 cases came to $10 each, or $2,500,000. When totaled, the world's losses were even more incomprehensible—perhaps 20,000,000 or 30,000,000 people died. Oddly enough, approximately two-thirds of American losses were between ages twenty and forty, people in the prime of their lives. In terms of equal time periods, this meant the influenza plague was five times more deadly than the trench warfare of World War I.[62]

Samuel Crumbine continued his health work after the war, but the spirit of reform had died. When the legislature failed to fund the Venereal Disease division of the department of health and thus provided no state match for federal funds, Crumbine sought an opinion from the state attorney general. The official ruled that venereal disease was communicable and money appropriated for research into causes of communicable diseases included this type and the doctor could provide his matching funds. As noted previously, he played a major role in getting the Tri-State Sanitary District established. He helped organize the Kansas Public Health Association and served as its vice president and his vaccination program in Wabaunsee County was a great success. Politically, though, it was a reactionary period as demonstrated in the state legislature with its penurious appropriations and its attack on the working man with the establishment of the Kansas Court of Industrial Relations for the arbitrary settlement of labor–management relations. Crumbine did manage, however, to continue his wartime crusade against venereal disease for a time.[63]

When the Court of Industrial Relations failed to resolve the critical coal strike in the fall of 1919, Governor Henry J. Allen mobilized the state militia and called for volunteers to mine coal. When the soldiers moved in, the prostitutes promptly followed. Crumbine advised the governor on December 4 that health officers were reporting an increase in venereal disease in the coal area of southeastern Kansas. The governor asked the board secretary to dispatch someone to help the local health authorities round up the prostitutes and make certain they received treatment if needed. Crumbine had anticipated this and already had requested the United States Interdepartment Social Hygiene Board to send him a skilled investigator. C.A. Bantleon had arrived, ready to work, and entrained for the Pittsburg area. Immediately, the population began to expand again at the State Industrial Farm for Women.[64]

Crumbine described Dr. C.J. Montgomery, health officer for Cherokee County in the coal district, as "one of our more resourceful" men. One day "Monty," as he liked to be called, began looking for two "wild girls," as he called them. He finally caught them when a farmer notified him they were camped out in his straw stack. He "mounted his trusty Ford," went out and captured them, and the "two chickens" spent the night in jail, ending up in the camp for infected women. Monty conducted his own educational campaign with signs on the neighboring highways, one of them taken from a board of health *Bulletin*: "If a Chicken Smiles at You—Safety First." On Sunday evenings motorists took a leisurely drive on the highways in Cherokee County to see what new "educational" signs Monty had erected recently.[65]

The crisis in social diseases in the coal area convinced Crumbine that he needed to attack the problem at its roots; there was a vital need to educate the youth of Kansas with social hygiene information. When he sent a letter to 535 high school superintendents across the state in the summer of 1920 describing his plans for this education, the response was gratifyingly positive. The program he subsequently established included two women, Lo Ree Cave of Hays State Normal School and Buena Burr of Manhattan to lecture to the girls and two former YMCA secretaries, C.A. Hall and Paul Moser, to talk to the boys. The discussions were prepared to include time for a question–answer period. The board of health also published two pamphlets, "Keeping Fit" for the boys and "The Girls' Part" for the young ladies. Mrs. Burr also tried to reach the mothers with group discussions. The program had the active support of women's clubs across the state. The three-year plan was highly successful although it met with some formidable opposition in puritanical Kansas, especially in some communities, even though the support of the superintendents was most favorable. But the presence of local gossips can always stir up resistance through vilification and falsification, especially when a hitherto taboo topic such as social hygiene education is involved, and the board of health became the focus of their attention. When Crumbine investigated the complaints, he was told that the board was "meddling in purely personal and community affairs." The opposition became strong enough to persuade the legislature in 1923 to drop the appropriation for the board's Division of Venereal Disease control. Thus died a truly pioneering effort to establish a reasonable sex education program in Kansas. The state had just successfully experienced the Progressive Movement and established some of the leading reform programs in the nation. Now, in the grip of the reactionary Big Red Scare and the Roaring Twenties, they were reacting against new ideas.[66]

This was a preview of Crumbine's disastrous problems in 1923, and perhaps the sex education experience also contributed to his tribulations that year. The Industrial Court had proven to be very unpopular in many quarters but it was a Republican measure so W.Y. Morgan, the GOP candidate for governor in 1922, supported the concept. The Democratic candidate, Jonathan Davis, campaigned in opposition to the court. He also promised tax reduction and thus farmers, who wanted tax relief, joined organized labor, which wanted the court abolished, and elected Davis.[67]

Democrats seldom win the governor's race in Kansas and when they do, they are hungry for the spoils of office. Davis, especially desiring patronage to reward his supporters, ruthlessly demanded a 40 percent turnover in the personnel of the board of health. Crumbine was outraged over this high-handed order because the departments of agriculture and health had always been nonpolitical and thus sacrosanct from political meddling. For nineteen years the doctor had made all health appointments, subject to board approval, and no state official was more insistent on competence

Kansas—I'm not sure this is just the sort of advertising I am wanting

Crumbine Reforms [Kansas State Historical Society]

as the sole criteria for office. This was a shocking request and the doctor adamantly refused.[68]

The governor immediately appointed six new members of the nine-man board of health, for the obvious purpose of having them replace Crumbine. Three of the six displaced members had been reappointed by Allen in 1922 but the senate journal did not indicate they had been confirmed, and there were questions on whether that move was necessary on reappointments. Allen named the other three as interim appointments because the legislature was not in session to confirm them. Davis informed four of these six that he was removing them from the board of health because they had not been confirmed by the senate. Dr. J.T. Axtell, Newton hospital administrator, was one of the other Davis appointees that was not challenged. He was a reappointee and Davis assured Axtell that he planned no change in the position of the board of health's secretary. But when strong rumors began to circulate that Crumbine would be fired, Axtell undertook a campaign in support of retaining him as secretary. This angered Davis and he sent Axtell "a red hot letter of dismissal" because of this "partisan political activity." "By writing letters to your friends," the governor sternly rebuked him, "you have aroused partisan feeling until you have succeeded in injecting politics into the board of health affairs. . . . Now changes are imperative for the good of the service." This observation appeared to be a non sequitur but these mental lapses did not bother Davis. The governor appointed Dodge City doctor Robert C. Klein in his stead.[69]

This left one Allen appointee, Dr. H.L. Aldrich of Carney, on the new Davis board. When the group met, Crumbine asked them if he would be retained or fired as rumor was insisting because he would like to arrange his business affairs accordingly. The board elected a new president and vice president but waffled on the question of whom it would choose for secretary. Because of the huge groundswell of opinion against the firing of Crumbine, the decision was made to postpone the issue until the annual meeting on June 27. The state's leading newspaper reported that the board would "probably" decide on Crumbine's future at that time.[70]

When serious rumors began surfacing about Crumbine's fate, Mervin T. Sudler, dean of the University of Kansas Medical School, immediately wrote his good friend that he had read a story in the *Kansas City Star* that the doctor was to be removed from his position. "Is there anything your friends can do to meet this pitiful situation,?" he queried. "In this position you have made a national reputation as a health officer. . . . Governor Davis must have the good of the state at heart and if we can just prove to him the great value of your service and the great loss that it would be . . . that this action might not be taken." Crumbine replied that he had "received an intimation this morning that the Governor is somewhat wavering in his purposes and that a little pressure at this time would be of great value." He believed that if Dr. Sudler and "a number of other good friends would write in a proper and dignified letter to the Governor expressing yourself in the way you have in your letter to me . . . it would be a big help." Sudler also wrote Henderson S. Martin, whom he thought might have some political influence about the matter, and he agreed it was deplorable. But ultimately Martin proved unable to alter the course of political events.[71]

A groundswell of reaction against firing Crumbine arose across the state. The Kansas Medical Society sent the governor a resolution supporting the doctor, as did most of the other medical organizations, as well as the Kansas Health Officers Association. Civic groups, women's clubs, and 300 Dodge City women, wrote Governor Davis in protest over such action. O.D. Walker, board of health member and former president of the Kansas Medical Society warned Davis that "no man one-half Dr. Crumbine's caliber in Public Health today is looking for a job" and, besides, he was irreplaceable. All to no avail. The Davis board of health elected its own officers. The remaining six members of the old board met, decided they were a quorum, and Crumbine submitted his resignation to them, saying he was accepting a position with the American Child Health Association. He decided not to fight for his job. The subsequent damage to public health progress in the state was not worth salvaging his pride. He said:

> I wish to thank the people of Kansas for their generous cooperation which has contributed much to whatever success has been achieved in public health and, finally, my sincere thanks to the ex-governors of Kansas who have always given their state board of health the fullest cooperation and freedom of action in its many-sided duties and who have never attempted the dictation of appointments in the department as reward for party service.
>
> My regret in severing my relation with public health work in Kansas is largely mitigated by the knowledge that the integrity of the organization will be preserved under the leadership of a health officer of training and experience.

The board of health accepted his resignation, "deeply deploring our loss of a great man." His administration of the department "has been marked by keen judgment, unfailing courtesy, absolute honesty, and skill of a rare order amounting almost to genius."[72]

When Crumbine attended the national health officers meeting in Washington, he invited the organization to hold their 1924 conference at Topeka. After hearing the subsequent news of his sordid treatment and ouster from office the organization withdrew its acceptance and decided to meet elsewhere if Crumbine were not going to be a health officer. The old board chose Dr. N.O. Nyberg as its new secretary. He was a World War I veteran who graduated from the Atlanta School of Medicine, specializing in public health and receiving war experience in sanitation before becoming health officer for Wichita. The issue probably would not have continued except for politics. "Crumbine was given to understand that he could stay on the job and reign peacefully if he would permit Carl Peterson to name all but three of the forty employees of the board." This he refused to do. Peterson, state Democratic central committee chairman, was determined to get possession of these jobs as they paid salaries ranging from Crumbine's $4,000 annually, and two jobs in the $3,300 range, down to $1,000. Governor Davis refused to accept the election of Nygard and convened a meeting of his new board. On June 7 they elected Dr. Leon Matassarin as executive secretary. Davis informed a newspaper reporter that "all Kansas is humiliated at the disgraceful spectacle that has been perpetrated during the last few days by Republican office holders in their efforts to retain of the patronage of the state board of health." Appointments to the state board of health had never been under the "patronage" of any administration until 1923.

At this point the executive council in charge of state house offices ordered the state health offices closed until the state supreme court made a decision on the legitimacy of the two boards. In addition, Topeka Postmaster Charles S. Sessions refused to deliver mail to either board until that decision was announced. Everyone seemed to agree with this sensible solution. Then the governor refused to approve Nyberg's bond for office of secretary but did that for Matassarin. Peterson named W.F. Freeman, president of the state federation of labor, as Registrar of Vital Statistics and hired two new stenographers, one of whom replaced Violet, Samuel Crumbine's daughter. The Democrats captured control of the board of health offices by obtaining the keys from the statehouse janitor. The statehouse mechanic refused to change the locks on the doors so they obtained the services of a locksmith on Kansas Avenue to do it.[73]

Both sides chose counsel for the looming legal battle. Samuel Crumbine immediately asked Attorney General Charles B. Griffith to bring a quo warranto proceeding in the state supreme court to place Nyberg in charge of the board of health. Davis issued a proclamation calling on the public to support their governor and for Griffith to withdraw his legal request, denouncing him for his betrayal. In turn, when Griffith discovered that Matassarin had taken possession of the board of health offices, he charged the governor with "bad faith ... in a few minutes of red-hot conversation" with the chief executive. The supreme court ordered the offices of the board of health closed until they could decide on the quo warranto proceedings.[74]

Employees of both boards began gathering around the state house. Robert Stone, Topeka lawyer, accompanied by Drs. Crumbine and Nyberg, entered the health offices area. They were met by Edward McKeever, Topeka lawyer, and W.H. Carpenter, "well-known" Democratic lawyer from Marion. Both sides avoided a clash with the Crumbine forces retiring to the attorney general's office and the Matassarin lawyers adjourning to the governor's private office for consultation. Crumbine issued a bitter statement denouncing "this action in disturbing the orderly work of an organized state department [that] should make Kansas hang her head because of the methods used in browbeating help" and observing that it was "the most disgraceful political incident in the history of the state."[75]

At this point Dr. R.C. Lytle of McPherson, the remaining Allen appointee and "one of the outstanding Democrats" of that part of the state, resigned from the board of health, saying:

> I have felt from the first that politics should play no part in this board of health matter. I am a friend of Dr. Crumbine's. I am a friend of the governor's.
>
> I believe that if the governor had been left alone in this matter, and been allowed to use his own judgment, he would not have been a party to the disgraceful tactics and the show of partisan selfishness which recently has been demonstrated in Topeka. . . . I have informed the governor that I am too busy to try to work in harmony with such men as seem to be using their influence to the discredit of my ethical training and convictions.[76]

One week later the supreme court refused to oust the Allen appointed members of the board of health, thus constituting the new board as these six plus three legitimate Davis nominees and confirming Nyberg's election. During the court proceedings Attorney General Griffith created "a sensation" when he announced that state bank commissioner and secretary of the Democratic state central committee Carl Peterson would be prosecuted for perjury if his affidavit was permitted to go into the court records. His sworn statement declared that "rough house" tactics were not used in the Democratic effort to revamp the board of health and that he did not play "a leading part" in taking possession of its offices.[77]

Governor Davis immediately issued a public statement that "the court of public opinion . . . is the final and highest court, in all public matters." He drew a far-fetched parallel between this issue and the Dred Scott decision of 1857 when the United States Supreme Court held Scott to be a slave and not a U.S. citizen with rights to sue in federal courts. The public later reversed that decision by approving the 13th Amendment and "history usually repeats itself," he said. Three days later Davis elaborated on this theme, calling for the election of a Democratic legislature. "Able lawyers tell me they cannot understand this decision," he asserted, so "how can I, a farmer, be expected to understand it." He did know, however, that it meant that "the wish of the nearly twenty thousand majority of Kansas voters" for him to direct the executive affairs for the state was thereby set aside and "the appointees of my predecessor shall sit in judgment and decide." He revealed his true feelings when he continued:

> As a matter of fact, Dr. Crumbine had needed moving for several years by reason of the fact that . . . in utter disregard for the interests of the taxpayers, he drew two salaries from the state, which the legislature found necessary to stop [untrue] and because of the fact that he defeated a meritorious bill regarding the control of venereal diseases because

he was not left alone to use his own autocratic will in the administration of the law. He showed an utter disregard for the taxpayer from the time he became connected with the department until he left it. He has been a sublime egotist, ready to admit at all times that he is the greatest man in the state.

Thus ended one of the most tempestuous and sordid episodes in the bizarre history of Kansas politics.[78]

One authority quotes Tom McNeal of the *Kansas Farmer*, under the title "Crumbine Hired and Fired," that the doctor held the idea

that health matters were sacred from profane political interference. So just to show him that there ain't no such word as sacred a little group of supergod politicians stepped up and said "You're fired." Hoover hired Crumbine in the U.S. Public Health Service. At a big national health meeting, held recently in Kansas City we heard the chairman of the meeting tell health people from all over the United States that Kansas had done a wonderful thing in releasing this man to America. Hats off to the blunders of the supergod politicians.[79]

The results were politically devastating for Governor Jonathan Davis. He was bombarded with letters and editorials "until it seemed that he had not a friend in the state legislature in either party." Years later Crumbine appeared on the same program with Davis's widow, speaking to a state women's group. "She told me," he reported, "that she had warned the governor that he was making a very great political mistake, and doing a terrible injustice, which he would later regret, then she added, 'and he did.'" But his regrets came sooner rather than later.[80]

The protests came from near and far. Dr. Oliver D. Walker of Salina wrote the governor that with Crumbine's departure, "we would be in very truth, the 'Nestor' of public health matters in our state." L.B. Gloyne, commissioner of health and sanitation in Kansas City, informed the doctor that he "had left a mark on Kansas history." He expressed the hope that his new job would have so many joys connected with it that he would "entirely forget the treatment that a small group of Kansans gave you." W.S. Frisbie of the Association of American Dairy, Food and Drug Officials observed that Kansas "has suffered a direct loss in your resignation" and he hoped his new position "will afford an opportunity to prosecute with vigor the lofty ideals which you have maintained throughout your term in office." E.B. Black of Black and Veatch consulting engineers of Oklahoma City congratulated Crumbine "on the stand you took in the recent controversy with the Governor ... and ... am genuinely sorry for the State." Bloomington, Illinois health director Harold B. Wood was "dumbfounded" over the episode but noted that Crumbine had "done so much for the welfare of your state and have so materially advanced the public health of the entire country" because his educational methods had extended "beyond the borders of Kansas."[81]

By this time Samuel Crumbine had earned a most enviable reputation in public health work. He was currently, or had been at one time, elected to a governing position in the State and Provencial Boards of Health, the American Public Health Association, the National Association for the Study and Prevention of Tuberculosis, the American Association of Food and Dairy Officers, and the National Health Council, becoming secretary of the latter as recently as 1921. Membership, and especially holding office, in these organizations symbolized the epitome of goals for public health officers anywhere. He and his office had pioneered in the proper handling of oysters, roller towels, common drinking cups, a traveling health car, attacks on the housefly, the first federal rural infant mortality study, public sex education, and the second child health division in the nation. But his international reputation did not awe Jonathan Davis.

There were immediate repercussions among the outstanding personnel of the board of health. In July Dr. B.K. Kilbourne resigned as director of the Division of Venereal Diseases. Dr. William Levin resigned in August as director of the Public Health Laboratory and Dr. Helen A. Moore left as director of the Division of Child Hygiene that December. W.G. Davies resigned as Registrar of Vital Statistics in June 1924. F.E. Rowland, for fourteen years the assistant food and drug inspector, was removed by the board of health in June 1924. By that time a newly constituted board of health with a majority of Davis appointees adopted a resolution to discharge or hire personnel at the discretion of a majority of its members. Nine employees were soon replaced. In addition to Rowland these included state epidemiologist C.H. Kinnaman, replacement for the venerable Sippy who left when Crumbine resigned. The board of health had now become politicized. Kinnaman had been lured away from the Rockefeller Foundation to come to Kansas and was terminated at the same time Governor Davis was simultaneously seeking a $2.5 million grant from the Rockefeller Foundation to make improvements in the state medical school. Such was the nonsensical course of Kansas politics in this crisis.[82]

Crumbine's departure led to a minimizing of outside funding for health work in Kansas. The U.S. Public Health Service and the International Health Board were reluctant to commit money to the state after this sordid episode and, of course, none came from the Sheppard–Towner program. Crumbine and the board of health had received funding from the Rockefeller Foundation to establish six demonstration units to assist these counties in creating a full-time health officer. In 1925 the legislature refused to appropriate $10,000 in matching funds for this work and the units were closed down. Lack of this funding, meager legislative appropriations, and the loss of key people, especially the dynamic leadership of Crumbine, led to the department being characterized by "apparent lethargy."[83]

Numerous national organizations sought the services of Samuel Crumbine and five major ones offered him a salary that would double his current income in Kansas. At the urging of Herbert Hoover, Secretary of Commerce, who telegraphed "urge your acceptance of important position with our association," he accepted the offer of the American Child Health Association to become executive secretary of its public health department. On June 5, 1923, he sorrowfully left Kansas for New York City, leaving behind a huge legacy in public health advances in his state. Whatever the bitter feelings over the politicalization of the department of health, he could take great pride in having moved his agency from one of a moribund state to one of the finest of its kind in the nation.

# Six

# THE CIVILIZED EAST

Early in their marriage Samuel and Katherine agreed to take an annual vacation. During the crisis in the summer of 1923 they had to postpone this but they did travel that year—to the big metropolis. Samuel left in early June and Katherine and Violet joined him in December to begin a new life for themselves. The last decade of his active career appears anticlimactic after his enormous contributions to public health before 1923. But he had more fields to conquer, more service to give his nation. At age sixty-two, when many men begin thinking seriously about retirement, he was moving to a completely different life with a new profession to explore. He hated to leave Kansas, his "home," for the rigors of life in a huge metropolis, with its compacted apartments and tenements, its crowded streets and sidewalks, but he saw challenges. He also would face situations he never foresaw nor wanted because he was accustomed to being the star and now he would be thrust into a galaxy of national stars in the American Child Hygiene Association (ACHA).[1]

A product of doctors, nurses, and health officials, the ACHA stressed the importance of improving the health of the mother and her preschool child. The organization sought to promote prenatal care, pasteurization of milk, and extension of vital birth certifications to reduce infant mortality. It had its origins in the American Association for the Search and Prevention of Infant Mortality (AASPIM), found in 1909. This group viewed its mission as coordinating the work of voluntary organizations dedicated to the improvement of baby care and the reduction of infant mortality.

Among other activities, it was a powerful lobby in persuading Congress to establish the Children's Bureau in the department of labor in 1912. Directed first by the great Julia Lathrop, followed by Grace Abbott, this agency encouraged states and municipalities to increase their public health work directed at mothers and children. The Sheppard–Towner Act of 1921 expended its activities. Late in his presidency, in 1909, President Theodore Roosevelt called a White House conference on child health and delegates there recommended creation of such an administration. Opposition to the idea centered around the conservative view that such a bureau would invade both parental and states' rights and no action resulted for another three years. Although AASPIM members supported the eugenicists ideas, popular in some quarters at that time but later discredited by association with Nazi Germany, the Americans had as their goal the mental and physical quality of humankind and they published a monthly, *Mother and Child*, to promote this principle.[2]

The Child Health Organization (CHO), on the other hand, was founded in the spring of 1918 and stressed health education for children in the schools by inspiring teacher participation to implement its policies. Both the CHO and the ACHA stressed voluntarism and relied on private philanthropy for financial support. A third group, the Children's Bureau in the department of labor then headed by Grace Abbott, sought to encourage states, counties, and municipalities to concentrate on and improve their public health work for children. All of these organizations benefited from the conscription statistics of World War I that highlighted the number of draft prospects rejected for health deficiencies. One-third of these men were rejected for health reasons that could have been rectified earlier, a subject that remained very much on the minds of Americans in the postwar decade. Public health officials, such as Samuel Crumbine, reminded people that most of these deficiencies could have been corrected through adequate health care during childhood.[3]

Following the war, a dichotomy arose between the groups. The Children's Bureau emphasized economic need as the motivation for child labor and working mothers. Poverty they saw as the root cause of poor child health. Although greatly interested in child welfare, Herbert Hoover believed, on the other hand, that these problems could be remedied through diffusion of health knowledge. He differed sharply with those in the Children's Bureau who stressed that socioeconomic conditions should have priority over the dissemination of knowledge. Hoover had gained an international reputation at the beginning of World War I with his work on relief for Belgian children then under German occupation. After the war he added to his renown in helping famine-plagued Russia and in directing the American Relief Administration to help feed and clothe European children. His background, one admirer wrote after the war, meant that it was "possible to appeal for help in child work . . . in the name of democracy instead of the old and long abused name of charity."[4]

Despite his objection to child labor, Hoover the engineer continued to identify ignorance as the basic cause for poor health in American youngsters. His obsession would increase as the Great Depression emerged. "Mothers fed their children the wrong things," he believed, wrote Professor James Giglio, "skimping on milk and fresh fruits. The community [also] was derelict because it failed to ensure milk purity and did not concern itself enough with other aspects of infant welfare." Hoover became president of the American Child Hygiene Association in 1921. As President Warren Harding's secretary of commerce, he "sought long term social and economic stability, the elimination of waste, and the conservation of resources through the application of expert skills and cooperative approaches." He immediately began to consolidate the work of the organization with that of the Child Health Organization because he agreed basically with the philosophy and approach of both and wanted to promote efficiency by eliminating the overlapping work of the two. After numerous conferences, the American Child Health Association (ACHA) was created with the merger of the two in 1923, a move that resulted from "Mr. Hoover's tact, his logic, and his enthusiasm as to a future." The new organization had its headquarters in Washington, D.C., and its administrative offices on Seventh Avenue in New York City with Hoover as its president.[5]

Courtney Dinwiddie, formerly of the National Child Health Council, served as its general executive and Edgar Rickard was secretary. Rickard had proven his mettle as Food Administrator in 1918 and would continue as Hoover's right-hand man in the 1920s. Dinwiddie coordinated the five staff divisions of medical service headed by Richard Bolt, Crumbine in public health relations, health education under Sally Lucas Dean, George T. Palmer in research, and public relations managed by Arthur Tomalin. Richard A. Bolt, in charge of health services and later to gain a reputation in public health in Cincinnati and the University of California, had been "taken into the confidence of Mr. Hoover" and Dinwiddie to discuss filling the position of executive secretary of public health relations. Well aware of Crumbine's work in Kansas and with the State and Provincial Health Officers Association, Bolt "strongly recommended" the Kansan to his superiors. As the train sped Crumbine to his new position, doubts raced through the doctor's mind but he countered them with the thought that he could bring the perspective of a state health officer to the new organization, "advise them how to deal with such officials, warn them of the uninformed and sometimes hostile attitudes of the public, especially when people's 'personal prerogatives' and their 'sacred superstitions' are assailed or threatened." He argued that he must make himself "useful, above all be yourself, express your opinion only when it seems worthwhile, and always be a good listener, then you may learn something." Good advice but difficult to accept as Crumbine was never a patient listener. He was a doer. He hated committee meetings and when he had learned the plan of action, he would say "splendid, I'll get started right off," and walk out while colleagues were calling out, "wait the meeting just assembled!"[6]

The association had inherited a number of ongoing programs, such as Child Health Demonstration Areas and the month before Crumbine's arrival, the American Child Health Association initiated its May Day program. This ceremony had its origins in the National Baby Week observance, calling attention to the "dos" and "don'ts" of baby care, which by 1916 had drawn the support of millions of mothers. In addition, in May 1919 President Woodrow Wilson called the second White House conference on Child Health as a "closing activity of the special 'Children's Year'" to urge a child health program, to no avail. Congress, in the throes of a postwar reaction, did nothing. "No other ACHA activity commanded as much attention as May Day—Child Health Day," noted one authority, but Congress remained unmoved. Mrs. Aida de Costa Breckinridge, wife of Henry Breckinridge, Woodrow Wilson's assistant secretary of war was an attractive, aggressive woman. She conceived the idea and assured its success with her publicity campaign.[7]

Herbert Hoover stressed the popular "Child's Bill of Rights," a copy of which hung in Crumbine's office. It read:

> The ideal to which we should strive is that there should be no child in America that has not been born under proper conditions; that does not live in hygienic surroundings; that ever suffers from undernourishment; that does not have prompt and efficient medical attention and inspection; that does not receive primary instruction in the elements of hygiene and good health; that has not the complete birthright of a sound mind and sound body; that has not the encouragement to express in fullest measure the spirit within, which is the final endowment of every human being.

This motto became the association's goal for its annual May Day observance and for all of its other activities and goals.[8]

New York City staged a parade in 1923 to mark the occasion, provided speakers, and memorialized the mayor with a resolution proclaiming Child Health Day. "We made it May 1st to offset the red (left-wing) business more or less," Crumbine said. "The union chaps were most cooperative." With AFL support, they finally persuaded Congress to make May Day the Child Health Day. Breckinridge promoted it as "one of festivity for children who danced around maypoles and presented plays." Adults, in turn, explored ways to improve their children's health. Leading magazines, such as *Colliers, McClures, Good Housekeeping, Literary Digest,* and *Women's World,* emphasized the day in their editorials and a good deal of ACHA materials found their way onto their pages. Woolworth's department store chain also paid for a full-page promotional in "some twenty-two journals." Breckinridge arranged for the distribution of 3,000,000 child health care booklets nationwide through department stores, altogether a remarkable publicity campaign. The event continued to be celebrated in schools for years and was annually noted in the *Congressional Record*. The celebration challenged cities and communities to analyze the health conditions of their children. By 1927 governors of thirty-two states proclaimed the day as a holiday, as did President Calvin Coolidge. He called upon "the people of the United States . . . to unite that day in observances of such exercises as will acquaint the people . . . with the necessity of a year-round program for . . . children's health." In October 1927 the AFL had a resolution introduced, which Congress accepted on May 14, 1928, writing the Child Health Day into the Federal Calendar[9]

Mrs. William Brown Meloney had replaced Theodore Dreiser as editor of *The Delineator*. She wrote Crumbine after he moved to New York City to assume administration of the division of Public Health Relations, that she had "never felt so happy" about the American Child Health Association as she now did. "I am certain you are going to accomplish a great work with it," she said, "and I want to help you in every way that lies in my power." Crumbine, of course, welcomed all assistance of this caliber, especially with that journal's potential for publicity.[10]

The American Child Health Association was a voluntary organization and publicity constituted its major weapon in its fight to improve the health of children. In contrast, Crumbine noted, official organizations have to limit their activities to those that have public support. In addition, their budgets "are rarely . . . ample . . . for the solution of pressing . . . problems . . . even more infrequent for pioneer work." Volunteer agencies, though, have much greater flexibility, can pioneer in new fields, as he knew, "and prepare the way for the official agency to take over the project when public approval permits health practice to catch up with health knowledge." As the doctor pointed out on other occasions, however, the effectiveness of publicity and public education was difficult to assess. He used Fire Prevention Week as an example of the difficulty of explaining to taxpayers how cleanup campaigns prevented fires. Nothing happened as there were no fires, but there might have been without the preventive work. By the same token, parents and politicians "may have had difficulty identifying the benefits of disease prevention for individual children," but public health officials were well aware of the effects, just as firemen appreciated cleanup campaigns.[11]

With his work during the war years, Hoover gained a reputation as a great humanitarian and brought much favorable publicity to his postwar program to help children. Under his leadership, from 1923 to 1935, the American Child Health Association raised some $5 million for community services to help children. Crumbine's original role was to bring his acquaintance with public health officials from across the nation and their confidence in his abilities and achievements to bear on improving the health of children. Early in 1923 he was named field secretary of the Conference of State and Provincial Authorities of North America and, when his retirement from the Kansas board subsequently made him ineligible for the position, members then named him a permanent honorary member of the conference. This gave him added stature for his new role in promoting child health.[12]

After forty years in Kansas it was difficult to pull up roots and begin anew in a strange environment. Crumbine lived at the nearby YMCA until the family joined him before Christmas. He wrote a friend in Massachusetts "confidentially" that he felt very much like the New England lady who moved to New York City and, when asked how she liked it, responded that "I feel like a cat in a strange garret." In a letter to a Topeka friend he was even more frank:

> My presence here seems all so strange and unreal. Somehow I feel as if I am just passing through New York and will be back in good old Topeka in a day or two. It's too crowded and too congested here. It takes me twenty-five minutes to negotiate the distance from Thirty-first street to Fifty-seventh street—so I must exercise, so I walk, or rather push, run, dodge and edge my way from my office to the Fifty-seventh Y.M.C.A. where I am temporarily located.
>
> How I long for the open spaces and the green fields of Kansas. Even the dandelions and jimson weeds would be a welcome sight, but most of all I miss my host of Kansas friends. But I am coming back some day. Topeka is to remain my home—my final resting place.

But he was enthusiastic about his job and eventually adjusted to life in the big city, especially after wife and daughter joined him and they could make a home in the five-room apartment at 3537, seventy-eighth street in Jackson Heights (Queens) in New York City. They found the city "filled with jangling crudities," but rode the subway and buses, "swallowed gasoline fumes, and fought the crowds with flinty resignation." "Oh, we were soft at first," he said, "but we toughened up in no time. A Kansan can get used to anything." Even the civilized East.[13]

The problem of gathering vital statistics on children proved to be an ongoing one for Crumbine. He helped Kansas lead the way in resolving this important quest but too few states followed his lead. Between 1923 and 1926, Philip Van Ingen, a pediatrician and American Child Hygiene Association secretary, assisted a dozen state health departments in updating their process of birth registrations. Prodded by Crumbine, the Birth Registration Area covered the entire nation by 1932.[14]

An organization such as the ACHA required significant funding and much of this came from the American Relief Administration's (ARA) Children's Fund, for which Congress initially appropriated $100,000,000 to finance Hoover's work with the American Relief Administration after World War I. When this amount was exhausted, Hoover and his aides founded a private ARA in New York City with subsequent donated funds invested in stocks. The dividends and interest provided the chief financial source for the ACHA. Edgar Rickard headed the ARA, assisted by journalist Richard Barr Baker, Walter Hines Page's son Frank, and Christian Herter, later President Dwight Eisenhower's secretary of state. Hoover delegated publicity activities to this group to "sell" the ACHA as "the central authoritative source of child health information."[15]

As might be expected, antagonisms developed between the leaders of the two merged groups. Dr. Philip Van Ingen, secretary of ACHA, was soon "very nearly frothing at the mouth" because he believed the Child Health Organization people were trying to run the new show. Sally Jean, on the other hand, thought the child hygiene work was rather useless. But more importantly, the division soon boiled down to the question of which faction would dominate and control the group's philosophy: Hoover's efficiency experts or the professional staff of medical people. The latter believed the ARA's function was to raise money to support their work and the ARA people wanted to eliminate "wasteful administrative financial control" that the medical people had created. Hoover supported the ARA position and as long as the ACHA needed his reputation to support them, he would determine the principles and goals. Hoover believed that Sally Jean's "Professor Happy's Official Rule Book [for good health to be] claptrap," and Page and Rickard deemed Dinwiddie to be a weak administrator. Professor Happy was a clownish promoter of hygiene for children. When the ACHA officers persuaded Hoover to continue as chief officer this meant Hoover had won the battle over approach, as least temporarily.

The fund-raising drive of 1923, when Crumbine joined the organization, was a dismal failure. The ARA goal of $384,769 was to be met by appeals to its former 150,000 contributors but only 600 of them donated $7,515 at a solicitation cost of $12,000. The failure of this drive could be attributed to intense competition for charitable organizations to contribute to worthy causes at that time, "it was perhaps easier to appeal to people's compassion for victimized European children than to seek funds for less understood goals at home," and the ARA was returning to the proverbial well too often. Economizing now became the order of the day and appeals to private foundations, such as the Laura Spelman Rockefeller Memorial Fund saved the day.

Secretaries, stenographers, and other administrative staff were subsequently reduced and all operations were shifted to New York City to achieve an annual rent reduction. Dinwiddie resigned as general executive secretary and Crumbine, who made a favorable mark on his superiors immediately, won a promotion to that position in an acting capacity. When the executive committee, prodded by Van Ingen, disapproved Jean's request for a separate budget and limited autonomy, she and a number of her staff submitted their resignations soon afterward.[16]

In his first two years with the association Crumbine made such a positive impression that he won the support of Rickard and other key Hoover aides. Rickard wrote to the "Chief" [Herbert Hoover], that "the more we see of Crumbine the more we all believe he is the proper man to head up this concern. The whole morale of the office of the A.C.H.A. has been changed under his direction." The 86 Cities survey and follow-up constituted the major success at that point of the association and it was imperative that his good relationship with the nation's public health officials be continued. "Crumbine is the only man who can satisfactorily see that this relationship is maintained on the splendid basis which he has already established," Rickard added. As one source has noted, "Crumbine was a gifted publicist whose flair for popularization appealed to Hoover." Even during World War I Hoover relied heavily on good public relations. Also Crumbine was obviously loyal to the "Chief." Rickard reported to Hoover that he understood that "any suggestion of yours is a positive order." The first major change came in December 1924 when Hoover named Crumbine "acting general director" and asked Dinwiddie "to help him take over the work."[17]

Hoover was not yet through with reorganization. As conflicts between groups of administrators continued, Hoover again threatened to withdraw from the organization, and they persuaded him to serve another term. With this victory, Hoover continued to cut staff, trim the 1925 budget, and complete his administrative changes. The association projects had expanded in two years to the point that a change in management was necessary, especially if Hoover's philosophy was to dominate. Hoover and his trusted administrators were considering naming A.J. Chesley and Crumbine as "Joint Managing Directors." Crumbine believed that his most important immediate task was to continue the 86 Cities project though, and he was convinced he could not do justice to that program and assume additional administrative tasks because the former required "personal contact and continual abstention from the Central Office." He preferred that Chesley become the chief manager, but Edgar Rickard concluded that he was thus "considering the welfare of the organization probably before his own advancement." Crumbine's aim, Rickard believed, "was to make clear his ideas of the direction which the A.C.H.A. should aim," stressing the importance of the 86 Cities program. Retaining Chesley in the association failed to materialize, though, and Crumbine became General Director on May 16, 1925. Hoover was convinced that a thorough national child health survey should be the top priority. In announcing his appointment, Hoover declared that he was "delighted that we have been able to secure the services of Dr. Crumbine." The doctor, in turn, justified Hoover's faith by convincing the executive committee and staff that, if the Children's Fund was financing the ACHA, its officers should determine their policies, exactly the attitude Hoover wanted from him.[18]

The ACHA began publishing the *Child Health Bulletin* in 1925. This was a small quarterly containing a half-dozen short articles and news concerning child health issues from around the world. Each issue also contained an updated bibliography to keep readers abreast of current literature in their field. The June 1925 issue carried a brief resume of the new director and observed that Samuel Crumbine had led Kansas

> to the forefront of the states in effective health administration. The progress made in health under his administration is in reality a record of the development of public health in the United States and is an earnest of what may be expected of his work for the American Child Health Association.

The story expressed confidence that "under his able leadership rapid gains will be made in the achievement of its high aims."[19]

Hoover believed that Americans had "adequately assumed responsibility" for orphans and crippled and sick children. He wanted the ACHA to help children in general with improving their health by offering advice and making help available to parents and professionals through interested organizations already established throughout the nation, a true bureaucrat's ambition. First, though, the situation must be evaluated. The Demonstration Areas program, already begun before Crumbine arrived, was a good example of his approach. Mansfield and Richland County, Ohio; Fargo, North Dakota; Rutherford County, Tennessee; and Athens, Georgia, four areas with comparable death rates and also a commitment to improve public health on a sustainable basis, were selected for experiment. A squad of experts spent six months in each area examining the health of children at ages one, five, ten, and fifteen, with control groups so that progress could be measured. Another part of the program established centers where pregnant women could be examined and yet another that instructed them in feeding and caring of babies. Toddlers could also be examined and referred to physicians if necessary. In all areas, participants tried to involve physicians, nurses, teachers, and parents in emphasizing the importance of inoculations, health education, hot lunch programs, and improvement of water and milk supplies. By 1928 Fargo's infant mortality rate had declined to 36.7 per thousand compared to the national average of 69, and served as an example of what Crumbine believed might be achieved through this approach.[20]

One of the first charges Herbert Hoover had given the new organization was to investigate what communities were doing to promote better child health as part of the national survey he believed to be necessary. Crumbine's close relations with public health officials and his national reputation proved crucial in this study. He made preliminary contacts with local authorities in eighty-six cities with populations ranging from 40,000 to 70,000 "to arouse their interest and support." The U.S. Public Health Service had already surveyed eighty-three cities with a population of over 100,000. The doctor usually referred to this work as the 86 Cities survey. Five trained investigators worked to gather data on the "programs of public health work for children" in these cities and to publish their findings as part of Hoover's passion for facts. The questionnaire had eleven categories with which to rate the communities and their health work, including vital statistics, communicable diseases, preschool hygiene, sanitation, and health instruction. The 614-page report "aroused the communities to consider the efficiency of their work" as they averaged a score of only 50 percent. This became the association's most lasting contribution to the improvement of child health. "Your dream come true," Crumbine described it to Hoover, "the most important single contribution to public health administration in a decade." The information also often proved helpful for local health officers seeking adequate funding for their work. Crumbine estimated this program "set forward health practices at least a decade."[21]

This task led to the next obvious step and Hoover suggested the follow-up of evaluating school health activities. This work was, at best, only about a quarter-century old and there were no existing methods of measuring these programs or even the existence of uniform, acceptable standards for child health. Crumbine's staff subsequently spent eighteen months wisely in developing "modes of approach and methods of measurement." Then three squads of five workers each engaged in field work investigating seventy cities and gathering statistics. This effort resulted in the publication of several monographs outlining procedures by which educational institutions could evaluate their programs for comparison. In addition, schools established routine vaccination plans and regular physical examinations by school physicians. In conjunction with this work, a survey of preschool children ages two to six was conducted in 156 cities and in rural areas in forty-two states. This report, Crumbine noted, "sets forth the results of the most intensive survey of its kind ever attempted and provide(d) for the first time a national index of the extent to which we are protecting our children during the very important period between birth and the sixth year of life." The study, in turn, prompted many of the cities to continue their own investigations "and several reported it had increased the number of vaccinations and . . . immunizations . . . by public authorities."[22]

Early in 1924 a staff member attended a conference of Supervisors of Indian Education, which resulted in an invitation by the Office of Indian Affairs to investigate the public health services of these schools. When visiting the Chippewas, Crumbine asked the public health official on the reservation "why don't you train some of these Indian girls in nursing and let them minister to their own people?" As a consequence of this somewhat casual observation, the Minnesota legislature approved a grant of money for its department of health to inaugurate a permanent Indian public health nursing service and the training of Indian nurses of the Chippewa tribe. Among other schools the Haskell Institute of Lawrence, Kansas, and Anker Hospital in St. Paul also established prenursing programs to help meet the demand for increasing numbers of Indian nurses for the reservation schools. When Crumbine addressed the annual meeting of the American Child Health Association in 1927, he happily reported that new "modern health methods" on Indian reservations were "giving them new vigor and life [and] American Indians can no longer be called the vanishing race." Crumbine was much too optimistic over the situation of Native Americans, probably stimulated by his enthusiasm for this nursing program.[23]

Several years after the closing of the American Child Health Association in 1935, Crumbine wrote Senator Arthur Capper to solicit his assistance in a Save the Children Federation project. The group wanted to help the Navaho Indians in their problems with child health. Indian reservations, in addition to bad health usually suffered by poor people everywhere, invariably had a high rate of tuberculosis. The senator believed that this request placed him in an embarrassing position and he responded in true political fashion. The tribe was "a somewhat controversial" topic in Congress, he noted, as the federal government had already appropriated a large sum to help the members, in addition to the trust fund held for them. Capper had heard the rumor that some members of the tribe had "almost a half million dollars in banks on deposit to their credit." With the new program, "private solicitation of funds will undoubtedly be involved" and the senator doubted the wisdom of his taking an active role in the project. "I am sure you will understand my situation in this connection," he added gratuitously. The Save the Children Federation later awarded Crumbine a special citation for his work, especially with Puerto Rican children and "his study of child needs in the Mountains" of the rural South.[24]

Samuel Crumbine made a major contribution to public health with his campaign for pure milk. The 86 Cities survey revealed that about 25 percent of the nation's children drank no milk and much that they did consume, he knew, was contaminated. Thus when communities began emphasizing increased consumption, the problem of securing pure milk multiplied. As one authority has noted, the child health movement went "hand in hand" with the drive for better milk. "There is no branch of human activity in which science has wrought more beneficial changes than in the protection of market milk," Crumbine once observed. From the beginning of written history milk had always been considered the most perfect single food.[25]

Scientists and health authorities made considerable progress in improving American milk from the early nineteenth century when "swill milk" was being sold in cities of the Northeast. This milk came from cows housed in sheds and fed on the watery waste products left over from the production of distilled liquors. A practice brought over from England, it became popular in the Northeast as pasturage there shrank in the 1820s and distillers made their products available at a low price to dairymen distressed by the shortage of grazing land. By the late 1830s, one authority estimated that swill milk represented 50–80 percent of milk consumed in the large northeastern cities. Temperance forces attacked this product, not only for its origins but also by stressing it as a public health issue. The increased competition from western grain farmers led to many northeastern agrarians selling their land and migrating westward. Those who remained tended to turn to dairy farming and the increase in this dairy industry finally brought an end to swill milk, but not to milk contaminated by unsanitary practices. Dairymen commonly failed to clean mud and manure off the flanks and udders of their cows and it fell into the milk. If they washed their cans, it often was with dirty water. They never cooled the milk but left it in the cans along the roadside pickup points. Once in the city, milk was usually vended from these containers, often dipped with common ladles. Unscrupulous dairymen occasionally adulterated their milk with water of dubious sources, while others tried to mask spoilage by adding sugar, molasses, bicarbonate of soda, chalk, and other adulterants after skimming the cream. Health officials increasingly turned their attention to this serious health hazard, which increased in conjunction with the national concern over adulteration of foods and other drinks.[26]

In the mid-nineteenth century, scientists began to suspect that milk might be the carrier of certain epidemic diseases. The study of bacteriology demonstrated clearly the normal bacterial flora of the udder and microorganisms that could gain entrance to milk. As early as 1857 Gale Borden emphasized the importance of clean milk, but as late as 1896 a study made for the commissioner of health in the nation's capital showed clearly the role of market milk in causing sickness in children and in disseminating epidemics. Cattle diseases, such as bovine tuberculosis, were spread to people through milk, causing authorities to insist on more sanitary production of milk and elimination of diseased animals. A major breakthrough came from studies by bacteriologist Herbert W. Conn who found that bacteria commonly found in milk multiplied rapidly if the milk was not cooled soon after it was drawn. Health reformers began demanding that milk be tested for the number of bacteria it contained to determine if it was old, dirty, or handled unhygienically.[27]

The general public slowly became aware of the connection between milk and epidemics after 1895 when typhoid broke out in Stamford, Connecticut, affecting 386 of the town's 15,000 inhabitants. Most of the victims were under ten years of age, causing authorities to suspect contaminated milk. Tests proved them correct. That same year outbreaks occurred in Providence and Buffalo and public health researchers commenced publishing reports connecting milk with epidemics. The press also helped in this campaign by emphasizing that, unlike waterborne typhoid, "those spread by milk were not largely confined to the poor." Getting the attention of the middle classes usually was a crucial prelude to effective reform.[28]

These and studies by Crumbine and others produced the principles of producing wholesome market milk: (1) pasteurization (heated to approximately 145°F, held there for about thirty minutes, then cooled to 50°F) should be required where practicable; (2) sanitary methods of production should be required; (3) cooperation between producers and health officials are most conducive to improvement; and

(4) in the absence of local milk control, the state must assume responsibility. At this time, though, the technology of inspecting milk was rather primitive and regulations were easily circumvented. Herbert Hoover was particularly concerned over this problem because so many infants died of diarrhea and enteritis acquired from contaminated milk, especially during the summer months. Samuel Crumbine undertook a national survey in 1925 to determine how well these principles were being implemented. He sent an automobile on tour with a trunk fastened to a frame protruding from the rear. The trunk was a small laboratory and Charles F. Crisman, a chemist, was the driver. Crisman's itinerary included communities where there were high infant mortality rates and those that had no milk control program but needed one. Crisman first obtained the interest and support of the health and agricultural authorities of each state before he arrived. He also secured the services of a bacteriologist, a veterinarian, and inspectors from these authorities. Dairies were randomly selected and a bottle ready for delivery was chosen at each site. The milk poured through a cotton disk inevitably left a residue of filth, "in many instances appalling," according to Crumbine. The dairymen, confronted with the evidence were "frequently appalled and the test would be repeated for them." "When the harm he is perpetuating is impressed on him." the doctor noted, "he usually promises to mend his ways." The accompanying veterinarian examined the cows for tuberculosis. As Crisman observed, many dairymen appreciated this service as it saved them the fee for a milk plant inspector who might charge $100–500 for the same work.[29]

This mobile laboratory visited state after state. A representative of the child health organization then followed up with meetings with women's clubs, school officials, dairymen, and interested citizens to stimulate concern in establishing local milk supervision centers. Large dealers began allying themselves with health authorities because they realized fighting the regulations was futile and, on the other hand, strict enforcement could force their small competitors out of business. By 1930, some 250 communities were enforcing the Standard Milk Ordinance, as reported by a White House conference investigation, but "the implementation of milk reform came slowly, especially in the mid-sized and small cities where the fight for clean commercial milk continued well into the 1930s."[30]

Milk producers created another problem during World War I when they developed what became known as "filled milk," by mixing skimmed milk with coconut oil. This was a highly profitable enterprise for the producers because they could extract and sell the expensive cream and the filled milk concoction could be passed off as evaporated or condensed milk. It tasted, looked, and smelled the same as whole milk and could be distinguished only by chemical analysis. By 1920, the United States produced 85 million pounds of this composite.

Some producers labeled the product as filled milk, others did not. Retailers placed the 16.5 oz cans on shelves beside evaporated milk and many customers purchased it without reading the label, assuming they were buying whole milk. After the cream was removed for sale, filled milk was produced for $3.50 per case and retailed for $5, the amount condensed milk demanded. Reformers and dairymen persuaded congressmen that the practice should be terminated. Not only was this a fraud on the American consumer but, like the filled cheese process three decades previously, it was seriously hurting the reputation and sales of pure American milk in Europe.[31]

When congressmen first sought to restrict filled milk, they decided to bring it under the purview of the pure food law. But, they were warned, this was unwise because if filled milk was properly labeled, and it often was, the pure food law would not ban it because the statute prohibited foods not truthfully labeled as to contents. Congress had exclusive control, though, over the regulation of interstate and foreign commerce, and had recently been successful in banning the transporting of women across state lines for immoral purposes. Reformers decided to use this approach. They introduced a bill in the House of Representative to ban filled milk from interstate and foreign commerce.

During hearings and committee discussions it was pointed out that Congress had the power to *regulate*, not *prohibit*, the flow of commerce, so another reason must be found for the ban, in addition to fraud; otherwise the prohibition might not survive the gauntlet of constitutionality. Dr. Elmer V. McCullom of Johns Hopkins University, "probably the greatest expert on nutrition in the world" a congressional committee noted, provided a solution to the dilemma. When the cream was removed, this also removed the "vitamines" (as they were then spelled) from the milk, especially A. Vitamins had just been discovered and nutritionists were placing great emphasis on their importance to proper diet. Thus filled milk would not only be a fraud but would also deny infants and young children the nutritional balance they required in their diet.[32]

By the time Congress acted, eleven states had already banned the product. Royal Copeland, a New York health official who rode his reputation in this field into a U.S. Senate seat, for instance, had persuaded New York City and Brooklyn to prohibit it. On May 25, 1922, the House of Representatives voted 250 to 40 to ban filled milk from interstate and foreign commerce if it was filled with any substance other than pure milk. Congress had a particularly busy agenda at this time and the Senate did not consider the measure until March of the following year. Senators were concerned that the House proposal would also ban milk that doctors in some instances had altered the content by special prescription for infants with gastro-intestinal problems. The Upper House, therefore, amended the bill they received to omit the ban on types of filled milk prescribed by physicians and clearly labeled as such. This type must be shipped in interstate commerce only to doctors, wholesale and retail druggists, orphan asylums, hospitals, and similar institutions. The Senate then approved the measure without a roll call vote, the House agreed to the change, and President Warren Harding signed it into law in March 1923.[33]

Harvey H. Wiley quickly expressed his opinion of the regulation in an article in *Good Housekeeping* that summer. He believed the law was a good one but the Senate amendment was unwise. The exception clause was inserted at the instigation of a filled milk manufacturer in Cleveland. His S.M.A., or Synthetic Milk Adapted, contained cod liver oil to protect infants against rickets and against convulsions. Wiley saw "no real necessity" for the addition to the bill as its only advantage was "the possibility of introducing it into orphan asylums and other aggregations of children where it might be used . . . without the formality of a physician's prescription." Reformers, however, believed they had achieved a significant success in eliminating the basic problem.[34]

The law successfully drove filled milk out of the market place temporarily and was not tested until a decade and a half later. During the Great Depression milk producers saw a market for cheap filled milk and Carolene Products began production of Milnut to satisfy the demand of people who were desperate to stretch their pennies. The government prosecuted, the defense pled the due process clause, and the case reached the Supreme Court in 1938 where the statute was sustained, with the court denying the argument that a statutory definition of "adulterated" food was an arbitrary denial of due process.[35]

In addition to the milk problem, the ACHA was deeply concerned over the perennial issue of midwifery. One of ACHA's early meetings was devoted to the subject of midwives, the women who delivered as high as 50 percent of farm babies in some areas and perhaps 90 percent of Southern black babies. During one session, a heated debate followed the observation that many of these women were "densely ignorant . . . and inept" because they followed principles of ancient superstitions. When some urged their abolishment, others, such as S. Josephine Baker and Abraham Jacobi, a nationally known pediatrician, argued that they were necessary as no substitutes were available. Dr. Helen Moore had been "devoted" in her labor for Crumbine in Kansas and he asked her to join the American Child Health Association and work on this problem in the South. He later assured her that her "work with colored midwives was outstanding and no doubt saved many lives since then." Crumbine directed this study of the Negro midwife problem in Louisiana, Kentucky, North Carolina, South Carolina, Texas, and Virginia. "Conditions almost beyond belief" were revealed and state departments of health eliminated the worst cases of ignorant midwifery, requiring midwives to take special courses to practice their profession and licensing those who qualified.[36]

Soon after Crumbine's promotion to general director, Herbert Hoover convinced him that he could do much to promote public health in the United States through radio addresses and programs. This new medium was becoming increasingly popular during the Roaring Twenties and was highly effective if the right combination could be found between entertainment and being informative. Hoover wrote him about his "lifelong friend" from Stanford days, Charles K. Field of San Francisco. For altruistic reasons, Field had devised a "morning broadcast service" for hospital patients and shut-ins and was enjoying his work immensely. Radio carried Field's "Cheerio" program and it "had most extraordinary results throughout the Midwest." Hoover believed that various associations for nurses, hospitals, the American Medical Association, and the American Child Health Association might organize a committee to advise and assist Mr. Field in his endeavors. Hoover thought that this broadcasting service gave "better distribution of general information to parents, doctors, and people generally about the A.C.H.A. than we can ever do through newspapers," and he was undoubtedly correct. Out of this suggestion grew Crumbine's famous and popular Cheerio program. The NBC network carried it from the eastern seaboard to the Rocky Mountains and it became highly successful because of its artful balance between entertainment and disseminating information.[37]

Every weekday morning at 8:30 the National Broadcasting Company "cast the bread of optimism" across the nation. NBC donated the time as the program accepted no sponsors and the American Child Health Association provided $10,000 annually for expenses. Field was not compensated. The latter wanted to keep his identity secret "as he felt his idea was more influential when it emanated from 'an imaginary person' instead of a name and address." Secrecy was maintained until November 1928. After Herbert Hoover won the presidential election that month, Field's enthusiasm over his friend's victory knew no bounds and this became obvious in his broadcasts. The media soon discovered his identity and exposed him.[38]

The weekly topics Crumbine discussed on Cheerio ranged far and wide on child health. They included "Food for Babies," "Food and Drink in Hot Weather," "The Gifted Child," "Preparing for Baby," "Learning to Talk," "The Toddler," "Air and Sunshine," "The Happy Child," "Adopting a Child," "Care of the Teeth," and "Discipline," all common sense discussions for helping to raise healthy children.

Discussions on discipline always generated a good deal of heat but often little light during the Roaring Twenties. Corporal punishment, according to Cheerio, was "usually the equivalent to an acknowledgment of failure of the parents." The father's attitude must have been influenced by his being taken from the table and whipped for not eating his food when he was a boy, he reported. Failure to understand the child's motives normally led to "a complete breakdown of discipline." The parents should have "a meaningful set of rules" and corporal punishment should come only as a last resort and "without anger." Children must be taught respect for authority but "the child must understand that he is loved and wanted above everything else."[39]

A nurse wrote to thank Cheerio and Crumbine for his talk on "Learning to Sleep." The aunt of a seven-year-old boy told her their home was revamped by it: "everyone calm and happy instead of ready to scratch one another's eyes out." She related that "a fool radio program" wrought the change. One morning the mother heard some doctor from the American Child Health Association talking about the amount of sleep a child required. "As a result, little Ned is going to bed every night with the window open" at 7:30 and sleeps until 7:00 AM, "instead of getting up at 5:30" and waking the entire household and the nurse said they owed this to Dr. Crumbine.[40]

Another listener was enthusiastic over Crumbine's broadcast on the topic of child psychology, in which he used a seven-year-old girl as his example. Her father's second marriage had changed her "into a little fiend." An understanding teacher had probed deeply "and eventually straightened out the kinks in her little mind and she became a sane, and nice child." The writer had witnessed a similar situation when her friend died. The husband soon remarried and the couple had a baby "(much too promptly)." The couple was deeply devoted to their child and badly neglected Tommy, a twelve-year-old from the first marriage. Tommy started playing "hookey," smoking cigarettes, "and finally robbing stores." After hearing the doctor's broadcast, the friend persuaded the father to let her raise Tommy. It proved to be a difficult task but her "faith in Dr. Crumbine [was] strong enough to keep on." Tommy's teacher had reported a positive change in his attitude "and here at home he obeys cheerfully and tries to do what is right." She had much progress to make with him yet, "but thanks to Dr. Crumbine and you, Cheerio, we've made a start."[41]

The Great Depression eventually forced an end to Cheerio and the American Child Health Association. Funding was cut from the American Relief Association's Children's Fund, their major source, and the ACHA could not continue without it. The diminution of funding was gradual and two years before its demise an analysis was made of 735 letters Cheerio received from listeners. The study was preceded by the announcement that Cheerio would be discontinued unless a sufficient number of listeners requested its continuance. This threat prompted a flood of "several thousand letters" that same day. The missives were analyzed according to an arbitrary system of defining the social and economic status of the writer. Of the 735 letters received the first day after the announcement, 128 were classed as "A," the highest ranking, 653 as "B," and 14 in class "C," the lowest. The analyst concluded from these responses that "these broadcasts have been of inestimable value." Many of them he noted, came from physicians and physician's wives "who, by the way are always critical of what they call 'public propaganda.'" Others came from preachers, teachers, presidents of social and civic organizations, "and perhaps best of all *mothers*." The letters conveyed the almost universal expression of considering the information given over the broadcasts as "authoritative and dependable."[42]

Four months after becoming President of the United States, Herbert Hoover called a White House conference on Child Health and Protection. He wanted a national study made of the status of child health with recommendations for further action, in other words, requesting a continuation of the work of the ACHA. He charged T.L. Seward with organizing the event and Seward wrote Crumbine about the "Chief's" enthusiasm over the concept. Secretary of Interior Ray Lyman Wilbur, a physician and former classmate at Stanford, and Seward met with Hoover and Seward reported:

> Your chart was spread on his desk and the plans for the conference were built around it. . . . The Chief is eager to start to work to organize the special projects, appoint the committees, get going.
>
> I have agreed to carry the responsibility [of organizing]. But if I had not known you and your staff would direct and aid me I should have shrunk from the task the Chief has given me.[43]

Hoover opened the conference on July 29, 1929, with a keynote speech stressing its purpose to be to "strengthen mother's hand." He cited 10 million deficient children out of 45 million in America who were undernourished. He stressed to the assembled delegates the importance of their mission:

> The greatest asset of a race is its children, that their bodily strength and development should prepare them to receive their heritage which each generation must bequeath to the next. These questions have the widest of social importance, that reaches to the roots of democracy itself. By the safeguard of health and protection of childhood we further contribute to that equality of opportunity which is the unique basis of American civilization.[44]

Wilbur presided over the sessions that followed. Participants included President William Green of the AFL, Surgeon General Hugh Cumming, Secretary of Labor James L. Davis, social worker Grace Abbott representing the Children's Bureau of the Department of Labor, Dr. Samuel McC. Hammil, Henry E. Bernard, a former U.S. Food Administrator, Crumbine, and others with expertise or interest in child health. They discussed topics of research and some 12,000 authorities on child welfare were appointed on national committees to investigate such areas as health programs in elementary schools, medical care for children, medical examinations, school clinics for children, adequate milk supplies, dependent children, community nurses, and child labor. Publications of these committee reports constituted the major consequences of the conference. These included "Health Protection for the Preschool Child," "Health Trends in Secondary Education," and "An Evaluation of School Health Procedures." Unfortunately, the results of the White House conference were just beginning to bear fruit when the Great Depression settled over the country and Americans became engrossed with their personal economic woes to the neglect of most other problems.[45]

Puerto Rican Children [Courtesy of the Clendening History of Medicine Library, University of Kansas Medical Center]

The results of this conference, though, impressed Hoover with the need for more rural health units. In his annual message to Congress on December 3, 1929, he recommended a program of federal aid to states to establish a health unit in every county in the United States, a desperately needed reform, especially in certain poverty-stricken areas. Congress did nothing so he repeated the request a year later on December 2, 1930. Again no action from Congress, so he reiterated the plea on December 8, 1931. This time the House of Representatives passed the measure but when it reached the upper chamber, Democratic Senator Elmer Thomas of Oklahoma defeated it with a filibuster. At that point in the depression the Democrats were opposing all positive measures that Hoover proposed, to make him look bad in the upcoming elections. This political vengeance, unfortunately, killed a most worthwhile program that would be of great value to rural areas, including Oklahoma.[46]

The year following the White House conference President Hoover sent Crumbine on a special mission to investigate the health condition of children in Puerto Rico, a lovely tropical island in the Caribbean some thirty miles wide and a hundred miles long. This American "commonwealth," already blighted with extreme poverty, was hit particularly hard by the Great Depression when its major money crop of sugar was devastated by collapsing economic conditions. Most important, without a show of American sympathy, Puerto Ricans might be more receptive to independence movements and follow the lead of other Latin American countries, which were politically restless at the time. Theodore Roosevelt, Jr., recently appointed governor by President Hoover, was deeply concerned over the many "underfed and malnourished children he observed in his travels around the island," and requested an investigation and assistance to address the problem. Roosevelt was the island's first American governor "to look at people instead of statistics." He wrote in a newspaper article in 1929, saying that in "riding through the hills, I have stopped at farm after farm, where lean, underfed women and sickly men repeated again and again the same story—little food and no opportunity to get more."[47]

When Roosevelt received his appointment as governor he found that, "economically the island was in bad case." It had grown rapidly to 1.6 million population, becoming one of the most densely populated areas per arable square mile in the world. The fertile coastal plain was controlled by the big sugar companies. Hunger, "almost to the verge of starvation," was common. The main diet of the common people, salt codfish, rice, and beans, was imported, the most productive land being devoted to the production of sugar. Roosevelt saw his first task as economic rehabilitation of the island. But in individual terms, the governor noted, when he asked a man how many there were in his family, the response was "Sir, I have twelve mouths."[48]

The national press publicized Roosevelt's remarks widely in December 1929. On December 13 Hoover sent Crumbine a note calling his attention to the condition of "Porto Rican children. There seems to be a very genuine case for some systematic service," the president added, and he "would like very much" for the doctor to investigate the situation.[49]

Samuel, Katherine, and a staff including Amy Tapping and Dr. Harold H. Mitchell sailed for Puerto Rico with Crumbine especially thrilled over the assignment because he loved action and new adventures. This duty especially appealed to his interest in saving lives and reforming systems. They arrived on January 6, 1930, and met with Governor Roosevelt who assured them of full cooperation from government agencies. After preliminary surveys, they decided on a two-phase inquiry: (1) determine the urgent need for temporary relief, and (2) assess requirements for permanent improvements in child health and protection. They soon recommended an emergency relief fund of $100,000 and this was forthcoming from the American Relief Administration's Children's Fund. The committee subsequently awarded $1,000 to the insular department of health for emergency medical supplies, $24,000 for milk to be supplied to children under age two at eighty stations across the island, and $75,000 for school lunches for needy school and preschool children.[50]

The second phase encompassed a three-month intensive study of conditions affecting child health. The island had a long history of poverty and peonage for a majority of its rural citizens, magnified by the anemia-producing diseases of hookworm and malaria. These conditions, in turn, produced "the fertile soil for the white plague" and was further compounded by the phenomenon "of fertility of the poorer classes in the rural population." The census of 1920 revealed that 43 percent of the populace was fourteen years of age and under and this constituted a high percentage of the nonproductive population. A comparison of infant mortality rates was revealing: while the rate in the United States declined from 71 to 69 per 1,000 in the years 1925–1929, it increased from 148 to 179 in Puerto Rico during the same period.[51]

After "painstaking inquiry" covering all portions of the island, the committee reached some sound but very obvious observations and conclusions. First, due to unemployment and a very low wage scale, most rural people suffered from poverty and there was "extreme destitution" of thousands in the larger cities. Common labor wages ranged from 60 to 80 cents per day. This pitiful rate dropped significantly the next year when the price of sugar, the island's major export, declined and the going wage became 40–60 cents. With work in the cane fields being available only six months of the year at best, and with a family ranging from four to ten mouths to feed, this meant "a precarious existence" for the laboring classes at best.[52]

Second, a majority of rural and a "considerable minority" of urban Puerto Ricans suffered from hookworm and other intestinal parasites. Hookworm was endemic, imported by African slaves decades earlier. At the turn of the century Bailey K. Ashford had identified the Puerto Rican hookworm and connected it with the cause of anemia of the natives. He used two wards in the Ponce hospital to study hookworms sufferers and he and Dr. W. W. King of the Marine Hospital Service wrote a pioneering report on their findings. Progress in combating the disease was slow because of lack of financial support until it captured the attention and support of the Rockefeller Sanitation Commission in 1910.[53]

By the time Crumbine arrived two decades later, conditions had improved, but surveys showed that 50–100 percent of the rural population still suffered from hookworm as did 15–50 percent of the urbanites. When the San Felipe hurricane hit on September 13, 1928, the bureau of rural sanitation undertook more aggressive steps to control this problem by building sanitary latrines. This was followed by treatment of the infected and an educational program of prevention. The process required a six- to eight-month cycle to complete and Crumbine's staff found some headway was being made to reduce the problem but with current funding and personnel it would take years to conquer it. The problem of unemployment and low wages, combined with a malnourished population produced a vicious cycle of lowered resistance to disease.[54]

Thirdly, this cycle created the optimum conditions for the spread of tuberculosis, which was currently of epidemic proportions. The mortality rates from consumption per 100,000 had increased from 221 in 1925 to 301 in 1929. During those same years, by contrast, the rate in the problem state of Louisiana had dropped from 111 to 86.9. In two of the larger Puerto Rican cities the mortality rate was five times that of New York City, one of the worst cities in America. From a sampling, 79 percent of the urban children under eight and 78 percent of the rural ones tested positive to the tuberculin test. The entire island provided 410 beds for tubercular cases while the effective American standard was one bed for each annual death from the disease.[55]

Fourth, illegitimacy had been "one of the great social evils" of the island for ages. The census of 1920 showed one-third of the marriages were "so-called consensual," making for loose family ties and frequent abandonment of children. The American staff reported "many thousands" of such waifs in Puerto Rico. They also noted that the country was seriously overpopulated with 400 per square mile causing "intense congestion and overcrowding in the larger cities, a problem magnified by the hordes of deserted children." Being a Roman Catholic country, birth control measures were unacceptable.[56]

The American Child Health Association issued several recommendations to attack the troubled situation, all of which, of course, required money to implement. A frontal assault on tuberculosis should be launched at once. Health districts should be combined and hospitals built with 350–450 beds in each unit. Heating was no problem on the island and thus the hospitals could be constructed rather cheaply for an estimated $25,000–$40,000 each. But Puerto Ricans had reached or surpassed their financial limitations, both on the insular and municipal levels, and they needed outside assistance to do more to fight the epidemic. Even the Rockefeller Foundation, which had "spent a fortune" in combating epidemics there, and the Red Cross were stretched to their limits in giving. Finally, the investigators recommended Puerto Rico be divided into twenty sanitary or health districts and that these be sufficiently funded, a needed recommendation but again, one that would cost money that was unavailable.[57]

Through Crumbine's initiative, the ACHA created the Porto Rico Child Health Committee to solicit private financial support. The committee assumed control of the milk feeding and school lunch programs. Unfortunately, by March 1931 the committee had received only $100,000 in donations, far below the projected necessary $3 million. The effects of the Great Depression were beginning to hit home in America. When Hoover's reelection bid failed disastrously in November 1932 and the insular government was unable to appropriate any matching funds, the ARA's Children's Fund was forced to withdraw its financial support.[58]

Samuel Crumbine revisited the island for two months the following year: (1) to check the progress of the activities established the previous year; and (2) to begin implementing a full-time health service for the island. On this trip he discovered that conditions had "worsened, if possible," because of a drought and "the extremely low price of sugar." Only the "tobacco section" of the island had shown improvement during that year because of good crops and "fair prices." The eighty operating milk stations had improved conditions in the areas they served, cutting the death rate of children under two years almost in half. Great progress! He also found cause to celebrate the increase in numbers of day nurseries "where jobs in the factories can be secured for the mothers, and a school where illiterate mothers are taught to read and write." This second trip convinced the doctor that "the only way out for these people is to attack the disease link of the vicious cycle." They had to be relieved of their disease burden to help them gain their economic independence. Crumbine believed anything less would be a violation of the principles of May Day. Improving health programs require funding and this problem again reared its ugly head. The Children's Fund of the American Relief Administration had appropriated $500,000 for Puerto Rican assistance, instructing the American Child Health Association to spend $100,000 annually for the next five years. But an estimated $7,500,000 would be necessary. The Roman Catholic church of New York had pledged $1,500,000, which meant another $5,000,000 must be raised elsewhere. It could not be found because the Great Depression required that American money be kept at home for domestic relief.[59]

Following the crash of the New York stock exchange in 1929, the worst depression in history settled over the United States. Factories closed, banks failed by the thousands, unemployment rose to a shocking 25 percent. Relief lines grew geometrically and relief stipends declined drastically. Those in New York City, for example, dropped to 50 cents per day for a family. How did a man feed his family on 50 cents? Samuel Crumbine advised a healthy breakfast of cereal and milk with a light lunch of a sandwich and a glass of milk. The lower the income, the greater reliance on bread and milk, along with cheaper vegetables such as potatoes, cabbage, and turnip greens. The United States Bureau of Economics drew up "a ration of last resort" in 1932 that cost as low as $4.50 weekly. This was helpful, assuming that a family had that amount available.[60]

As Hoover began to concentrate on national politics increasingly in the late Roaring Twenties, philanthropic sources slowly dried up. The ACHA lost the support of the Laura Spelman and Commonwealth Fund. Then the Children's Fund of the American Relief Administration announced in 1931 that it was "gradually retiring" from relief work. The American Child Health Association's Executive Committee called in financial experts who advised that further revenue support for the organization was impossible to obtain. At the December 1932 executive committee meeting Crumbine recommended the liquidation of the publication and promotion division, the first serious cutback. This department was headed now by Aida Breckinridge, whom Crumbine, Hamill, and Van Ingen "loathed" because she "constantly" went over Crumbine's head to appeal directly to Hoover when she disliked the doctor's decisions and also for her "excessive spending" on promotion.[61]

Crumbine reported a serious "slump" in 1933 in both membership dues and sales of literature. Despite this financial pressure, that same year the ACHA began publishing *Spyglass*, a children's publication for which, Crumbine noted, there "seems to be a recognized and vital need for this type of material." Designed for fifth and sixth graders, the journal provided eight "large, well-illustrated" pages of information on health, history, geography, and civics. While this was a marvelous project, it consumed scarce dollars and was unprofitable as public schools were also feeling the financial pinches of the Great Depression.[62]

The staff was gradually reduced from seventy-three to twenty-three by early 1935. Rickard noted at that point that the organization was not accomplishing much and a "job-holding spirit" was prevalent. The executive committee, reviewing the consultant's report concluded that the ACHA "had served a useful purpose" but it should be liquidated. On August 13, 1935, Samuel Crumbine was forced to announce the termination of the work of his agency. This brought many letters of condolences. The secretary of the association summed up Crumbine's contributions:

> He never lost his courage in the apparent failure of an effort. His unruffled persistence usually resulted in success. In all the work of the Association, he was a tactful coordinator, smoothing out the little rough spots occasionally arising. He never allowed a molehill to grow into a mountain. Apparent mountains seemed to become molehills. No one familiar with the Association will ever forget what it owes to Dr. Crumbine.[63]

By that time what little philanthropy that was available was needed elsewhere and the voluntarism of the Hoover persuasion was yielding to the philosophy of the necessity of an expanded role of the federal government. Rickard had recommended merger with the National Tuberculosis Association, but Crumbine opposed this because of probable elimination of competing positions, including his own. No alternative appeared. The end was inevitable and it came swiftly.[64]

Again the loss of a job. Again the decision of what to do. He had begun a new career when he was sixty-two but now he was seventy-three. It was definitely time to consider seriously the idea of retiring. Offers of employment, of course, came from many directions as people wanted to utilize his experience and reputation. Colleagues urged him to accept the enticing University of Kentucky's request, for example, that he establish a School of Public Health on that campus. This time, though, he decided to retire and spend more time enjoying life with his wife and daughter's family. Violet had married Charles Christman and they settled nearby on Eighty-first street in New York City.[65]

He was too full of ideas and energy to sit still for very long and, as he noted, "nature abhors a vacuum." He "found it rather dreary not to have some compelling interest other than playing golf and reminiscing." In 1938 he became executive vice president and health consultant of the private Save the Children Federation. He and the federation concentrated on the South's mountain regions on the theory that this area had the highest birthrate in the country and these underprivileged children constituted an important source of population that sorely needed attention. The region, he observed, comprised an area one-and-one-third times as large as New England and "thousands" of the inhabitants in the mountain counties had inadequate medical hospitals or public health services. As urban areas improved their health conditions rural communities, in turn, fell farther behind comparatively, and these children continued to suffer from what were termed the "rural diseases." These conditions were more desperate in the rural South than in the rural North. The mortality rates for these Southern children were staggering: in 1916 one North Carolina mountain county had an infant mortality rate of 80.4 per thousand births, and for a lowland county in that state it was 48.1. In Mississippi, by contrast, the rate for white children was 61.2 while that for Negro children was 107.3. By comparison it was 40 in Kansas.[66]

The objective of the organization was to provide these youngsters of Appalachia "with enough clothing and shoes to get them to school and to give them at least one hot lunch" daily. Crumbine made two trips through the area during the next two years and was "amazed at the things I saw," he wrote a friend. "It was almost inconceivable that such a condition exists in our land of 'plenty and opportunity.'" As with the Puerto Rican youngsters, he prepared a classic report on southern children and it subsequently was adopted as a textbook in many universities for courses in public health. In addition, he was active as a public health consultant for the Paper Cup and Container Institute until his death.[67]

Another part of the mountain crusade involved sending visiting nurses into the region. At a luncheon meeting of the federation, Crumbine shared the podium with one of the nurses, whom he believed to be typical, who discussed her experiences. She related that she was taken on a six-mile ride into the hills as a "brought-on woman" to assist in a childbirth. Neighbor women watched as they wanted to see how "a brought-on" worked as a midwife. They taunted her as the fireplace light was insufficient for her to see, yet it was always "good enough for the granny women." She maintained her night-long vigil, however, sewing baby clothes from a bundle of rags until the boy was born at dawn and she felt vindicated. Both she and Crumbine pleaded for financial support to bring these isolated people into "the currents of present day American life, but to no avail."[68]

In 1939 he wrote the surgeon in Cleveland who had operated on him for a duodenal ulcer, that he remained in good health, "have practically no gastric disturbances, eat pretty much what I like," although he did "try to be careful." In 1943 he again wrote a friend that his health was "as good as when I lived in Dodge City . . . and that is saying a good deal."[69]

In his spare time he played golf once or twice a week until he was eighty-five with a retired YMCA secretary, a former chemistry professor, and a hydro engineer

Drinking Cup Award [Kansas State Historical Society]

who lived nearby. He "played an uncommonly hasty game, proceeding in a kind of shuffling trot from stroke to stroke, and en route keeps a lookout for faulty sanitation, such as clogged-up drains, stagnant water traps, and excessive spitting." He knew golf was good for him physically but "is it good for the soul? Sometimes I wonder when I try to remember how many strokes it took me to get out of a certain sand-trap." He and Katherine also enjoyed a Western movie occasionally, good, bad, or indifferent.[70]

He congratulated an old Dodge City friend for his reaching his ninetieth birthday and noted that Katherine "has had a bad time for the last two years, although for the past six months is feeling pretty good again." He expressed pleasure that their grandson Warren took Naval Officers Training School while attending Northwestern University and would soon receive his commission as an ensign.[71]

The Kansas Society of New York City honored Crumbine on his eightieth birthday with a testimonial dinner at the Waldorf-Astoria Hotel. A news report at the time described him as "a slight man with grey hair and gold-rimmed spectacles ... [who] looked younger than his eighty years." The theme, of course, was public health and speakers included Governor Payne Ratner, Kansas-born explorer Mrs. Osa Johnson, and Nassau County Health Commissioner Earle G. Brown, who had

served as head of the Kansas board of health following Crumbine's departure. Former Governor Henry J. Allen, the last Republican chief executive whom Crumbine
served under, was toastmaster. It was here that the plaque honoring him for his
work in abolishing the common cup was unveiled. Due to wartime scarcities, the
plaque, which was to be cast in bronze, remained in its plaster-of-Paris mold until after the war when it was displayed in the department of health offices at the
statehouse in Topeka. At this time his picture was placed in the Harvard Medical
School as a tribute to his contributions to public health. In addition, 1940 marked
the Crumbines' fiftieth anniversary and good friends and former colleagues gave
them a Golden Jubilee gold and red leather-bound book in which to preserve con-
gratulatory letters and cards. That evening Violet and her family hosted another
party for them, making it the "fourth most memorable and happy of our fifty years
of married life," the others being their marriage day and the births of their two
children.[72]

In June 1946 his Nassau County friend Earle Brown, introduced him as speaker of
the annual meeting of the Kansas Public Health Association in Wichita. It was here
that he presented his "Historical Background of Public Health in Kansas." This was
"an incomplete address," he explained to a friend, "because my time was limited."
But it was sufficient to remind the organization's members that he had been a great
pioneer in that state's campaign to improve public health and they established what
became a prestigious annual prize, the Crumbine Award, to someone who had made
a significant contribution to public health.[73]

Samuel Crumbine published his autobiography when he was eighty-six. He and
Katherine worked on it for three years and, as he expressed it, "we lived our lives
over again" in their reminiscences. The experience also left a nostalgic longing for the
Kansas prairies. Dorrance of Philadelphia published it in 1948 amid wide publicity
and good reviews. Herbert Hoover thanked him for a copy and assured him that
"I am going to like it because of my affection for you." As usual, reviewers found
differing interpretations or views to stress. The one for *Saturday Review of Literature*
thought "the most interesting pages [to be] those that tell of those pristine times when
the official notice in the local paper asked people, 'especially the ladies,' . . . not to be
profane when they don't get the letters they want." One former colleague appreciated
the emphasis the book placed on cooperation and the manner in which he had "tied
the work of the state health department into the educational institutions and into the
attitudes and thinking of the medical profession." The *Kansas City Times* praised the
story of "the man who accomplished so much in the face of public disapproval, and
the active and often aggressive opposition of many interests."[74]

"AJC, Under the Whispering Willow" columnist for the *Topeka State Journal*,
observed that the appearance of *Frontier Doctor* had many Kansans reminiscing and

they were pleased to reprint one of their 1909 stories discovered by Dr. Karl A. Menninger when he began rummaging through "his mother's old papers":

> If Dr. Crumbine, secretary of the state board of health had never done anything else of value his discovery of an efficacious remedy for chigger bites would entitle him to a prominent place in the eternal hall of fame. It's nothing more expensive than hyposulfite of soda, a chemical which is more familiarly known to photographers as "hypo." An application of a solution of this salt and water is sure death to the most onery creature that ever disturbed the peace of men.
>
> All hail to Dr. Crumbine.[75]

In 1952 the Kansas Public Health Association asked Crumbine to come to their annual banquet to present his award in person. They hoped to have the previous award winners there for this special occasion because it would now be a medal designed by "Prof Taffit of the University of Kansas." Later that year they added a ribbon to the medal "to remind you of the Kansas Sunflower." Elmer V. McCullom of the Johns Hopkins University School of Hygiene & Public Health, and a native Kansan, was that year's recipient. Crumbine described him as "one of the worlds [*sic*] greatest scientists, the discoverer of vitamins A B & D and many of the mineral elements so essential to good nutrition."[76]

Unfortunately McCullom was unable to attend the meeting because of ill health. Crumbine wrote him that while the medal could "add nothing to your high prestige and international fame," he wanted to think that the scientist had accepted it in absentia "as a token of the esteem and affection of the people of Kansas for their native son" and for his "distinguished services in the field of nutrition." Crumbine was "highly honored" that he had received the award and the meeting had been one that he would "long remember. . . . It would have been perfect if you had been there."[77]

In November 1952 the American Medical Association requested that he participate in a documentary for television that they were broadcasting on NBC, along with "other pioneer health educators." They would forward the "substance" of the remarks he should make but wanted him to "put the thoughts into your own words." The various contributions would be coordinated by "Marshall-Hester Productions" of New York City and any expenses incurred would be borne by the AMA.[78]

Crumbine made his last trip to Kansas in 1954. When he returned to New York City he wrote the director of the sanitary division of the Kansas state board of health with a suggestion: why not take the sludge from sewage treatment and use it as a fertilizer, enhanced perhaps with potato peelings that are rich in minerals. "Eventually the filth of a city may be a real source of revenue," he noted, "while our rivers are cleansed and the threat of world famine be set back a thousand years. Does that sound fantastic?" he asked. "Well, I think it is less so than the telephone and radio." He had read an article in the March 1953 health bulletin from Connecticut on the concept of recycling of sewage sludge. Later he saw an editorial in the *Journal of the American Public Health Association* on the same topic, noting that this product was lacking in potassium and thus required some addition. Finally, he noted with pride that the city of Wichita was currently selling its sludge and, "in some months," receiving as much as $800 for it. He had seen them all, from fly swatters to television and at age ninety-one he was still thinking and promoting public health.[79]

Meanwhile Katherine's health was failing and for several years Samuel had been doing the housework. Then in March 1954 she died. As so often happens when a couple have loved so deeply and for so long, he soon followed her. Samuel J. Crumbine died at his home on July 12, 1954, and his body was returned to Kansas to rest forever in Mount Hope Cemetery in Topeka, site of his great achievements in public health.

# SEVEN

# CONCLUSIONS

This quiet, soft-spoken man had unlimited courage to fight for his beliefs. A relatively small man, he enjoyed asserting his authority but, unlike many personalities of this type, he did so to make people follow the law, not merely to obey Samuel Crumbine. As a contemporary writer noted, "he doesn't look for trouble . . . he looks for things that are wrong, and then he buckles on, instead of a red sword and a sash, the lawbooks of Kansas, a microscope, and an outfit of analyzing utensils, and marches right up the hill and finds out about it." Relentless in pursuit of reforms he deemed necessary, Crumbine seldom viewed things in black or white. He saw shades of gray in public affairs, as does any successful politician. As historian Thomas Bonner observed, he "used threats of force which were balanced by suave diplomacy behind the scenes," like his contemporary Theodore Roosevelt. He did his utmost, for instance, to educate merchants to the requirements of the law before prosecuting them if they chose not to comply with the regulations. He carefully explained the need for, and provisions of, the statute before implementing the regulations.[1]

The epitome of the capable, conscientious public servant, within a short time after becoming secretary of the Kansas state board of health, Crumbine had "pushed his state forward a hundred years in half a decade." He accomplished this through ardent persuasion, preceded by careful education of the public and the politicians. He was a born educator, explaining concepts in terms of common sense, and his rural audience usually understood his message, unless superstition interceded. He could take scientific principles of disease and translate them to his agrarian constituency as well as to his medical colleagues. He did much to shape modern society's concern for cleanliness. Functioning in a state that was chronically short on public funding, with legislators convinced that it was more important to help cattle, and horses, and hogs than little babies and children and mothers, he gradually educated them to accept his occasionally startling new viewpoints. This was an ongoing campaign where it often appeared that the fiscal battle won in the last legislative session had to be fought all over again in the next one. But Kansas was not alone in this. Fiscal support for maternity, infant, and child welfare, for example, faced obstacles in most state legislatures where males had difficulty viewing this great need in proper perspective. Very importantly, Americans failed to attack the problems of child health and maternity care at their social and economic roots, as did European reformers. Here is where Herbert Hoover erred.

Samuel Crumbine succeeded in keeping public health out of partisan politics. Health departments across the nation typically were "dominated more by patronage and political considerations than by concern for economic or administrative efficiency." He managed to keep politics out of his department, but was helped in this by being a well-known Republican and by the Democrats electing only one governor during his two-decade tenure. He convinced these governors, except the one who ended his Kansas career, to support his work. He played no significant role as dean of the school of medicine at the University of Kansas except during the legislative sessions where he won scarce dollars to support his struggling school and eventually established it on a sound and successful foundation.[2]

A continuing theme in American public health history, "possibly the most striking one is the constant alternation between apathy and sharp reaction to periodic health crises." Crumbine's important role in the apathy side of the cycle was to intervene with snappy slogans, hard-hitting reports, blazing headlines, startling statistics, common sense rules for healthier living. He was adept at creating "sharp reaction to periodic health crises," when he needed the political support of a governor or funding for an emergency from a frugal legislature.[3]

Another recurrent theme "is the clash between individual liberty and the public welfare." The conflict occurred often in the categories of quarantine and vaccinating. Crumbine successfully convinced entire counties to vaccinate their school children. He first won his colleagues' approval when he used a common sense approach to the problem of quarantine in the smallpox epidemic at Pratt in 1900. Although people became restive after weeks of dealing with the Spanish flu pandemic of 1918, he was able, with the power of the governor supporting him, to retard the spread of that dread disease. In addition, he successfully employed his common sense approach to convince people to stop using a common drinking cup and a far better alternative—the paper cup—then made its appearance. He managed to convince parents that milk, "the almost perfect food," might carry a contamination that could kill their child.

Besides his "firsts," he achieved great strides in combating adulterated food and drink and the spread of tuberculosis, and his drive for better water and sewage systems, improved child hygiene, and an annual school for health officers, for full-time county health units, for records of vital statistics, all were copied in other states. He once observed rather arrogantly that "Kansas leads and the other states follow." He knew he copied progress in other states and he did not believe that he achieved these advances alone, but his recommendations for using common sense brought the obvious into focus for the public to comprehend, both in Kansas and for the nation. He had the great gift every teacher aspires to of making the complex understandable in simple terms.

Crumbine was successful in replacing ineffective folklore and superstitious ways of "doctoring at home." Sometimes this presented his greatest challenge—to persuade parents to take their sick children to a doctor before it was too late. It was difficult to convince people that they could communicate diseases through their breath, through their sputum, through unsanitary care of their children, through giving them contaminated food and drink. With the hysteria of the Great Crusade and powerful support of a wartime government, he was highly effective in eliminating venereal disease under his jurisdiction, hitherto an unmentionable topic in polite circles. He was unable, however, to breach the taboo against teaching sex education to teenagers, despite the dangers of neglecting social hygiene during the peacetime period that followed.

His most important legacy in Kansas, certainly in his eyes, was the department of health he molded over a two-decade period. It had been completely nonpartisan, if not humble, under his direction and above the political fray, but this did not survive his departure. He had performed amazingly well in centralizing the board's powers while maintaining support from local units. It became the single state agency with authority over both state health matters and for dealing with the federal government on public health issues. It became a model health board for other states to emulate. Through acquiescence or delegation, its authority over health matters statewide was complete. It failed in only one significant area actually, when Crumbine's salesmanship failed to convince Kansans overwhelmingly of the need for social hygiene education. He was a successful administrator in using federal standards to force increased appropriations for the state legislature but he also used his resources wisely. A 1916 survey of state boards of health concluded that Kansas received more and better health care per capita of money expended than any other state. Governor Davis's assault crippled the board of health and it took years for Crumbine's successors to restore its vitality without his leadership.

Crumbine made public health exciting. He had the ability to take raw statistics and turn them into flaming headlines. He rallied the state's medical profession to support his department, while keeping authority over them centralized in his hands. Free enterprisers had gone their untrammeled way throughout the nineteenth century and could not understand this reformer wanting to regulate their ways of conducting business. At first willing to challenge him, these free spirits soon acknowledged his leadership skills and became increasingly reluctant to clash with him. He loved doggerel and used it effectively to promote his causes. His common sense advice and pragmatic approach was welcomed by the public because it seemed reasonable even if sometimes contrary to their cultural teachings. Sleep with your windows open! Swat the fly! If your well and your roof leak, fix your well first! Keep the food and drink clean for your baby! Quarantine those with infectious diseases! Don't Spit on the Sidewalk! All these ideas seemed to be so obvious, to him, and to the public, after he educated them. Some of his crusades, such as that against the fly, appear superficially quixotic, but actually they helped raise public awareness of the danger of germs present everywhere and the need for cleanliness.

On the other hand, he faced difficult battles for most of his career, especially in promoting the cause of children. Presidents called White House conferences on child health once every decade during his active public health work but implementation of the resulting recommendations proved difficult, and usually impossible. America considers itself to be a child-oriented society but its legislative action in support of child health care falls far short of its rhetoric. Any success in this category usually has been through voluntarism.

It should also be noted that Crumbine, like his contemporaries in public health, sometimes succeeded too well. Cleaning up the environment too successfully can prevent children from acquiring immunities, such as milder polio viruses, and thus become more susceptible when a virulent strain appears. The experience of Franklin D. Roosevelt exemplifies this problem. He was raised in a highly protected environment and never built up the necessary immunities. One sometimes has to be slightly sick to avoid becoming seriously ill.[4]

This doctor from Pennsylvania who transplanted himself to the prairies of the Great Plains found his life's calling when he found himself in charge of protecting the people's health. And his greatest legacy to his state and nation was a new type of public health system, one that tried both to maintain health and to promote it. While the one Crumbine created in Kansas did not survive his departure intact, his contributions as one of the pioneers in the field had lasting impact. Many adults in today's world owe much, some of them perhaps their existence, to the doctor of common sense. As historian Gerald Grob notes, the decline in infant mortality rates results in an increase in life expectancy and an increase in morbidity rates in older people, a trade-off any society would gladly accept. Demographers labeled this the second epidemiological revolution, to which Samuel Crumbine contributed significantly, the first being the ancient transition from a hunting-gathering society to an agricultural one.[5]

It is lamentable that scholars in public health studies in recent decades have ignored this noble figure. It was not always so. During his career, eastern cities such as Boston, New York, and Philadelphia, and dozens of newspapers east of the Mississippi River recognized his pathbreaking work. His annual school for public health officials attracted candidates from the eastern seaboard and elsewhere. Scientists from Harvard, MIT, Johns Hopkins, and other leading universities from coast to coast utilized his ideas and publications to learn and to emulate. His great achievements deserve the same recognition today that they received during his lifetime.

# NOTES

## PREFACE

1. Paul Starr, *The Social Transformation of American Medicine* (New York: Basic Books, 1982), p. 128.

2. Thomas Neville Bonner, *The Kansas Doctor* (Lawrence: University of Kansas Press, 1959), p. 170.

3. Starr, *Social Transformation*, pp. 134–140; "good and bad doctors" quote from James T. Patterson, *The Dread Disease* (Cambridge, MA: Harvard University Press, 1987), p. 17.

4. Nancy Tomes, *The Gospel of Germs* (Cambridge, MA: Harvard University Press, 1998), pp. xiv, xv.

## CHAPTER ONE

1. Robert Lewis Taylor, "Men of Medicine," 5 (1949): 59; Samuel Jay Crumbine, Ailien Mallory story in series 18, biographical summaries folder, Crumbine papers; Martin Kaufman, Stuart Galishoff, and Todd L. Savitt (eds.), *Dictionary of American Medical Biography*, Vol. I (Westport, CT: Greenwood Press, 1984), p. 168. Foodservice and Packing Institute Inc. has a brief biography of Crumbine at http://www.fpi.org/HistoryofCrumbine.htm. Biographers are forced to rely heavily on his autobiography, Samuel J. Crumbine, *Frontier Doctor* (Philadelphia, PA: Dorrance, 1948), written at the incredible age of eighty-five.

2. Crumbine, *Frontier Doctor*, pp. 13–14.

3. Ibid., pp. 11, 15.

4. Quote from *Greenville (Pa) Record-Argus*, August 10, 1948; Diploma, series 23, Soldiers' Orphans School folder, Crumbine papers.

5. Crumbine, *Frontier Doctor*, p. 57.

6. Starr, *Social Transformation*, p. 65; Kenneth M. Ludmerer, *Time to Heal* (Oxford: Oxford University Press, 1999), p. 66.

7. The "fifty-fifty chance" encounter quote is from Richard Harris, *A Sacred Trust* (Baltimore, MD: Penguin Books, 1962), p. 5; overabundance of doctors from Starr, *Social Transformation*, p. 64.

8. Starr, *Social Transformation*, pp. 45, 60, 63–64, 85, 90–91.

9. Crumbine, *Frontier Doctor*, pp. 16–18.

10. Ibid., p. 19.

11. Ibid., pp. 20–21.

12. Ibid., pp. 21–22; Allen Greiner, "Pushing the Frontier of Public Health," *KU Med* (1999): 22; series #21, drugstore folder, Crumbine papers; Taylor, "Men of Medicine," p. 59. The beard quote is from William R. Kercher, "Dr. S. J. Crumbine and His Work," *Kansas Magazine* (November 1910): 27. The modern spelling of Spearville is used here.

13. Kansas medical practice laws, as in most other states, were primitive. To practice medicine, one had to have attended "a reputable school of medicine" and receive approval from his medical association, whether allopath, homeopath, eclectic, or whatever. Crumbine says in his memoirs that he received his degree in 1885 and then moved to Dodge City. When he and the other five doctors in Dodge City finally registered with the Kansas Board of Health in 1891, he listed February 1883 as his date of degree and noted he had six years experience in medicine at that time, with five and a half of them in Kansas. The Cincinnati School of Medicine lists his graduation date as 1889. I have accepted the latter as accurate.

14. College "Prospectus" for 1889–1890, copy from Cincinnati Medical Heritage Center.

15. Stanley Vestal, *Dodge City, Queen of the Cowtowns* (London: Peter Nevill, 1955), pp. 11–12. The reporter quoted from David K. Strate, "Up From the Prairie" (Dodge City: Cultural Heritage and Arts Center, 1974), p. 19. Settlers in Western Kansas said "there is no law west of Newton and no God west of Dodge."

16. C. Robert Haywood, *The Victorian West* (Lawrence: University Press of Kansas, 1991), pp. 85–86; Crumbine, *Frontier Doctor*, pp. 70–71.

17. Odie B. Faulk, *Dodge City, the Most Western Town of All* (New York: Oxford University Press, 1977), is a serious and fascinating story of the town during its "hey day." C. Robert Haywood, *The Merchant Prince of Dodge City* (Norman: University of Oklahoma Press, 1998), is a good scholarly account of Robert M. Wright.

18. These doctors and their degrees are listed in Department of Health, Report, 1891, p. 168.

19. Crumbine, *Frontier Doctor*, pp. 25–31.

20. Ibid., pp. 24, 28–29.

21. Enjoying tobacco was not unusual for physicians as many of them, and military personnel, smoked. It was not until after World War II that the *Journal of the American Medical Association* ceased accepting cigarette advertising and the dangers of smoking were being

publicized. Some doctors, however, continued to smoke for many years thereafter, unable to break the habit.

22. Series 19, newspaper clippings folder, Crumbine papers.

23. Samuel J. Crumbine to the Meade Workshop, January 8, 1952, series 16, post–American Child Health Association folder, Crumbine papers.

24. Crumbine, *Frontier Doctor*, pp. 128–129.

25. Crumbine typed the "dude" story on the back of handwritten pages of his epigrams, found in series 11, poetry folder, Crumbine papers.

26. Crumbine, *Frontier Doctor*, pp. 74–75.

27. Unidentified news clipping in series 23 oversized, public health folder, Crumbine papers.

28. Crumbine, *Frontier Doctor*, p. 68. Wellman's story is in an unidentified news clipping, "Ford in Crumbine Fete," series 23 oversized clippings, public health folder, Crumbine papers.

29. Robert Lewis Taylor, "Swat the Fly," *New Yorker*, 5 (1949): 61.

30. T.L. Pfalster, "Doc Crumbine of Dodge City," series #21, biography summaries folder, Crumbine papers; Crumbine, *Frontier Doctor*, pp. 63–64.

31. K.D. Curtis, "Doctor Crumbine of Dodge City," *TV Guide* (November 2, 1963).

32. Vestal, *Dodge City*, pp. 262–265.

33. Crumbine, *Frontier Doctor*, p. 64.

34. Ibid., pp. 58–60.

35. Ibid., pp. 37, 39–40.

36. Ibid., pp. 66–67.

37. Ibid., p. 70.

38. Series #21, drugstore folder, ledger for Crumbine and Dorsett, Crumbine papers; *Dodge City Times*, August 2, 1888; Eleanor Fry, "Spearville, City of Windmills," *Speareville News*. In a letter to the editor, *Dodge City Globe*, February 5, 1948, Crumbine detailed these prices compared with current ones. The "large and lucrative practice" quote is from *Kansas: Biography*, Vol. III (Chicago, IL: Standard Publishing, 1912), p. 710.

39. *Dodge City Times*, September 12, 1890; *Dodge City Democrat*, October 4, 1890; Crumbine, *Frontier Doctor*, p. 76.

40. Crumbine, *Frontier Doctor*, pp. 44–47. He used this analogy later in an article for *Hygeia*, 13 (September 1935), p. 804, entitled "Diphtheria—The Big Bad Wolf," expressing the wish that parents would take care of their children as well as these "dumb" animals did theirs.

41. Ibid., pp. 60–62.

42. Ibid., pp. 74–75; Taylor, "Men of Medicine," p. 61.

43. Crumbine, Frontier Doctor.

44. Ibid., pp. 87–91.

45. Ibid., pp. 97–100; Patrick Brophy, "The Weltner Institute and Magnetic Healing in Nevada, Missouri," in *Mystic Healers and Medicine Shows*, Gene Fowler (ed.) (Santa Fe, NM: Ancient City Press, 1997), pp. 111–126.

46. Crumbine, *Frontier Doctor*, pp. 103–104.

47. Unidentified news clipping, series 12, organizations with accompanying documents and newsclippings, Crumbine papers.

48. Samuel J. Crumbine to Prof. J.B. Rine, April 1, June 5, 1951, series 16, post–American Child Health Association folder, Crumbine papers.

49. Crumbine, *Frontier Doctor*, pp. 260, 270.

50. Ibid, pp. 108–109.

51. Tomes, *The Gospel of Germs*, chap. 1, especially p. 33; Bonner, *The Kansas Doctor*, p. 53.

52. Harriet S. Pfister, *Kansas State Board of Health* (Lawrence: University of Kansas Governmental Research Center, 1955), pp. 15–17.

53. *Kansas Senate Journal*, 1885, p. 132; Kansas, *Laws*, 1885, chap. 129; Bonner, *Kansas Doctor*, pp. 25–29, 78–79.

54. Kansas, *Laws*, 1885, chap. 129.

55. Department of Health, *Report*, 1886, pp. 15, 69–75.

56. Pfister, *Board of Health*, pp. 18–21.

57. Bonner, *Kansas Doctor*, pp. 82–83, quotes at p. 121; Department of Health, *Report*, 1894, pp. 1–14; Larry Jochims, "Medicine in Kansas, 1850–1900," master's thesis, Emporia State University 1977, p. 133; John Duffy, *The Sanitarians* (Urbana: University of Illinois Press, 1992), p. 153; Kansas, *Laws*, 1893, chap. 74.

58. Crumbine, *Frontier Doctor*, pp. 109–110; Kercher, "Crumbine and His Work," p. 27.

59. Crumbine, *Frontier Doctor*, pp. 110–111.

60. Letter quoted in series #18, biographical summaries folder, Crumbine papers.

61. Eastern Star Grand Chapter of Kansas, obituary (Topeka, KS: Hall Lithro, 1954), p. 231.

62. Crumbine, *Frontier Doctor*, p. 113.

63. Tomes, *The Gospel of Germs*, p. 104, for quote on physicians' beards. Gail Bederman, *Manliness and Civilization* (Chicago: University of Chicago Press, 1995), is good on the American distinction between manliness and masculinity in the nineteenth and early twentieth centuries.

64. *Topeka Daily Capital*, June 3, 1904; Department of Health, Biennial Report, 1903–1904, p. 14; Crumbine quote from Allen Greiner, "Pushing the Frontier of Public Health," *KUMed*, 49 (1999): 23.

## CHAPTER TWO

1. R. Alton Lee, *Farmers versus Wage Earners* (Lincoln: University of Nebraska Press, 2005), chap. 3, "The Apogee of Liberal Labor Legislation," discusses this movement in Kansas.

2. John Duffy, *The Sanitarians* (Urbana: University of Illinois Press, 1992), chap. 5.

3. R. Alton Lee, *A History of Regulatory Taxation* (Lexington: University Press of Kentucky, 1973), chaps. 3 and 4.

4. James Harvey Young, *The Toadstool Millionaires* (Princeton: Princeton University Press, 1961), pp. 214–224, quote at p. 220.

5. Oscar E. Anderson, Jr., *The Health of a Nation* (Chicago: University of Chicago Press, 1958), pp. 136, 149–52, 165.

6. Louis Fuller, *Crusaders for American Liberalism* (New York: Collier Books, 1961), is good on the Muckrakers and chap. 13 covers Upton Sinclair.

7. Samuel J. Crumbine, long hand notes, series 1, subseries 2, "Public Health Issues: Notes on Health Beginnings in Kansas" folder, Crumbine papers; Samuel J. Crumbine, "A Few Highlights in the History of Sanitation," *Modern Sanitation* (April 1954): 4.

8. Crumbine, "Highlights in the History of Sanitation," p. 4.

9. C.F. Menninger to Samuel Jay Crumbine, August 25, 1953, series 16, significant correspondence folder, Crumbine papers.

10. The "den of lions" quote is from Crumbine, "Highlights in the History of Sanitation," p. 6.

11. The "center of health related decisions" quote is from Mary Rowland, "Dr. Crumbine in Topeka," *Bulletin of Shawnee County Historical Society* (November 1980): 89; Department of Health, Bulletin, July 1905, p. 2.

12. Samuel J. Crumbine, "Means and Measures to Popularize Food and Drug Control," series 9, publications folder, Crumbine papers.

13. *Kansas City Star*, January 30, 1910.

14. Anderson, *Health of a Nation*, p. 77; Kansas, *Laws*, 1889, chap. xxix. The house passed the measure without recorded vote, the senate approved it 21-0, Senate, Journal, 1889, p. 963.

15. *Topeka Daily Capital*, August 20, 1891.

16. Thomas Neville Bonner, *The Kansas Doctor* (Lawrence: University of Kansas Press, 1959), p. 125; William R. Kercher, "Dr. S.J. Crumbine and His Work," *Kansas Magazine* (November 1910), p. 27.

17. *The Merchants Journal*, August 22, 1908.

18. *Topeka Daily Capital*, June 23, 1907; *The Merchants Journal* (Topeka), September 22, 1906.

19. C. Robert Haywood, *The Victorian West* (Lawrence: University Press of Kansas, 1991), p. 188; for examples of oyster suppers in a small town, see R. Alton Lee, *T-Town on the Plains* (Manhattan, KS: Sunflower University Press, 1999), p. 55.

20. Samuel J. Crumbine, *Frontier Doctor* (Philadelphia, PA: Dorrance, 1948), p. 121–122.

21. Board of Health, Bulletin, February 1908; Samuel J. Crumbine, "The Historical Background of Public Health in Kansas," series 1, subseries 2, pp. 9–10, Crumbine papers.

22. Robert Lewis Taylor, "Swat the Fly," *New Yorker*, 5 (1949): 62–63; James Harvey Young, "From Oysters to After-Dinner Mints: The Role of the Early Food and Drug Inspectors," *Journal of the History of Medicine and Allied Sciences*, 42 (January 1987): 48.

23. *Emporia Gazette*, August 19, 1908.

24. Ibid., July 26, 1906, February 7, 1907.

25. F.D. Coburn, "Samuel J. Crumbine," *American Magazine*, 72 (June 1911): 182; *Topeka Daily Capital*, February 4, 1907.

26. Bonner, *Kansas Doctor*, pp. 126–129; *The Merchants Journal*, February 8, 1908.

27. *Kansas Senate Journal*, 1907, p. 387; *Kansas House Journal*, 1907, p. 750; Kansas *Laws*, chap. 381.

28. *Emporia Gazette*, January 26, 1907; Kansas, Laws, 1907, chap. 266; *Kansas Senate Journal*, 1907, p. 153; *Kansas House Journal*, 1907, p. 406; Kansas, Laws, 1907, chap. 382.

29. *The Merchants Journal*, September 22, 1906.

30. 225 U.S. 501.

31. 249 U.S. 427.

32. *Topeka Daily Capital*, March 14, May 5, 1907.

33. *Wichita Eagle*, unidentified date, Crumbine papers, series 23, oversize, pure food folder.

34. David K. Strate, "Up From the Prairie" (Dodge City: Cultural Heritage and Arts Center, 1974), p. 23; Taylor, "Swat the Fly," p. 28. For a story on the opposition of the state's druggists to the passage of the law in 1907, see *Topeka State Journal*, February 4, 1907.

35. *Lawrence Times*, May 4, 1907.

36. *Independence Reporter*, May 25, 1907.

37. *Topeka Daily Capital*, July 1, 1915.

38. *Emporia Gazette*, April 5, 1906.

39. *Topeka Daily Capital*, July 17, 1906.

40. Ibid., December 3, 1908.

41. Board of Health, Bulletin, January 1908; *Topeka Daily Capital*, September 1908.

42. Young, "From Oysters to After-Dinner Mints," p. 32; "Single Service News by the Cup Reporter," Paper Cup and Container Institute, New York, September 1948.

43. *Emporia Gazette*, July 28, 1908.

44. James Harvey Young, "Botulism and the Ripe Olive Scare of 1919–1920," *Bulletin of the History of Medicine and Allied Sciences*, 50 (Fall 1976): 375, 378, 391.

45. Naomi Rogers, "Germs With Legs," *Bulletin of the History of Medicine and Allied Sciences*, 63 (Winter 1989): 600–601. Nancy Tomes, *The Gospel of Germs* (Cambridge, MA: Harvard University Press, 1998), pp. 101–102, rightly describes the housefly as "by far the worst of the insect enemies" and observes the dilemma of farm wives wanting fresh air and sunshine without flies in the days before screen wire.

46. Crumbine, "Historical Background of Public Health," series 1, subseries 2, public health issues folder, pp. 2–4, Crumbine papers.

47. Quote and poem from Bonner, *Kansas Doctor*, p. 135; Board of Health, Bulletin, 1905; Rogers, "Germs With Legs," p. 601.

48. "The Common Housefly," series 6, "swat the fly" folder, Crumbine papers.

49. Ibid.

50. Kansas, *Laws*, 1907, chap. 383; Harriet S. Pfister, *Kansas State Board of Health* (Lawrence: University of Kansas Governmental Research Center, 1955): 46.

51. Kercher, "Crumbine and His Work," p. 31.

52. Andrew McClary, "Swat the Fly," *Preventive Medicine*, 11 (1982): 373–377. Andrew McClary, "Germs Are Everywhere," *Journal of American Culture*, 3 (1980), suggests that these same journals popularized cleanliness, adequate sunlight, and healthy posture in much the same manner.

53. Allen Greiner, "Pushing the Frontier of Public Health," *KUMed*, 49 (1999): p. 23; *Salina Evening Journal*, July 1, 1913.

54. *Topeka Daily Capital*, July 7, 1915.

55. Bonner, *Kansas Doctor*, p. 138; *Topeka Daily Capital*, May 24, 1923.

56. Crumbine, *Frontier Doctor*, pp. 161–163.

57. Rogers, "Germs With Legs," pp. 613–614; Kenneth M. Ludmerer, *Time to Heal* (New York: Oxford University Press, 1999), pp. 34–35.

58. Tomes, *Gospel of Germs*, p. 241.

59. J. Floyd Telford to Samuel J. Crumbine, October 25, 1910; Kansas Bureau of Health, Report, 1910, pp. 149–152.

60. Board of Health, Reports, 1906, pp. 77–78. Clayton Koppes, "The Industrial Workers of the World and County Jail Reform in Kansas," *Kansas Historical Quarterly*, 41 (Spring 1975), is a good account of this public health problem and what, if anything, was done to correct it.

61. The following investigations and records are in Board of Health, Reports, 1908, pp. 15–53.

62. Crumbine, *Frontier Doctor*, pp. 184–186.

63. Koppes, "County Jail Reform," pp. 77–78.

64. Duffy, *The Sanitarians*, pp. 201–203; "running water purifies itself" from Gerald N. Grob, *The Deadly Truth* (Cambridge, MA: Harvard University Press, 2002), p. 188.

65. Samuel J. Crumbine, "The Pollution of Underground Waters," *Transactions of the Kansas Academy of Sciences*, 23–24 (1909–1910): 170–176. See William L. Bowers, *The Country Life Movement in America, 1900–1920* (Port Washington, NY: Kennikat Press, 1974), chaps. 5 and 6 for these agrarian attitudes.

66. Crumbine, "Highlights in the History of Sanitation," p. 7.

67. Ibid.

68. *Kansas City Times*, July 25, 1915.

69. Crumbine, *Frontier Doctor*, pp. 132–133; Taylor, "Swat the Fly," pp. 28–29. Modern scientists, who know that bacteria in water multiplies exponentially unless refrigerated immediately, may question the results reported by Crumbine in this study because of the many variables present.

70. Unidentified newspaper clipping, series 23 oversized, Crumbine papers.

71. Ibid.

72. *Topeka Daily Capital*, March 30, 1910.

73. Bonner, *Kansas Doctor*, pp. 141–142.

74. Ibid.

75. Crumbine, *Frontier Doctor*, pp. 137–139.

76. *Topeka Daily Capital*, May 2, 1911; Kansas, *Laws*, 1913, chap. 204.

77. Cecil Howes, "This Month in Kansas History," *The Kansas Teacher* (October 1948), 104–105. This story appears to have been copied from *Kansas City Times*, June 4, 1946.

78. Series 11, quotations folder, Crumbine papers.

## CHAPTER THREE

1. Barton H. Barbour, "Westward to Health," *Journal of the West*, 28 (April 1989): 40, 43.

2. Thomas Dormandy, *The White Death: A History of Tuberculosis* (New York: New York University Press, 1997), pp. 117–121; Samuel J. Crumbine, *Frontier Doctor* (Philadelphia, PA: Dorrance, 1948), p. 142.

3. Crumbine, *Frontier Doctor*, pp.142–143; *Emporia Gazette*, August 11, 1906; F.D. Coburn, "Samuel J. Crumbine," *American Magazine*, 12 (June 1911): 182.

4. Board of Health, Reports, 1910, pp. 101–102.

5. Thomas M. Daniel, *Captain of Death* (Rochester: University of Rochester Press, 1997), chap. 9.

6. Crumbine, *Frontier Doctor*, pp. 143–145; Robert Taylor, "Swat the Fly," *New Yorker*, 5 (1949): 32.

7. Nancy Tomes, *The Gospel of Germs* (Cambridge, MA: Harvard University Press, 1998), pp. 117–124.

8. Ibid., pp. 145–146; *Topeka Daily Capital*, December 4, 1908; *Health Education in Kansas*, 9 (June 1946).

9. *Topeka Daily Capital*, December 4, 1908; Marion M. Torcha, "The Tuberculosis Movement and the Race Question, 1890–1950," *Bulletin of the History of Medicine*, 49 (Summer 1975): 152.

10. George Rosen, *Preventive Medicine in the United States, 1900–1975* (New York: Prodist, 1977), p. 29; J. Aurthur Myers and James H. Steele, *Bovine Tuberculosis Control in Man and Animals* (St. Louis, MO: Warren H. Green, 1969), pp. 127, 157; Charles Wood, "Science and Politics in the War on Cattle Diseases: The Kansas Experience, 1900–1940," *Agricultural History*, 54 (January 1980): 91.

11. *Emporia Gazette*, June 5, 1908.

12. A.S. Alexander, "Testing Cows for Tuberculosis," *Country Life in America*, 14 (October 1908): 585.

13. Mark Aldrich, "Train Wrecks to Typhoid Fever," *Bulletin of the History of Medicine*, 75 (Summer 2002): 281–282.

14. G.V. (Trudy) Martin, "Dr. Crumbine's Health Bricks," *International Brick Collectors Association Journal*, 5 (Spring 1987): 4; Frank M. Chase, "The Man Who Made it Safe to Take a Drink," *The Dearborn Independent* (October 15, 1921): 10; "The Evolution of Railroad Sanitation," *The Pullman News* (Chicago, September 1923).

15. Samuel J. Crumbine, "A Few Highlights in the History of Sanitation," *Modern Sanitation* (April 1954): 8–9; "Dr. Crumbine Tells How He Banned the Common Cup," *Single Service News by the Cup Reporter* (New York: Paper Cup and Container Reporter, September 1948).

16. Crumbine, "Highlights in the History of Sanitation," p. 9.

17. Tomes, *Gospel of Germs*, pp. 132–134.

18. Ibid., pp. 9–10.

19. htpp://ww2.lafayette.edu/~library/special/dixie/dixie.html.

20. Ibid.; David Webb, "Kansas Characters," Kansas Heritage Center, 1985; Hugh Moore to S.J. Crumbine, December 4, 1935, series 16, ACHA folder, Crumbine papers.

21. S.J. Crumbine, "The Common Drinking Cup," Kansas Portraits by the staff of the Kansas Historical Society, p. 219.

22. Tomes, *Gospel of Germs*, p. 95. The author notes, p. 117, that the new business technique of advertising "represented a veritable gold mine of persuasive techniques" in the campaign against tuberculosis. Kansas, *Laws*, 1909, chap. 122.

23. Martin, "Dr. Crumbine's Health Bricks"; Daniel, *Captain of Death*, pp. 90, 93–94; Tomes, *Gospel of Germs*, p. 118.

24. Daniel, *Captain of Death*, chap. 10.

25. *Topeka Daily Capital*, May 20, 1916.

26. Board of Health, Reports, 1912, pp. 86–87, 97–98.

27. William R. Kercher, "Dr. S.J. Crumbine and His Work," *Kansas Magazine* (November 1910): 31.

28. Ibid., p. 32; *Topeka State Journal*, September 19, 1905; *Emporia Gazette*, August 23, 1909.

29. Crumbine, *Frontier Doctor*, pp. 153–55; Thomas Neville Bonner, *The Kansas Doctor* (Lawrence: University of Kansas Press, 1959), pp. 144–145.

30. *Topeka Daily Capital*, July 19, 1908.

31. *Topeka State Journal*, April 1, 1916.

32. Crowder, "Evolution of Railway Sanitation"; Crumbine, "Highlights in the History of Sanitation," p. 10. The order was printed in Kansas Board of Health, Bulletin, June 1911.

33. HTTP.Inventors. About.com/library/inventors/blkitchen.htm.

34. *St. Louis Republic*, April 9, 1911.

35. *Kansas Senate Journal*, 1911, p. 222; *Kansas House Journal*, 1911, p. 911; Kansas, *Laws*, 1911, chap 295; *Topeka Daily Capital*, March 9, 1911.

36. Martin J. Fitzpatrick, "Tuberculosis in Kansas," *Journal of the Kansas Medical Society*, 43 (September 1957): Kansas, *Laws*, 1913, chap. 302.

37. *Topeka State Journal*, June 15, 1914.

38. *Kansas City Star*, December 10, 1915; *Topeka State Journal*, December 20, 1915.

39. *Topeka Daily Capital*, September 20, 1914.

40. Thomas M. Daniel, *Pioneers of Medicine and Their Impact on Tuberculosis* (Rochester: University of Rochester, Press, 2000), p. 11.

41. *Topeka State Journal*, April 20, 1915.

42. Crumbine, *Frontier Doctor*, pp. 146–147.

43. *Topeka State Journal*, March 7, 1913; Kansas, Board of Health, Bulletin, April 1913. For con men working similar schemes in Europe at the time, see Barry Smith, "Gullible's Travails," *Journal of Contemporary History*, 20 (1985).

44. Cleo E. Strickland, "Tuberculosis in Cherokee County," county study, 1953, copy in Kansas State Historical Society; Crumbine, *Frontier Doctor*, p. 148.

45. Crumbine, *Frontier Doctor*, p. 149.

46. Ibid., pp. 150–151. Samuel J. Crumbine essentially repeats this story in "The Historical Background of Public Health in Kansas," series 1, subseries 2, pp. 6–7, Crumbine papers; Fitzhugh Mullan, *Plagues and Politics* (New York: Basic Books, 1989), p. 86.

47. Strickland, "Tuberculosis in Cherokee County," pp. 7–11.

48. Quote from Mary Wood-Simons, "Mining Coal and Maiming Men," *The Coming Nation*, Girard, KS, November 11, 1911; Commission of Labor and Industry, Annual Report, 1935.

49. Ibid., pp. 12–14.

50. Ibid., pp. 15–17.

51. *Topeka Daily Capital*, July 15, 1914. See James Harvey Young, *The Medical Messiahs* (Princeton: Princeton University Press, 1967), chap. 6, for nostrum advertising.

52. Ibid., April 21, 1915.

53. *Topeka State Journal*, June 4, 1914.

54. "Borrowing" story from *The Merchants Journal*, December 20, 1913; series 23, oversized newspaper clipping, state board of health folder, Crumbine papers; Bonner, *Kansas Doctor*, p. 120.

55. *Topeka Daily Capital*, April 9, September 16, October 6, 1915.

56. Crumbine, "Historical Background of Public Health," pp. 14–15.

57. Bonner, *Kansas Doctor*, p. 132; series 19, newspaper clipping, Crumbine papers.

58. *Topeka Daily Capital*, January 19, 1913; *Emporia Gazette*, February 26, 1913; Board of Health, Report, 1914, pp. 24–25.

59. Series 11, newspaper clippings, poetry folder, Crumbine papers. Someone mislabeled the one with the poem as "*Topeka State Journal*, Mar. 11, 1913," but it was printed in the *Wyandotte Daily Cricket*, March 12, 1913.

60. *University Daily Kansan*, March 13, 1916; *Topeka State Journal*, March 11, 1913. The charges and findings were reprinted in *Kansas Senate Journal*, 1913, pp. 817–818. See also Bonner, *Kansas Doctor*, p. 134.

61. *Emporia Gazette*, March 4, 1913; *Topeka Daily Capital*, March 13, 1913, May 7, 1916; Board of Health, Reports, 1914, p. 33. The point about his running for governor is from *The Food Law Bulletin*, March 2, 1908.

## CHAPTER FOUR

1. Charles R. King, "Childhood Death: The Health Care of Children on the Kansas Frontier," *Kansas History*, 14 (Spring 1991): 26–30.

2. Ibid., "most medical care" quote at p. 26; Glenda Riley, *The Female Frontier* (Lawrence: University Press of Kansas, 1988), p. 83; "high value on child life" quote from George Rosen, *A History of Public Health* (New York: MD Publications, 1958), p. 350.

3. Richard A. Meckel, *Save the Babies* (Ann Arbor: University of Michigan Press, 1998), pp. 3, 103.

4. Ibid., pp. 5–6.

5. Samuel J. Crumbine, *Frontier Doctor* (Philadelphia, PA: Dorrance, 1948), pp. 188–189.

6. *Topeka Daily Capital*, December 4, 1908.

7. Anne Hardy, "Straight Back to Barbarism: Anti-typhoid Inoculation and the Great War, 1914," *Bulletin of the History of Medicine*, 74 (Summer 2000): 268–269.

8. George H. Hodges to S.J. Crumbine, January 2, 1915; John J. Sippy to S.J. Crumbine, January 5, 1915; Governor Arthur Capper correspondence, 27-08-01-04, box 1, folder 7, KSHS.

9. Susan S. Novak, "Killed by the Cure," *Kansas Heritage*, 10 (Spring 2002): 18.

10. Crumbine, *Frontier Doctor*, pp 190–191. The author can remember as a sixth grader in Morris County in 1942, the entire school population receiving free diphtheria and smallpox vaccinations.

11. Samuel J. Crumbine, "Moving Forward in a United Front Against Diphtheria," *Child Health Bulletin* (New York: Child Health Association, 1926): 2.

12. Crumbine, *Frontier Doctor*, pp. 199–200.

13. *Topeka State Journal*, October 4, 1916.

14. Meckel, *Save the Babies*, p. 135.

15. Kansas Board of Health, Reports, 1914, p. 62.

16. Kansas, *Laws*, 1915, chap. 269; Board of Health, Bulletin, May 1916, p. 117.

17. *Topeka Daily Capital*, February 13, 1915.

18. Department of Health, Bulletin, 1913, p. 141.

19. *Topeka Daily Capital*, May 23, 1913.

20. Elizabeth Fee, *Disease and Discovery* (Baltimore, MD: Johns Hopkins University Press, 1987), p. 14; *Topeka State Journal*, December 19, 1914.

21. *Topeka Daily Capital*, July 13, 1913.

22. Meckel, *Save the Babies*, p. 122.

23. *Topeka Daily Capital*, September 11, 12, 1914.

24. Ibid., May 2, 1915.

25. Ibid, July 2, 1915.

26. Crumbine, *Frontier Doctor*, p. 212.

27. *Topeka Daily Capital*, August 15, 1915, this same story quoted the other newspapers.

28. Board of Health, clippings, undated, unpaged, KSHS.

29. Ibid., p. 127; Meckel, *Save the Babies*, pp. 144–145.

30. *Topeka State Journal*, July 10, 1915.

31. *Topeka Daily Capital*, July 14, 1915.

32. Ibid., July 27, 1915.

33. *Topeka State Journal*, October 6, 1915.

34. *Topeka Daily Capital*, March 5, 1916; Martin S. Pernick, *The Black Stork* (New York: Oxford University Press, 1996), is a gripping story of the Haiselden saga.

35. *Topeka Daily Capital*, February 28, 1918.

36. Ibid., April 3, 1916.

37. Ibid., March 5, 1915.

38. Honore Willlsie, "Save the Seventh Baby—Whose Business Is It?" *The Delineator* (April 1918): 18, 46, 150–151.

39. *Topeka Daily Capital*, February 1, 1916.

40. Ibid, March 18, 1916.

41. Suellen Hoy, *Chasing Dirt* (New York: Oxford University Press, 1995), p. 134.

42. Kansas Department of Health, Bulletin, 1911; Samuel J. Crumbine to Ralph R. Scoby, July 29, 1952, series 16, post–American Child Health Association folder, Crumbine papers.

43. Gerald N. Grob, *The Deadly Truth* (Cambridge, MA: Harvard University Press, 2002), p. 191. It should be noted that paralytic polio "was a disease directly associated with improved sanitation and housing" because children in less sanitary surroundings were more likely

to have been exposed to various strains of poliovirus and thus build up immunities. Ibid., pp. 189–190.

44. *Topeka Daily Capital*, July 12, 18, 1916.

45. Ibid., March 17, 1919.

46. Ibid., March 16, 1919.

47. Ibid., March 20, 1919.

48. Ibid., May 24, 1919.

49. Ibid., September 11, 1921.

50. Ibid., September 18, 1915; Crumbine, *Frontier Doctor*, pp. 216–217.

51. Board of Health, Bulletin, March 1921, pp. 60–61; Frank M. Chase, "Taking Health to Kansas in a Railroad Car," *The Dearborn Independent* (October 8, 1921): 12.

52. Topeka Daily Capital, November 4, 1922.

53. Meckel, *Save the Babies*, pp. 189–190.

54. Elizabeth G. Reilinger, "Child Health and the State" (Ph.D. dissertation: Cornell University, 1980), pp. 28–29; Joseph M. Hawes, *The Children's Rights Movement* (New York: Twayne, 1991), pp. 55–56; Jonathan Engel, *Doctors and Reformers* (Columbia: University of South Carolina Press, 2002), p. 15; Meckel, *Save the Babies*, pp. 207–209.

55. S. Josephine Baker, "The First Year of the Sheppard-Towner Act," *The Survey*, 52 (April 15, 1924): 89–90.

56. Board of Health, Report, 1922, pp. 41, 47, 76; 262 U S 447; John Duffy, *The Sanitarians* (Urbana: University of Illinois Press, 1992), p. 258; Reilinger, "Child Health", pp. 36–37.

57. Robert P. Hudson, "Hoxie's Bad Dream: Early Medical History in Kansas," *Journal of the Kansas Medical Society*, 71 (March 1970): 126.

58. Paul Starr, *The Transformation of American Medicine* (New York: Basic Books, 1982), pp. 112–123, is good on the background of changes in medical training; Robert P. Hudson, "Abraham Flexner in Perspective: American Medical Education, 1865–1910," in Judith Walzer Leavitt and Ronald L. Numbers (eds.), *Sickness and Health in America*, 3rd ed. (Madison: University of Wisconsin Press, 1997), p. 200. The "pocketbook" quote is from Kenneth M. Ludmerer, *Time to Heal* (Oxford: Oxford University Press, 1999), p. 5. See also Martin Kaufmann, *American Medical Education* (Westport, CT: Greenwood Press, 1976), chap. 11.

59. Lawrence H. Larsen and Nancy J. Hulston, *The University of Kansas Medical Center: A Pictoral History* (Lawrence: University Press of Kansas, 1992), p. 3. Thomas Neville Bonner, *The Kansas Doctor* (Lawrence: University of Kansas Press, 1959), pp. 72–73.

60. R. Alton Lee, *The Bizarre Careers of John R. Brinkley* (Lexington: University Press of Kentucky, 2002), p. 106; Larsen and Hulston, *Medical Center*, p. 3; Kansas, *Laws*, 1901, chap. 254.

61. Larsen and Hulston, *Medical Center*, p. 4; Bonner, *Kansas Doctor*, p. 146.

62. Hudson, "Hoxie's Bad Dream," p. 126.

63. Helen M. Sims, "The Wahl Years at the University of Kansas Medical Center, 1919-1948," (University of Kansas Alumni Association, 1983), pp. 8–11; Hudson, "Hoxie's Bad Dream," p. 126.

64. Larsen and Hulston, *Medical Center*, p. 27.

65. Frank Strong to S.J. Crumbine, November 30, 1909; E.S.J. Bailey to S.J. Crumbine, December 1, 1909; Frank Strong to S.J. Crumbine, June 27, 1910, series 13, school of medicine folder, Crumbine papers.

66. Bonner, *Kansas Doctor*, pp. 148–149.

67. Crumbine, *Frontier Doctor*, p. 193.

68. Bonner, *Kansas Doctor*, p. 150; *Kansas City Star* quote from Larsen and Hulston, *Medical Center*, p. 29.

69. Bonner, *Kansas Doctor*, pp. 151–152; Sims, "Wahl Years," pp. 12–13.

70. Elizabeth Fee, *Disease and Discovery* (Baltimore, MD: Johns Hopkins University Press, 1987), chap. 1.

71. Alan Greiner, "Pushing the Frontier of Public Health," *KU Med*, 49 (1999): 25; Samuel J. Crumbine to Frank T. Stockton, August 25, 1952, series 13, school of medicine folder, Crumbine papers. Dean Stockton was writing a history of the school and had asked for information.

72. Samuel J. Crumbine to Frank Stockton, May 8, 1953, Crumbine papers.

73. Ibid., February 26, 1953.

74. Earle Brown, elected secretary of the board of health in 1925, to Frank Stockton, April 21, 1953; Samuel Crumbine to Dean Stockton, April 27, 1953, Crumbine papers; Harriet Pfister, *Kansas State Board of Health* (Lawrence: University of Kansas Governmental Research Center, 1955), pp. 44–45.

75. Bonner, *Kansas Doctor*, p.157; Stanley R. Friesen and Robert P. Hudson, *Preventative Medicine* (Kansas School of Medicine, 1996); Kansas, *Laws*, 1911, chaps. 292, 293, 294.

76. News clipping with pictures of a crippled boy before and after, series 13, school of medicine folder, Crumbine papers.

77. *Topeka State Journal*, March 17, 1919.

78. Kansas, *Laws*, 1919, chap. 284; Ralph H. Major, "An Account of the Kansas School of Medicine" (University of Kansas Medical Alumni Association, 1968), pp. 19–20; Minnie S. Misslie, secretary to the chancellor, to S.J. Crumbine, June 30, 1919, series 13, school of medicine folder, Crumbine papers.

## CHAPTER FIVE

1. Robert W. Richmond, *Kansas: A Land of Contrasts* (Wheeling, IL: Forum Press, 1989), pp. 23–26; *Topeka Daily Capital*, May 19, 1917.

2. *Topeka Daily Capital*, July 15, 1917.

3. Samuel J. Crumbine, *Frontier Doctor* (Philadelphia, PA: Dorrance, 1948), pp. 217–218.

4. *Topeka Daily Capital*, August 23, 25, 1918.

5. S.J. Crumbine to Arthur Capper, May 13, 1918, Governor Capper Correspondence, 27-08-04-06, box 25, folder 6, KSHS.

6. *Topeka Daily Capital*, August 14, 1918.

7. Governor Arthur Capper correspondence, 27-08-03-03, box 15, folder 13; John Duffy, *The Sanitarians* (Urbana: University of Illinois Press, 1992), p. 225.

8. Allan M. Brandt, *No Magic Bullet* (New York: Oxford University Press, 1985), pp. 30–48.

9. Ibid., pp. 52–60. For operation of the draft laws, see Fred D. Baldwin, "The Invisible Armor," *American Quarterly*, 16 (Fall 1964): 432.

10. Donald Smythe, "Venereal Disease: The AEF's Experience," *Prologue*, 9 (Summer 1977): 66.

11. Ibid., pp. 65–66, 70.

12. Ibid., 65, 67.

13. Ibid., pp. 68–69.

14. Ibid., pp. 69–70, 72–74. The infection rates are from Baldwin, "Invisible Armor," p. 438.

15. John Duffy, *The Sanitarians*, p. 242.

16. Bonnie Bullough and George Rosen, *Preventive Medicine in the United States, 1900-1990* (Canton, MA: Science History Publications, 1992), pp. 43–44.

17. Brandt, *No Magic Bullet*, pp. 70–71.

18. Crumbine, *Frontier Doctor*, pp. 218–220.

19. Ibid., p. 220.

20. *Topeka Daily Capital*, December 20, 1917.

21. Governor Arthur Capper correspondence, 27-08-03-04, box 16, folder 39, KSHS.

22. Board of Health, Report, 1918, pp. 55, 65–66.

23. *Topeka Daily Capital*, March 18, 1917.

24. Ibid., August 20, 1917.

25. Ibid., June 9, 1917.

26. Ibid., June 16, 1917.

27. Ibid., July 2, 1918. Kansas newspapers labeled the American soldiers in France "Sammies," apparently copying the British term "Tommies" for their men. After repeated protests that they disliked "Sammy," the term "doughboy" came into vogue, much like "G.I. Joe" was used in World War II.

28. *Topeka Daily Capital*, August 3, 1917. For a discussion of the Supreme Court sustaining the Mann Act, see R. Alton Lee, *A History of Regulatory Taxation* (Lexington: University Press of Kentucky, 1973), p. 127.

29. Crumbine, *Frontier Doctor*, pp. 221–222.

30. Ibid., pp. 222–223. *Topeka Daily Capital*, November 6, 1917. The August 19, 1917 issue of the *Topeka Daily Capital* headlined its story on this with "State Opens War on the Vampires." Ronald Schaffer, *America in the Great War* (New York: Oxford University Press, 1991), p. 103, notes that federal detention centers had over 18,000 women submitted to them from 1918 through 1920.

31. David M. Kennedy, *Over Here* (New York: Oxford University Press, 1980), p. 83.

32. Samuel J. Crumbine, "The Historical Background of Public Health in Kansas," series 1, subseries 2, folder 1, public health issues, Crumbine papers.

33. Ibid.

34. Ibid., p. 222; Lawrence H. Larsen and Nancy J. Hulston, *Pendergast!* (Columbia: University of Missouri Press, 1997), p. 72. The following year the *Topeka Daily Capital*, March

16, 1919, headlined a story on murder, theft, and white slavery with "Kansas City is the Capital of the Criminal World."

35. *Topeka Daily Capital*, July 15, March 31, 1918.

36. In reference to McGee, Kansas Reports, 105 at 547s, November 18, 1919.

37. Crumbine, *Frontier Doctor*, pp. 225–226.

38. Ibid., pp. 226–231.

39. "A Study of the Causes of Delinquency of Women Quarantined at the State Industrial Farm for Women," series 1, subseries 2, Women's State Industrial Farm folder, Crumbine papers. This report contains a number of unidentified specific case studies.

40. Crumbine, *Frontier Doctor*, pp. 231–233.

41. Ibid., pp. 237–240. Nothing in the Crumbine papers identified this state.

42. Duffy, *The Sanitarians*, pp. 225, 233, 249.

43. *Wichita Beacon*, November 5, 1918.

44. *Topeka Daily Capital*, January 21, 1923.

45. Charles V. Chapin, A Report on State Public Health Work (Chicago: American Medical Association, 1977 reprint edition), pp. 23, 195, 192.

46. *Topeka Daily Capital*, March 7, 1920; August 8, 1922.

47. Thomas N. Bonner, *The Kansas Doctor* (Lawrence: University of Kansas Press, 1959), p. 160; "proved futile" quote from Gerald N. Grob, *The Deadly Truth* (Cambridge, MA: Harvard University Press, 2002), p. 225. Clark Miller, "The Great Flu Epidemic of 1918," *Heritage of the Great Plains*, 18 (Winter 1985): 25, claims that "Kansas had the honor of being the site of the first recorded outbreak of the epidemic in this country" at Camp Funston on March 5, 1918.

48. Duffy, *The Sanitarians*, p. 243.

49. *Topeka Daily Capital*, September 17, 18, 1918.

50. Ibid., September 26, 1918; Blue to Crumbine September 18, 1918; S.J. Crumbine to Surgeon General, September 19, 1918, Board of Health, Report, 1920, p. 13.

51. *Topeka Daily Capital*, September 26, 1918.

52. Crumbine, *Frontier Doctor*, p. 242.

53. Crumbine, *Frontier Doctor*, pp. 243–246; *Topeka State Journal*, n.d., series 8, subseries 2, newspaper clippings, Crumbine papers.

54. Bonner, *Kansas Doctor*, pp. 161–162.

55. *Topeka Daily Capital*, October 3, 19, 1918.

56. Ibid., October 13, 1918.

57. Ibid., October 10, 11, 12; Bonner, *Kansas Doctor*, p. 162.

58. *Topeka Daily Capital*, October 19, 1918; *Kansas City Kansan*, October 30, 1918.

59. *Topeka Daily Capital*, October 21, 1918; *Wichita Beacon*, October 16, 1918.

60. *Topeka Daily Capital*, October 23, 24, 26, November 2, 1918.

61. Ibid., November 21, 27, 28, 29, 30; *Wichita Beacon*, December 10, 21, 1918.

62. *Topeka State Journal*, January 21, 1919; the world death toll is from Grob, *Deadly Truth*, p. 224; the "two-thirds" figure is from Alfred W. Crosby, Jr., "The Influenza Pandemic of 1918," in June E. Osborn (ed.), *Influenza in America, 1918, 1976* (New York: Prodist, 1977), pp. 6, 13.

63. Mary Scott Rowland, "Managerial Progressivism in Kansas" (Ph.D. dissertation: University of Kansas, 1980), p. 116.

64. Crumbine, *Frontier Doctor*, pp. 254–255.

65. Ibid., pp. 225–226.

66. Ibid., pp. 255–258.

67. See R. Alton Lee, *Farmers versus Wage Earners* (Lincoln: University of Nebraska Press, 2005), p. 171.

68. Bonner, *Kansas Doctor*, p. 166.

69. *Topeka State Journal*, June 1, 1923.

70. *Topeka Daily Capital*, May 5, 18, 1923.

71. Mervin T. Sudler to Dr. Crumbine, April 19, 1923; S.J. Crumbine to M.T. Sudler, April 20, 1923; Henderson S. Martin to Mervin T. Sudler, May 2, 1923, series 6, Samuel J. Crumbine 1912–1916 folder, Crumbine papers.

72. Bonner, *Kansas Doctor*, p. 167; *Emporia Gazette*, June 5, 1923; copy of board of health letter in series 15, Crumbine Letters in Hoover Library folder, Crumbine papers. Interestingly, the Davis papers include a folder entitled board of health, but it does not contain one letter regarding this stupendous struggle.

73. *Topeka Daily Capital*, June 6, 8, 1923; Rowland, "Managerial Progressivism," pp. 132–133.

74. *Topeka State Journal*, June 8, 1923.

75. Ibid.

76. *Topeka Daily Capital*, June 12, 1923.

77. Ibid., June 12, 1923.

78. Ibid., June 16, 19, 1923.

79. Everett Newfon Dick, *From Horses to Horsepower: Life in Kansas, 1900–1925* (Topeka: Kansas State Historical Association, 1986), from *Kansas Farmer*, November 1, 1924.

80. Samuel J. Crumbine to "Ches," January 8, 1953, series 16, post–American Child Health Association correspondence folder, Crumbine papers.

81. O.D. Walker to Jonathan M. Davis, March 31, 1923; E.B. Black to S.J. Crumbine, June 8, 1923; B. Gloyne to S.J. Crumbine, June 6, 1923; F.S. Frisbie to S.J. Crumbine, June 4, 1923; E.B. Black to S.J. Crumbine, June 8, 1923; Harold B. Wood to Samuel J. Crumbine, June 19, 1923; series 16, board of health folder, Crumbine papers.

82. Board of Health, Report, 1924.

83. Rowland, "Managerial Progressivism," p. 134; Harriet S. Pfister, *Kansas State Board of Health* (Lawrence: University of Kansas Governmental Research Center, 1955), p. 49.

## CHAPTER SIX

1. Samuel J. Crumbine, *Frontier Doctor* (Philadelphia, PA: Dorrance, 1948), p. 274.

2. Elizabeth G. Reilinger, "Child Health and the State," Ph.D. dissertation, Cornell University, 1980, pp. 22–23. Richard A. Meckel, *Save the Babies* (Ann Arbor: University of Michigan Press, 1998), pp. 109–122, traces the early activities of the AASPIM.

3. James N. Giglio, "Herbert Hoover and the American Child Health Association" *Presidential Studies Quarterly*, 13 (Summer 1983): 431.

4. Quoted in Ibid., p. 432.

5. Ibid.

6. Ibid., pp. 274–275; Richard A. Bolt to Doctor Samuel J. Crumbine, August 9, 1948, series 16, Board of Health folder, Crumbine papers; quote from Robert Lewis Taylor, "Swat the Fly," *New Yorker* 24 (July 24, 1948): 34.

7. Reilinger, "Child Health," p. 29; Taylor, "Swat the Fly," p. 34.

8. *New York Times*, May 1, 2, 1923; Philip Van Ingen, "The American Child Health Association" (American Child Health Association reprint, 1936).

9. Giglio, "Herbert Hoover and the ACHA," pp. 441–442; ACHA, *Child Health Bulletin*, 4 (July 1928).

10. Marie M. Meloney to Dr. Crumbine, May 18, 1925, series 16, correspondence, ACHA folder, Crumbine papers.

11. Charles R. King, *Children's Health in America* (New York: Twayne, 1993), p. 151.

12. Samuel J. Crumbine, "What the American Child Health Association is Doing," address at the fourth annual meeting, May 9–11, 1927, p. 2; Joan Hoff Wilson, *Herbert Hoover: Forgotten Progressive* (Prospect Heights, IL: Waveland Press, 1975), p. 111.

13. S.J. Crumbine to Eugene R. Kelley, June 14, 1923, series 16, ACHA folder, Crumbine papers; *Topeka State Journal*, June 19, 1923, carried his nostalgic story on the jimson weed; "soft" quote from Taylor, "Swat the Fly," p. 33.

14. Philip Van Ingen, "Story of American Child Health Association," p. 31. Honore Willsie, "Save the Seventh Baby, Whose Business is it?" *The Delineator* (April 1918): 18 says that at that time only one-third of the towns in America had "adequate birth registration."

15. Giglio, "Hoover and the ACHA," pp. 431, 433.

16. Ibid., pp. 434–436.

17. Ibid., pp. 436–437; Herbert Hoover to Courtenay Dinwiddie, December 23, 1924, series 16, correspondence, ACHA folder, Crumbine papers.

18. Edgar Rickard to Herbert Hoover, January 31, 1925, February 10, 1925, news release of secretary of commerce, series 15, Crumbine Letters in Hoover Library folder, Crumbine papers.

19. ACHA, *Child Health Bulletin*, 1 (June 1925).

20. Giglio, "Hoover and the ACHA," pp. 437–438.

21. Van Ingen, "American Child Health," pp. 19–20; Giglio, "Hoover and ACHA," pp. 439–440.

22. Van Ingen, "American Child Health," pp. 20–22.

23. *New York Times*, May 9, 1927; Jack Yarmove, "One Man Health Crusade," *Coronet*, 19 (February 1946): 102.

24. Arthur Capper to Dr. S.J. Crumbine, July 22, 1948, series 16, correspondence, post–ACHA folder, series 12, Save the Children folder, Crumbine papers.

25. John Duffy, *The Sanitarians* (Urbana: University of Illinois Press, 1992), p. 207; Samuel J. Crumbine, "Diseases of Cattle Communicable to Man Through Milk," series 9, publications folder, pp. 1–2, Crumbine papers.

26. Meckel, *Save the Babies*, pp. 63–66.

27. Crumbine, "Diseases of Cattle"; Meckel, *Save the Babies*, p. 75.

28. Meckel, *Save the Babies*, p. 73.

29. ACHA, *Child Health Bulletin*, 8 (May 1932).

30. *New York Times*, May 17, 1925; Meckel, *Save the Babies*, pp. 69, 90.

31. Congressional Record, 67 cong, 4 sess., pp. 4981–4986.

32. Ibid., p. 7581.

33. Ibid., pp. 5545, 5556, 7583.

34. Harvey H. Wiley, "A Bad Spot in a Good Law," *Good Housekeeping*, 77 (August 1923): 88, 144–145.

35. *U.S. v. Carolene Products*, 304 US 144. Chief Justice Harlan Stone, writing for the majority, inserted the most famous footnote in constitutional history in the opinion. Footnote Four observed that the due process clause of the 14th Amendment applied the Bill of Rights also as restrictions on the states. Following this decision the Supreme Court proceeded to apply this concept over the next several years in case after case, eventually extending the first nine amendments to the states as well as to the federal government.

36. Van Ingen, "American Child Health," pp. 32–33; S.J. Crumbine to Helen A. Moore, February 18, 1949, series 8, subseries 2, correspondence on *Frontier Doctor* folder, Crumbine papers; Taylor, "Swat the Fly," p. 34. Crumbine's assistants had some difficulty persuading some of them that "a sharp axe placed under the bed of a patient would not materially alleviate hemorrhage."

37. King, *Children's Health*, p. 130; Herbert Hoover to Dr. S.J. Crumbine, October 23, 1925, series 15, Crumbine letters in Hoover Library folder, Crumbine papers.

38. *New York World*, November 22, 1928.

39. Notes on Visit With Dr. Lowrey, February 10, 1931, series 2, American Child Health Association, subseries Cheerio, Crumbine papers.

40. "A Former Nurse," Ibid.

41. Beatrice Wood, June 4, 1930, Ibid.

42. Mr. Houston to Dr. Crumbine, March 21, 1933, Ibid.

43. T.L. Seward to Dr. Crumbine, June 4, 1929, series 4, White House Conference on Child Health, Crumbine papers.

44. ACHA, *Child Health Bulletin*, 5 (September 1929).

45. Ethel Perrin, "American Child Health Association," *Journal of Health and Physical Education*, 4 (November 1933).

46. Raymond Lyman Wilbur and Arthur Mastich Hyde, *The Hoover Policies* (New York: Charles Scribner's Sons, 1937), pp. 67–74.

47. Parker Hanson, *Puerto Rico* (New York: Knopf, 1960), pp. 76–77.

48. Theodore Roosevelt, *Colonial Policies of the United States* (New York: Doubleday, Doran, 1937), pp. 107–108, 123.

49. ACHA, *Child Health Bulletin*, 6 (July 1930).

50. American Child Health Association, Report on Porto Rican Children's Health, pp. 8–14, series 5, Porto Rico folder, Crumbine papers.

51. Ibid., pp. 15–16.

52. Ibid., p. 17; American Child Health Association, news release, April 20, 1931, series 5, Porto Rico folder, Crumbine papers.

53. John Ettling, *The Germ of Laziness* (Cambridge, MA: Harvard University Press, 1981), pp. 124–127.

54. American Child Health Association, Report on Porto Rico, pp. 17, 19–20.

55. Ibid., p. 17.

56. Ibid.

57. Ibid., pp. 23, 29–32; Gordon K. Lewis, *Puerto Rico* (New York: MR Press, 1963), p. 98.

58. Giglio, "Hoover and the ACHA." pp. 445–446.

59. American Child Health Association news release, April 20, 1931, series 5, Porto Rico folder, Crumbine papers; ACHA, *Child Health Bulletin*, 7 (May 1931); *New York Times*, March 24, April 20, 21, 1931.

60. *New York Times*, January 24, 1932. The story was entitled "The Nutritive Value of Cheap But Wholesome Foods Set Forth to Help the Housewife Whose Pennies Must Feed Many Mouths."

61. Giglio, "Hoover and the ACHA," pp. 446–447.

62. ACHA, *Child Health Bulletin*, 9 (January 1933).

63. *New York Times*, November 24, 1935; Fred J. Kelly to S.J. Crumbine, November 22, 1935; S. Mc. Hamill to S.J. Crumbine, January 2, 1936, series 16, ACHA folder, Crumbine papers; Van Ingen, "American Child Health Association," p. 34.

64. Giglio, "Hoover and the ACHA," p. 446.

65. Samuel McC. Hamill to S.J. Crumbine, January 2, 1936, series 16, ACHA folder, Crumbine papers.

66. D. Clayton Brown, "Health of Farm Children in the South, 1900–1950," *Agricultural History*, 53 (1979): 170, 172.

67. Taylor, "Swat the Fly," p. 34; S.J. Crumbine to George W. Crile, December 18, 1939, series 16, personal correspondence folder, Crumbine papers; Crumbine, *Frontier Doctor*, p. 152.

68. Unidentified newspaper clipping, series 12, save the children folder, Crumbine papers.

69. Samuel J. Crumbine to George W. Crile, December 18, 1939; Samuel J. Crumbine to John J. Summersby, March 4, 1943, series 16, personal correspondence folder, Crumbine papers.

70. Crumbine, *Frontier Doctor*, p. 280.

71. S.J. Crumbine to John J. Summersby, March 4, 1943, series 16.

72. Crumbine, *Frontier Doctor*, p. 280; *New York Herald Tribune*, November 9, 1942; *Topeka Daily Capital*, July 19, 1943.

73. S.J. Crumbine to Helen A. Moore, February 18, 1949, series 8, subseries 2, correspondence on *Frontier Doctor* folder, Crumbine papers.

74. Herbert Hoover to "my dear Dr. Crumbine," September 16, 1948, series 15, Crumbine letters in Herbert Hoover Library folder; E.C. Bishop to Samuel J. Crumbine, December 31, 1948, series 8, subseries 2, correspondence on *Frontier Doctor* folder, Crumbine papers; *Kansas City Times*, September 23, 1948; *Saturday Review of Literature*, 32 (January 22, 1949): 23–24.

75. Series 23 oversized newspaper clippings, Crumbine papers.

76. V.M. Winkle to Samuel J. Crumbine, March 6, 1952; Evalyn Folk to S.J. Crumbine, June 25, 1952; Samuel J. Crumbine to "Ches," January 8, 1953, Ibid.

77. Samuel J. Crumbine to Elmer V. McCullom, May 24, 1952, Ibid.

78. W.W. Bauer to Samuel J. Crumbine, November 10, 1952, Ibid.

79. I.C. Pfalser, "Doc Crumbine of Dodge City," series 18, autobiographical summaries folder, Crumbine papers; Samuel J. Crumbine, "A Few Highlights in the History of Sanitation," pp. 5–6.

## CHAPTER SEVEN

1. William R. Kercher, "Dr. S. J. Crumbine and His Work," *Kansas Magazine* (November 1910): 29. Thomas Neville Bonner, *The Kansas Doctor* (Lawrence: University of Kansas Press, 1959), p. 171.

2. F.D. Coburn, "Samuel J. Crumbine," *American Magazine*, 72 (June 1911): 182. See also Alan Greiner,"Pushing the Frontier of Public Health" *KUMed*, 49 (1999); quote on politics from Elizabeth Fee, *Disease and Discovery* (Baltimore, MD: Johns Hopkins University Press, 1987), p. 16.

3. This theme and the following one are from John Duffy, *The Sanitarians* (Urbana: University of Illinois Press, 1990), pp. 2–3.

4. Gerald N. Grob, *The Deadly Truth* (Cambridge, MA: Harvard University Press, 2002), pp. 189–190.

5. Ibid., pp. 180, 217–218.

# BIBLIOGRAPHY

The Crumbine papers, deposited in the Clendening Library at the University of Kansas Medical Center, were indispensable for this study. The annual *Reports* and monthly *Bulletins* of the Kansas State Department of Health also were valuable as indications of what reforms Crumbine and his colleagues were pursuing at any given time. State government documents, such as papers of governors, legislative journals, statutes, and occasional court cases were helpful. There is a great amount of secondary works on the history of the public health movement in the United States. Those works I found most useful for this study were

## BOOKS

Anderson, Oscar E. *The Health of a Nation.* Chicago: University of Chicago Press, 1958.

Bederman, Gail. *Manliness and Civilization.* Chicago: University of Chicago Press, 1995.

Bonner, Thomas Neville. *The Kansas Doctor.* Lawrence: University of Kansas Press, 1959.

Bowers, William L. *The Country Life Movement in America, 1900–1920.* Port Washington, NY: Kennikat Press, 1974.

Brandt, Allan M. *No Magic Bullet: A Social History of Venereal Disease in the United States Since 1880.* New York: Oxford University Press, 1985.

Brophy, Patrick. "The Weltner Institute and Magnetic Healing in Nevada, Mo." In Gene Fowler (ed.), *Mystic Healers and Medicine Shows.* Santa Fe, NM: Ancient City Press, 1997.

Bullough, Bonnie and George Rosen. *Preventive Medicine in the United States, 1900–1990: Trends and Interpretations.* Canton, MA: Science History Publications, 1991.

Cassidy, James H. *Charles V. Chapin and the Public Health Movement.* Cambridge, MA: Harvard University Press, 1962.

Chapin, Charles V. *Report on State Public Health Work Based on a Survey of State Boards of Health.* Chicago, IL: American Medical Association, 1915, Arno Press reprint, 1977.

Crumbine, Samuel J. *Frontier Doctor.* Philadelphia, PA: Dorrance, 1948.

Crumbine, Samuel J. and James A. Tobey. *The Most Nearly Perfect Food: The Story of Milk.* Baltimore, MD: Williams and Wilkins, 1929.

Crumbine, Samuel J. and William O. Krohn. *Graded Lessons in Physiology and Hygiene.* Topeka, KS: State Printer, 1918.

Daniel, Thomas M. *Captain of Death.* Rochester: University of Rochester Press, 1997.

———. *Pioneers of Medicine and Their Impact on Tuberculosis.* Rochester: University of Rochester Press, 2000.

Dick, Everett Newfon. *From Horses to Horsepower: Life in Kansas, 1900–1925.* Topeka: Kansas State Historical Society, 1986.

Dormandy, Thomas. *The White Death.* New York: New York University Press, 1999.

Duffy, John. *A History of Public Health in New York City.* 2 vols. New York: Russell Sage Foundation, 1968, 1974.

———. *The Sanitarians.* Champaign: University of Illinois Press, 1990.

Dykstra, Robert R. *The Cattle Towns.* New York: Alfred A. Knopf, 1968.

Engel, Jonathan. *Doctors and Reformers.* Columbia: University of South Carolina Press, 2002.

Ettling, John. *The Germ of Laziness: Rockefeller Philanthropy and Public Health in the New South.* Cambridge, MA: Harvard University Press, 1981.

Faulk, Odie B. *Dodge City: The Most Western Town of All.* New York: Oxford University Press, 1998.

Fee, Elizabeth. *Disease and Discovery: A History of the Johns Hopkins School of Hygiene and Public Health.* Baltimore, MD: Johns Hopkins University Press, 1987.

Fleming, Donald. *William H. Welch and the Rise of Modern Medicine.* Boston, MA: Little, Brown, 1954.

Freidson, Eliot. *The Profession of Medicine: A Study of the Sociology of Applied Knowledge.* New York: Dodd Mead, 1970.

Friesen, Stanley R. and Robert P. Hudson. *Preventive Medicine.* Lawrence: Kansas School of Medicine, 1996.

Fuller, Louis. *Crusaders for American Liberalism.* New York: Collier Books, 1961.

Grob, Gerald N. *The Deadly Truth: A History of Disease in America.* Cambridge, MA: Harvard University Press, 2002.

Hardin, Victoria. *Inventing the NIH: Federal BioMedical Research Policy.* Baltimore, MD: Johns Hopkins University Press, 1986.

Harris, Richard. *A Sacred Trust.* Baltimore, MD: Penguin Books, 1969.

Hawes, Joseph M. *The Children's Rights Movement: A History of Advocacy and Protection.* Boston, MA: Twayne, 1991.

Haywood, C. Robert. *The Victorian West.* Lawrence: University Press of Kansas, 1991.

————. *The Merchant Prince of Dodge City*. Norman: University of Oklahoma Press, 1998.

Hoy, Suellen. *Chasing Dirt: The American Pursuit of Cleanliness*. New York: Oxford University Press, 1995.

Hudson, Robert P. *Disease and Its Control*. Westport, CT: Greenwood, 1983.

Jonas, Steven. *Medical Mystery: The Training of Doctors in the United States*. New York: W.W. Norton, 1978.

Kaufman, Martin. *American Medical Education: The Formative Years, 1765–1910*. Westport, CT: Greenwood Press, 1976.

Kevles, Daniel. *In the Name of Eugenics*. New York: Knopf, 1985.

King, Charles R. *Children's Health in America: A History*. New York: Twayne, 1993.

King, Lester S. *Transformations in American Medicine*. Baltimore, MD: Johns Hopkins University Press, 1991.

Krause, Elliott A. *Power and Illness: The Political Sociology of Medical Care*. Berkeley: University of California Press, 1993.

Larsen, Lawrence H. and Nancy J. Hulston. *The University of Kansas Medical Center: A Pictoral History*. Lawrence: University Press of Kansas, 1992

————. *Pendergast!*. Columbia: University of Missouri Press, 1997.

Leavitt, Judith Walzer and Ronald L. Numbers (eds.). *Sickness and Health in America*, 3rd ed. Madison: University of Wisconsin Press, 1997.

Lee, R. Alton. *A History of Regulatory Taxation*. Lexington: University Press of Kentucky, 1973.

————. *T-Town on the Plains*. Manhattan, KS: Sunflower University Press, 1999.

————. *The Bizarre Careers of John R. Brinkley*. Lexington: University Press of Kentucky, 2002.

————. *Farmers versus Wage Earners*. Lincoln: University of Nebraska Press, 2005.

Lewis, Gordon K. *Puerto Rico*. New York: MR Press, 1963.

Ludmerer, Kenneth M. *Time to Heal*. New York: Oxford University Press, 1999.

McKeown, Thomas. *The Role of Medicine: Dream, Mirage, or Nemesis*. Princeton: Princeton University Press, 1979.

McNeil, William. *Plagues and Peoples*. Garden City, NY: Anchor Press, 1976.

Meckel, Richard A. *Save the Babies: American Public Health Reform and the Prevention of Infant Mortality, 1850–1929*. Ann Arbor: University of Michigan, 1998.

Morantz-Sanchez, Regina Markell. *Sympathy and Science: Women Physicians in American Medicine*. New York: Oxford University Press, 1977.

Mullan, Fitzhugh. *Plagues and Politics: The Story of the United States Public Health Service*. New York: Basic Books, 1989.

Myers, J. Arthur and James H. Steele. *Bovine Tuberculosis: Control in Man and Animals*. St. Louis, MO: Warren H. Green, 1969.

Numbers, Ronald. *Almost Persuaded: American Physicians and Compulsory Health Insurance, 1912–1920*. Princeton: Princeton University Press, 1978.

Osborn, June E. (ed.). *Influenza in America*. New York: Prodist, 1977.

Patterson, James T. *The Dread Disease*. Cambridge, MA: Harvard University Press, 1987.

Paul, John. *A History of Poliomyelitis*. New Haven, CT: Yale University Press, 1971.

Pernick, Martin S. *The Black Stork: Eugenics and the Death of "Defective" Babies in American Medicine and Motion Pictures since 1915*. New York: Oxford University Press, 1996.

Pfister, Harriet S. *Kansas State Board of Health*. Lawrence: University of Kansas Governmental Research Center, 1955.

Ravenil, Mazych Porcher (ed.). *A Half Century of Public Health*. New York: Arno Press, 1970.

Reilinger, Elizabeth G. "Child Health and the State: The Evolution of Federal Policy." Ph.D. dissertation, Cornell University, 1980.

Reverby, Susan and David Rosner (eds.). *Health Care in America: Essays in Social History.* Philadelphia, PA: Temple University Press, 1979.

Richmond, Robert. *Kansas: A Land of Contrasts*. Wheeling, IL: Forum Press, 1989.

Riley, Glenda. *The Female Frontier*. Lawrence: University of Kansas Press, 1988.

Risse, Guenter B., Ronald L. Numbers, and Judith Walzer Leavitt (eds.). *Medicine Without Doctors*. New York: Science History Publications, 1977.

Roosevelt, Theodore, Jr. *Colonial Policies of the United States*. New York: Doubleday, Doran, 1937.

Rosen, George. *A History of Public Health*. New York: MD Publications, 1958.

————. *Preventive Medicine in the United States, 1900–1975*. New York: Prodist, 1977.

Rosenkrantz, Barbara Gutman. *Public Health and the State: Changing Views in Massachusetts, 1842–1936*. Cambridge, MA: Harvard University Press, 1972.

Rowland, Mary Scott. "Managerial Progressivism in Kansas." Ph.D. dissertation, University of Kansas, 1980.

Starr, Paul. *The Social Transformation of American Medicine*. New York: Basic Books, 1982.

Stevens, Rosemary. *American Medicine and the Public Interest*. New Haven, CT: Yale University Press, 1971.

Tomes, Nancy. *The Gospel of Germs: Men, Women, and the Microbe in American Life*. Cambridge, MA: Harvard University Press, 1998.

Vestal, Stanley. *Dodge City: Queen of the Cowtowns*. London: Peter Nevill, 1955.

Vogel, Morris and Charles Rosenberg (eds.). *The Therapeutic Revolution*. Philadelphia: University of Pennsylvania Press, 1979.

Vogel, Morris. *The Invention of the Modern Hospital: Boston, 1870–1930*. Chicago: University of Chicago Press, 1980.

Warner, John Harley. *The Therapeutic Perspective*. Princeton: Princeton University Press, 1997.

Whorton, James C. *Crusaders for Fitness: A History of American Health Reform*. Baltimore, MD: Johns Hopkins University Press, 1987.

Wilson, Joan Hoff. *Herbert Hoover; Forgotten Progressive*. Prospect Heights, IL: Waveland Press, 1975.

Young, James Harvey. *The Toadstool Millionaires*. Princeton: Princeton University Press, 1961.

## ARTICLES

Aldrich, Mark. "Train Wrecks to Typhoid Fever: The Development of Railroad Medical Organizations, 1850 to World War I." *Bulletin of the History of Medicine*, 75 (Summer 2001).

Alexander, A.S. "Testing Cows for Tuberculosis." *Country Life in America*, 14 (October 1908).

Baker, S. Josephine. "The First Year of the Sheppard-Towner Act." *The Survey*, 52 (April 15, 1924).

Baldwin, Fred D. "The Invisible Armor." *American Mercury*, 12 (Fall 1964).

Barber, Barton H. "Westward to Health: Gentlemen Health-Seekers on the Santa Fe Trail." *Journal of the West*, 28 (April 1989).

Brown, D. Clayton. "Health of Farm Children in the South, 1900–1950." *Agricultural History*, 53 (1979).

Burnham, John L. "American Medicine's Golden Age: What Happened to It?" *Science*, 215 (March 19, 1982).

Chase, Frank M. "Taking Health to Kansas in a Railroad Car." *The Dearborn Independent*, (October 8, 1921).

Coburn, F.D. "Samuel J. Crumbine." *American Magazine*, 72 (June 1911).

Crumbine, Samuel J. "Food and Drug Control Laws." *Reference Handbook of the Medical Sciences* (1914).

———. "The New Public Health." *Journal of Missouri Medical Association*, 13 (1916).

———. "The Pollution of Underground Waters." *Transactions of the Kansas Academy of Sciences*, 23–24 (1909–1910).

———. "The Socialization of Preventive Medicine Through the Public Health Nurse." *American Journal of Nursing* (1918–1919).

———. "A Study of One Thousand Reported Cases of Tuberculosis." *Journal of Outdoor Life*, 18 (1921).

———. "Health Progress in Wisconsin Cities." *Wisconsin Medical Journal*, 24 (1925–1926).

———. "Moving Forward in a United Front Against Diphtheria." *Child Health Bulletin*, 2 (September 1926).

———. "Two Suggestions for Raising the Status of Public Health Officers." *American City*, 35 (September 1926).

———. "Municipality's Part in Conserving Its Greatest Asset." *American City*, 44 (February 1931).

———. "Diphtheria—the Big Bad Wolf." *Hygeia*, 13 (September 1935).

———. "A Few Highlights in the History of Sanitation." *Modern Sanitation* (April 1954).

———. "Were the Good Old Days Really Good?" *Today's Health* (August 1954).

———. "Undulant Fever." *Child Health Bulletin*, 5 (November 1929).

———. "The Children of Porto Rico in 1931." *Child Health Bulletin*, 7 (May 1931).

———. "To the Stars Through Difficulties." *Child Health Bulletin*, 7 (November 1931).

———. "Milk-Borne Epidemic Diseases in the United States and Canada, 1924 to 1931." *Child Health Bulletin*, 8 (July 1932).

———. "Milk-Borne Epidemic Diseases in the United States and Canada in 1933." *Child Health Bulletin*, 10 (July 1934).

———. "Save Children From Diphtheria." *Child Health Bulletin*, 10 (July 1934).

Crumbine, Samuel J. and Dorothy F. Holland. "The Lost 16,000: Maternal Mortality and Race Betterment." *Child Health Bulletin*, 4 (March 1928).

Curtis, K.D. "Doctor Crumbine of Dodge City." *TV Guide* (November 2, 1963).

Fitzpatrick, Martin J. "Tuberculosis in Kansas." *Journal of the Kansas Medical Society*, 43 (September 1957).

Giglio, James N. "Voluntarism and Public Policy Between World War I and the New Deal: Herbert Hoover and the American Child Health Association." *Presidential Studies Quarterly*, 13 (Summer 1983).

Greiner, Allen. "Pushing the Frontier of Public Health." *KUMed* (1949).

Grob, Gerald, "The Social History of Medicine and Diseases in America: Problems and Possibilities." *Journal of Social History*, 10 (June 1977).

Hardy, Anne. "'Straight Back to Barbarism': Antityphoid Inoculation and the Great War 1914." *Bulletin of the History of Medicine and Allied Sciences*, 74 (Summer 2000).

Holt, L. Emmett. "The Child Health Organization of America." *Modern Medicine*, 11 (September 1920).

Howes, Cecil. "This Month in Kansas History." *The Kansas Teacher* (October 1948).

Hudson, Robert P. "Hoxie's Bad Dream: Medical History in Kansas." *Journal of the Kansas Medical Society*, 71 (March 1970).

Jochims, Larry. "Medicine in Kansas, 1850–1900." M.A. thesis, Emporia State University, 1977.

Kercher, William R. "Dr. S. J. Crumbine and His Work." *Kansas Magazine* (November 1910).

King, Charles R. "Childhood Death: The Health Care of Children on the Kansas Frontier." *Kansas History*, 14 (Spring 1991).

Koppes, Clayton. "The Industrial Workers of the World and County Jail Reform in Kansas." *Kansas Historical Quarterly*, 41 (Spring 1975).

McClary, Andrew. "Germs Are Everywhere: The Germ Threat as Seen in Magazine Articles, 1890–1920." *Journal of American Culture*, 3 (1980).

———. "Swat the Fly: Popular Magazines and the Anti-Fly Campaign." *Preventive Medicine*, 11 (1982).

Mallory, Aileen. "Dr. Crumbine Patched Up the Cowboys." *Persimmon Hill*, 12 (National Cowboy Hall of Fame and Western Heritage Center, 1982.

———. "Don't Spit on the Sidewalk." *Kansas Territorial*, 3 (1983).

Martin, G.V. (Trudy). "Dr. Crumbine's Health Bricks." *International Brick Collector Association Journal*, 5 (Spring 1957).

Miller, Clark. "The Great Flu Epidemic of 1918." *Heritage of the Great Plains*, 18 (Winter 1985).

Novak, Susan S. "Killed by the Cure." *Kansas Heritage*, 10 (Spring 2002).

Peck, Phoebe. "These Were the Giants." *Journal of the Kansas Medical Society*, 66 (March 1965).

Perrin, Ethel. "The American Child Health Association." *Journal of Health and Physical Education*, 4 (November 1933).

Rogers, Naomi. "Germs With Legs: Flies, Disease, and the New Public Health." *Bulletin of the History of Medicine and Allied Sciences*, 63 (Winter 1989).

Rowland, Mary. "Dr. Crumbine in Topeka." *Bulletin of the Shawnee County Historical Society* (November 1980).

Sims, Helen M. "The Wahl Years at the University of Kansas Medical Center, 1919–1948." University of Kansas Alumni Association, 1983.

Smith, Barry. "Gullible's Travails: Tuberculosis and Quackery 1890–1930." *Journal of Contemporary History*, 20 (1985).

Smythe, Donald. "Venereal Disease: The AEF's Experience." *Prologue*, 9 (Summer 1977).

Strickland, Cleo E. "Tuberculosis in Cherokee County." County Study in 1953, copy in Kansas State Historical Society.

Strate, David K. "Up From the Prairie: Dodge City." Cultural Heritage and Arts Center. 1974.

Stutzman, Howard E. "Samuel J. Crumbine: The Little Giant of Public Health." PostGraduate Medical Education, University of Kansas School of Medicine, 1960–1961.

Taylor, Robert Lewis. "Swat the Fly." *New Yorker*, 24 (July 17, 1948; July 24, 1948).

———. "Men of Medicine." *Postgraduate Medicine*, 5 (1949).

Torcha, Marion M. "The Tuberculosis Movement and the Race Question, 1890–1950." *Bulletin of the History of Medicine and Allied Sciences*, 49 (Summer 1975).

Van Ingen, Philip. "The Story of the American Child Health Association." American Child Health Association. 1936.

Webb, David. "Kansas Characters." Kansas Heritage Center. 1985.

Wood, Charles. "Science and Politics in the War on Cattle Diseases: The Kansas Experience, 1900–1940." *Agricultural History*, 54 (January 1980).

Wood-Simons, Mary. "Mining Coal and Maiming Men." *The Coming Nation*, Girard (November 11, 1911).

Yarmove, Jack. "One Man Health Crusade." *Coronet*, 19 (February 1946).

Young, James Harvey. "Botulism and the Ripe Olive Scare of 1919–1920." *Bulletin of the History of Medicine*, 50 (Fall 1976).

———"From Oysters to After-Dinner Mints: The Role of the Early Food and Drug Inspector." *Journal of the History of Medicine and Allied Sciences*, 42 (January 1987).

# INDEX

**About the Author**

R. ALTON LEE is Professor Emeritus of History at the University of South Dakota. He taught American history for the last thirty years of his career, specializing in American labor and constitutional history. After retiring in 1996, he moved to Kansas where he has been researching Kansas history.